BESTSELLERS

TOP WRITERS TELL HOW

Also by the author

Michael Joseph – Master of Words

RICHARD JOSEPH'S

BESTSELLERS

TOP WRITERS
TELL
HOW

SUMMERSDALE

First published 1997
Reprinted 1997

Summersdale Publishers
46 West Street
Chichester
West Sussex PO19 1RP
United Kingdom

A CIP catalogue record for this book is available from the British Library.

Text set in Baskerville.
Printed and bound by Creative Print and Design (Wales).

ISBN 1 84024 009 1

Cover design by Fiona Burnett
Cover photograph by Peter Russell

Contents

Preface

The origin of this book will be of interest to all would-be writers, for it had a most unconventional start.

I had been fortunate enough to have had a book published before *Bestsellers*; not a well-written book or even a bestseller it has to be said, but one that at the time had to be written. *Michael Joseph, Master of Words* was published in 1986 to coincide with the fiftieth anniversary of the eponymous, and well-known publishing company.

Master of Words, a biography of Michael Joseph, was written on a speculative basis. It was submitted to two publishers, both rejecting it after many weeks of 'consideration'. Months elapsed but then I had a break. A publishing company, part of the group that I was employed by, agreed to publish it. My joy was to last less than a week, for a ruling was introduced as a result of my book being accepted, stating that no book written by a serving director could be published by the group. If they published mine, a precedent would be established and that might cause problems in the future. Naturally, I was very terribly disappointed, but it was a point I could understand.

To my surprise, it took just two weeks to find another publisher. Before my first book was sent to the printer, Jane Tatam, then the publisher at Ashford Press Publishing, talked me into agreeing to interview a number of contemporary authors of bestsellers for my next book. Most authors would consider this commission to be a confirmation that a career lay ahead as a successful writer. I did not, but I did agree that the thought of interviewing top authors would be an exciting and unique experience.

No synopsis was required; instead, I was presented with draft copy of the jacket blurb. This was my brief and I had to create the book around it. There was no limit to the number of authors to be interviewed, but the book had to be substantial, about 100,000 words in length, and I was asked to complete the book within two years.

The jacket copy began:

> For every author who makes a million, there's a million authors who make very little; for a million authors who make very little, there's another million who never get published. So just what is that intangible quality that bestows fame and fortune upon the select few?

My publisher presented me with this and a contract to sign at the party to mark the publication of my first book. The location was memorable too; it was held at Foyle's Bookshop in Charing Cross Road, London.

At that celebration, my emotions ranged from extreme happiness at becoming a 'commissioned' author, to the angst of realization that I had taken on a task of awesome proportions. Little did I know then that future actions by my employer would exacerbate matters.

Six months after *Master of Words* was published, my employer bought Ashford Press Publishing. When I heard about this acquisition, it caused me some anguish, for once again it appeared that I would be prevented from getting my book published. Although this time I had a formal contract and a publisher known for supporting her authors, my fears were justified. Despite the support and encouragement, it was not going to be an easy task and for a time my enthusiasm wavered. Nevertheless, I received sufficient advances against future royalties to travel to America where I could meet those authors who seldom travelled to the United Kingdom. This did much to restore my drive to complete the interviews!

Bestsellers took longer to complete than first thought, mainly as a result of the time consumed securing the interviews. The date for the handover of the typescript was extended by mutual agreement but, by the time the project was finished, my publisher had been sold again. The new owner agreed to take on the contract; the schedules were again extended but, sadly, the new publishers found themselves unable to publish it and effectively ceased trading. I had to look for yet another publishing house and succeeded last year.

As you will now understand, these events took place over a period of ten years which explains why the interviews occurred some years ago. In reality, it matters not that such time has elapsed. The events that have led these authors to become so successful would not be affected; how they started, how they became authors of bestsellers and the background to their successes would not alter with the passing of time. I was fortunate too in the choice of authors as they remain household names.

These events show just how difficult it can be to get a book published. In these days of rapid changes in the world of commerce, especially publishing, no author can be absolutely sure that even with a signed contract, the book to which so much time has been devoted is ever going to be published.

Although the background details of these authors will not have changed, opinions and views expressed when we met might have been modified or changed during the intervening years. With the exception of the late Roald Dahl and James Herriot, most of the authors have seen the relevant chapter and thus have given their approval to what follows.

Richard Joseph

Introduction

Just for a moment can you be honest with yourself? Millions dream, at some time or another in their lives, of writing a book. The more ambitious of them dream of writing a bestseller. If you have shared such dreams, read on.

The reasons that drive us to write are, of course, far too numerous to list here. For many people, however, it is simply the wish to record their own personal experiences. For the more imaginative and ambitious, it can be the dream of writing a bestseller with, perhaps, the chance of enjoying ego-boosting fame from radio and television appearances. This harmless dream is, as I have said, one that millions harbour, but only very few achieve the reality. If they actually have the drive and dedication, it is possible to cross the first hurdle, completing the typescript, but few writers – as compared to the total number of people who write – ever have their work published. Why? Well, again the reasons are legion, and there are many excellent books available to advise would-be authors. But if a writer jumps that hurdle and is published, what are those intangible reasons by which one author is singled out from a million others for fame and glory?

To answer this question, I set out to interview twenty-three top contemporary authors. I posed a similar series of questions to each of them, and their replies, taken together, go a long way towards providing the answer. It is clear from my discussions with them, though, that each of us will draw different conclusions, depending on which replies impress us most deeply.

What sets these authors apart from others is that, collectively, they have sold over 1,000 million books.

The interviews are divided into three groups: General Fiction; Sex, Sagas and Romance; and Adventure Writers. I would hope that any aspiring writer will read all the interviews, and not just that with their favourite author, for the advice given by all the writers interviewed is extremely valuable.

What they had to say makes engrossing reading, not just for the devoted reader but also for the aspiring writer. Although much has been published about the lives of these authors, little, if anything, has been written that explains in detail how they became such popular writers, and what it was that gave them that big break. Most press interviews reduce this fascinating aspect to just a single paragraph.

I am sure that amongst the millions of readers of bestselling fiction, there must be a number who yearn to emulate their favourite author. The aspiring author, even if only half-serious about becoming a writer, will usually turn to the standard writers' reference books and magazines for guidance. Although these are excellent sources of information, they can cause further confusion. For example, Ruth Rendell is quoted in the November 1987 edition of the American magazine, *The Writer*, as saying, 'I wonder where I should be now if I had aimed to please a public rather than suited my own taste.' And in the same issue, there was conflicting advice from Samm Sinclair Baker, 'Write what you think will interest others, not just what pleases you.'

But what makes a book, whether written to please yourself, or others, a bestseller? Especially if it is a first book?

Most authors do not set out to write a bestseller, and those who write for a living never really know what the formula is. More importantly, no publisher will be so rash as to state that they know for certain, either. It is all too easy to put a book's success down to luck. True, luck is a part of the answer, but it is by no means the only reason. Attributing a book's success entirely to luck is an over-simplification.

To start with, original ideas make an important impact, and they must be such as to impress the reader. Any book has to be *wanted* by the public. Judging that aspect is the very crux of the mythical and magical formula, for the public's taste in reading is fickle. Then the typescript needs to be in the right publisher's hands at the appropriate moment. The publisher has to be motivated and in the right frame of mind to send it off to be 'read' by trusted experts. Then, if the publisher is interested, and always assuming that author and publisher can agree terms, the book will eventually be published. But what happens then to make it a bestseller?

That question, of course, begs others. What qualities do you need to become one of this élite group of people? Certainly, a good education is an advantage, but it is not essential. Being well-known in other careers, however, does appear to help writers achieve bestsellerdom.

And what is a bestseller, anyway? Well, they are not just those much-hyped works of lurid fiction by big names, often with a glamorous and seductive woman on the cover. Unknown authors, writing on esoteric subjects, are sometimes highlighted in the mass media.

In 1957, Michael Joseph, founder of the well-known publishing company of the same name, was rash enough to state the parameters of what, in the field of fiction and from the publishers' point of view, makes a bestseller. He considered that such a book had to sell over 50,000 copies in the original edition in hardback. But times change, and in that company's fiftieth anniversary publication, *At the Sign of the Mermaid* (published in 1986), there is a list of contemporary Michael Joseph bestsellers. And though no statements are shown indicating the number of copies sold, I am told by one of the authors listed, 'Miss Read', who writes those marvellous tales about village life, that none of her books ever sold more than 20,000 copies in hardback.

What makes one book become a bestseller? For example, has the author got to have a flair for advertising and public relations, like Jeffrey Archer, Arthur Hailey, Clive Cussler and James Herbert? Is word-of-mouth recommendation essential? And how effective is the publisher's advertising by comparison?

Let us also reflect for a moment on successes in the literary past. Bestsellers can be on any subject or theme. Historical novels like *Gone with the Wind*, even those with religious themes, like *The Robe*, humorous stories like those of P. G. Wodehouse, serious novels like *The Heart of the Matter* by Graham Greene, and romantic novels like Daphne du Maurier's *Rebecca* are all examples of successes in varied fields. And I am sure you can think of others.

Though the theme of your book may not be important, the timing of its publication most certainly is. So the first rule, surely, is to appreciate the public's taste for reading matter. The bestselling author of twenty years ago would probably be a failure today; and today's successful author might have been a failure twenty years ago. In the main, books should either satisfy some particular hunger in the reading public, or reflect a prevailing mood (although, obviously, there have been exceptions to this).

Having met these criteria does not, however, guarantee the writer the heady heights of stardom. For it is a feature of the publishing world that book sales periodically ebb and flow, sometimes ebbing to such an extent that publishers take fright and reduce the number of books being published. It is at these times that the unfortunate new author can suffer; few publishers will gamble heavily in such a situation. Sales of books are nowadays far more subject to market forces than in years past, and when publishers have sizeable numbers of books returned to them for credit by booksellers who have been unable to sell them, they become cautious.

Sadly, many people who actually start their first book fail to recognise the most elementary, and most important, point of their labours. Your book, if it is ever going to be published, must in some way coincide with the public's current reading interest. But, what *is* the public's taste? You may think you know, but even experienced writers can fall foul of the prejudiced few: the loony left, for example, the sexist and the racist amongst us. They can put paid to a well-thought-out book even before it is published. Cross their paths, and it does not matter how well it is written, how apt the plot and how well-portrayed the characters, the book will fail to become a bestseller, even if it actually gets published in the first place.

You will read that the novel that achieves the rank of bestseller must rise above the level of merely competent story-telling, good writing, and skilful characterisation.

It must make people laugh or cry, or both, as well as engaging and keeping their attention and exciting their imagination. It does not have to have a conventional happy ending, but it must be a satisfying one. Publishers will tell you that few bestsellers survive to become classics, the majority being ephemeral; they blaze like rockets in the sky and tomorrow they are forgotten.

Bringing sex into a book can, of course, help sales, but the subject will not by itself make your book a bestseller. On the other hand, a book that sets out to titillate and excite the reader will sell extremely well for a time, especially if the storyline is one with which readers of all types can easily associate. One exception is *Riders* by Jilly Cooper. Published in 1985, there were six editions in two years. The book was a huge success, not because of its size – it ran to over 900 pages – but because of the cover on the paperback edition, which depicted the taut, white-jodhpur-covered behind of a young girl rider, a riding crop in hand, and with a man's hand about to cup one buttock. This is a perfect example of what I mean. The cover suggests sex. One reviewer provided an apt comment, stating that *Riders* is a boring book, for 'there is a mounting about every seventy-five pages . . . but the cover undoubtedly helped the title to sell and it is still selling well today.'

This is not always true: look at those consistently read – and often hugely successful – Mills & Boon books. They seem to be ageless, and the stories in them can be, and are, read over and over again. I am told that they make extremely pleasant light reading with which to relax for a couple of hours. Perhaps there is a message here for the budding author!

So you want to write the book of your dreams? Well, the important thing to remember is to *do* something about writing it, rather than just dreaming about success. Few people ever do anything to further their writing ambitions and aspirations, whatever their dreams.

There is also the glittering incentive of winning a literary prize. There are many very good prizes awarded annually for all types of literature: novels, plays, non-fiction and short stories. For 1997, there are over 160 organisations offering awards and the prize money exceeds £900,000. Two prizes attract more publicity than others: the Booker Prize for fiction (worth £20,000) and the Whitbread Literary Awards (worth £31,000).

If you need further encouragement, remember that one in a million authors does not have to wait to win an award. Not so long ago, in 1987, Scott Turow, a thirty-five year-old, highly successful, American lawyer wrote his first novel on scraps of paper whilst commuting. This book, *Presumed Innocent*, which was rejected by twenty-five publishers before being accepted, broke many records. For example, it appeared in the *New York Times* bestseller list for fourteen weeks, four of them prior to publication! And over forty US publishers negotiated for the paperback rights, with the successful publisher agreeing to pay $3.9 million (about £2.1 million). Film rights were also clinched at $1.25 million and by the time it had been published in the United Kingdom, it had earned over £4 million . . . and Scott who, at twenty-one, had wanted to emulate James Joyce, commented that after the success of this novel, all he wanted to do was to save condemned men from the electric chair!

Serious would-be authors might ponder for a moment that Scott Turow struck his success at the age of thirty-five. Perhaps more importantly, he wrote his novel using his personal experience as a lawyer to formulate the plot and background. I do wonder, though, whether the fact that he was already a highly successful lawyer actually helped, and whether the book's title made any difference. You will find more discussion of such factors amongst the interviews that follow.

Anyone who has ever thought of becoming a writer would do well to note Arthur Hailey's comment:

> Get on with it. There are people who 'talk book', and there are people who 'write book'; talking writers, and writing writers.

PART ONE

GENERAL FICTION

Catherine Cookson DBE, OBE

Kate Hannigan, The Fifteen Streets, Colour Blind, The Mallen Girl, Tilly Trotter, and ninety further titles. Worldwide sales over 90 million copies.

The description that annoys Catherine Cookson more than anything else is the one that reviewers often use, namely that 'she is a writer of romance'. When I spoke to her, she most certainly did not subscribe to this view, believing with intense passion that she writes about social history, whilst telling a darned good story at the same time.

Her achievements are extremely impressive, for, quite apart from having had ninety-five books published over a period of forty-six years, she has received the Freedom of the Borough of South Shields, an honorary degree from the University of Newcastle, and the Royal Society of Literature's award for the Best Regional Novel of the Year. The Variety Club of Great Britain named her Writer of the Year, and she has been voted Personality of The North-East. But the honour that gave her the most pleasure was the OBE to which she was appointed in 1986.*

So how did she achieve this fame that today stretches around the world? Her books have now been translated into twenty languages, and according to an assessment made by her publishers and agents as long ago as 1978, her total sales had by then exceeded 87 million copies. *The Bookseller* (the trade journal of the book business) published a report that between 1980 and 1986 sales of her books topped 3,602,000 copies, placing her ahead of such writers as Danielle Steel, Alistair Maclean and Dick Francis. Today, the total exceeds 90 million copies.

Her biographical details are well recorded in her autobiography, *Our Kate,* and in her memoirs, *Catherine Cookson's Country,* but for those who do not know, or have not followed her writing career, she was born in Tyne Dock, in the heart of Tyneside, in 1906. The young Katie McMullen, as she was then known, spent her formative years in an environment of extreme poverty, embarrassment and bitterness. The utter and wretched humiliation she had experienced left a mental wound that was to take years to heal.

Unlike so many leading writers, she started life with many disadvantages. She was born illegitimate; endured deprivation and hardship; her mother was,

---

* In 1993 Catherine was appointed DBE in addition to the OBE; and D.Litt. in 1991 (Honorary).

at times, an alcoholic and occasionally violent; and from the age of thirteen she suffered from hereditary haemorrhagic telangiectasia. But above all, she had only the minimum of education. In this aspect, her early life differs significantly from the other authors interviewed and her ultimate success as a bestselling author makes her achievements all the more remarkable.

Katie left school at thirteen but, being street-wise, she had learned the language of the region, which is unique. Even today, the dialect is so strong that many outsiders cannot easily understand what is said. However, in her novels, inflection is used and only in rare cases does she use dialectic words. Few appreciate the culture of the north-east, which is steeped in history, and the character of its people.

* * *

In all her books, Catherine encompasses and portrays the real gritty ambiance of the region. It is this, and her complete understanding of the people and their problems, that indicate why her books have appealed to her readers for so long.

Amazingly, all her novels with the exception of two – one set in Fenland and the other in Manchester and London – are based in the north-east, set in the mines and shipyards, or the farms and surrounding countryside. But unlike other authors whose popularity has waxed and waned, her novels are still avidly read, though they can appear to be very similar to each other; and in recent years she has also written a number of children's books. Catherine did try to write books outside her area such as *The Fen Tiger* (written whilst enjoying a boat trip on the Fenland rivers of East Anglia, and published under the name of Catherine Marchant) – but conceeded that the results were never going to be readable or even published. This marked a turning-point in her life, for thereafter she realised that she was primarily a regional writer – proving the point that writers succeed more often when they write about what they know.

How, but more importantly, why, are her books still so phenomenally successful? When one reads how she started, the truth is even stranger. At the age of eleven, she knew she was destined to become a writer, an ambition fuelled by others who told her that she possessed the ability to describe events with a clarity and colour that totally captivated her listeners' attention. Catherine was quite open as to why:

I was a story-teller from the time I could talk, and if I could get an audience, if I could get someone to listen to me . . . I used to pass the time, telling myself wonderful stories about us living in a nice house with lino on the stairs . . . one of the best ones I've ever told was about the wee folk, the little green men talking to me.

The account of these little green men appears in her autobiography *Our Kate*:

> . . . 'Granda, you know that little man you tell me about, the one that sits on the wall in Ireland no bigger than your hand, you know him? With the green jacket and the red trousers and the buckles on his shoes, and the high hat and a shillelagh as big as himself, you remember, Granda?' 'Aye, what about him?' 'Well, I have seen him, Granda.' 'Ya have?' 'Aye, Granda. He was round the top corner.' 'Well, he said, "Hello, Katie."' 'He said, "Hello, Katie", did he? And what did you say?' '. . .I said, "Hello, Mister, me Granda knows you."' He wiped his tash with his hand while raising his white eyebrows, then he said, 'You know what you are, Katie McMullen, don't ya? You're a stinking liar. But go on, go on, don't stop, for begod! it will get you some place . . . either into clink or in the money.'

Nearly all young children enjoy telling a story, but for most it is a passing phase. Catherine practised the art seriously, even at an early age, but to become adept at the art, other talents are necessary. She added, 'I soaked up everything, everything people said, not only what they said, but how they said it.' Possibly this is the main reason why her books are consistent bestsellers. She explained:

> I'm a frustrated actress. I act all these characters. If I don't cry about them, if I don't laugh at their jokes, if I don't lose my temper and if I don't swear, it doesn't seem that I am writing them; someone else is. I act all these characters, I live these characters.
>
> And I never use four-letter words either, just all the 'damns' and 'blasts', and nor will I go into the dockyard atrocities of sex. I imply it and let the reader take it from there.'

As I have said, Catherine knew from a very early age that she was going to be a writer, though she denies having dreamt about it. When she was eleven she wrote a short story. It was called *The Wild Irish Girl*, and though the tale was rewritten many times it still kept the same theme. The heroine was being chased through the woods by a man who wanted to take her into his lodge, but though the details of the chase and the countryside were graphically detailed, she could not finish the story because she did not know what would go on once the girl got inside the lodge! Catherine sent it off to the *South Shields Gazette*, but it was returned after three days.

Catherine was also an avid reader from a very early age. *Rainbow Comic* and *Tiger Tim's Weekly* are two she recalled, but Grimms' *Fairy Tales* was her first serious, and much treasured, book; and as a teenager she read *T. P. & Cassell's Weekly* on a regular basis. What is clear from her biography is that she read everything she could lay her hands on. It was part of her learning process and vital if she was to become successful.

In her teens, she worked in a laundry as a checker. It was a tough job, but there was always room for humour. Catherine's desire to make people laugh prompted her to write a play which she thought was not only amusing but quite good as well. This she sent to a well-known writers' school, which promptly turned it down as being unsuitable for publication. But it was the way it was rejected that has stuck vividly in Catherine's memory: a cryptic message written by the reader, in vivid red ink, sideways across the back page: 'Strongly advise author not to take up writing as a career.'

That might have been enough to put most people off, perhaps, but not Catherine. The rejection may have deterred her from writing but it did not stop her reading. If there was one book that played a pivotal part in her career, it was Lord Chesterfield's *Letters To His Son.* (First published in 1774, though written nearly forty years earlier.) As she explained:

> He taught me history, mythology and geography. He seemed to take me all over the world and I soon realised that I had to read many more books before I could write.

Not all her life was spent in Tyneside. In 1929, she moved first to Clacton-on-Sea and later to Hastings where she became a manageress of a laundry in a work-house. For some thirty-six years she lived in Hastings. Catherine married Tom Cookson in 1940 but it was a marriage that was not to be blessed with children. It was also a time of great personal stress culminating in a mental breakdown, and only Catherine's inner strength brought her through the ordeal. No reader of her biographies can fail to be moved by the emotions and troubles she endured.

> I was never ambitious to be published, that's the odd thing. I wanted, candidly, to work out my breakdown. That was the main thing. It wasn't money and it wasn't my ambition to be published. I hid behind this façade of refinement [she pronounced this 'refeenment'] for so many years. I had lied about my upbringing and my relations and I knew I had to come clean. I thought that if I came clean, my breakdown would go and my mind would settle . . . I thought my early books would do the trick, but they didn't. It didn't do it until I

wrote *Our Kate*, which was published in 1969. It took twelve years to write . . . If anyone read those first drafts they would have shuddered, because the bitterness within me was so great.

'A very good way of cleansing one's soul,' I said. 'Yes, oh yes,' she retorted, 'if anyone can bear to read it.' But it was a catharsis.

* * *

When Tom had returned home from the war, he encouraged Catherine to start writing again. This time she tried writing short stories instead of plays, joining the local writers' group for encouragement. She soon became part of the organisation.

> I was secretary of this little first writers' group in Hastings. Members wrote about kittens, cats and dogs, and nice little bits of poetry. Many were published but I never got anywhere.
>
> I knew nothing about publishers and how they worked. I didn't even know about agents. You will find in my autobiography that it was Major Christopher Bush who gave me the name of an agent. [John Smith of Christy & Moore.] I wrote the first three chapters of my first book and sent them to him. He wrote back asking for the rest as soon as I had finished. He sent it to Macdonalds and Murray Thomson, who was a director of the firm, read the first two pages. 'Too grim', he said and threw it back at his secretary who took it home and read it all. Next morning, she told him that he had missed something — and that was that.

Secretaries play a much greater role in publishing than people imagine. (Another author I interviewed, Molly Parkin, had the same sort of luck.) But after her first novel, *Kate Hannigan*, was published in 1950, she realised that the support of her husband Tom had been important too. He was then a schoolmaster and his command of the English language was a tremendous help. I was surprised, though, to learn that *Kate Hannigan* very nearly didn't appear in the bookshops because Catherine's neighbours tried hard to stop the publication.

> You wouldn't believe it, but some of my neighbours tried to get it banned because I had dared, in the first two or three pages, to write about a baby being born — actually coming out of the womb. It was very detailed, because during the war, as a voluntary worker, I went into the hospital at St. Albans and saw a baby born.

It was banned in Ireland. It was too much for the Catholic Church and I was advised to cut down on this. I gave the reader a whole bottle of medicine, instead of a spoonful. I had to cut all that down.

I asked Catherine if she made much money out of this first book. It comes as a surprise to learn that her first royalty cheque amounted to £100. And she received the same amount for the next three books, though nowadays the advances she is paid are very different. It wasn't the money that pleased her, however. It was the thrill of having her first book published. But this was not her first effort.

You see, I had been writing plays up to then, about ladies and gentlemen. What did I know about ladies and gentlemen, I ask you? But I seemed to know. I had been writing three long plays after the war and prior to that I had been writing children's stories but I never thought about sending them away. It wasn't until after the war that I got the idea that I might have a hand at doing a novel.

When my first book was published, I went, as they say up here, doolally tap.*

It is very odd, but I never wrote for the money. I had my husband who was a grammar schoolmaster; the salary was not great but I could make sixpence go as far as somebody else could make half a dollar... I just wanted to write.

Right from the very beginning I was reviewed in *The Times*, and *The Times Literary Supplement*. John Betjeman wrote about it too... that he could smell the river and so on. I got very good reviews until I started making money. It's always the way, they don't review you once you are successful, but I can't grumble at the reviews I got for my early books.

I've never given myself credit for writing the books, but I've given myself credit for promotion. Because for the last thirty years, whenever I've had a letter I've answered it personally, that is, up to recently when my husband has answered them for me. My husband is my private secretary and I dictate to him. I have a filing system which my secretary maintains, and I have a card system because many of the people who write to me have been doing so for twenty-five years or more. People of all ages write to me, from great-grandmothers to twelve year-old children who are doing projects in school.

---

* *Doolally Tap* originates from around 1900 when time-expired soldiers in India were sent to Deolalie, a sanitorium in Bombay, to await a troop-ship to take them home. *Tap*: Hindustani for fever. The long wait led to boredom, resulting in some very bizarre behaviour.

Is this, I wondered, the clue to her consistent and phenomenal success? Publishers and many bestselling authors agree that the best method of promoting book sales is 'by word of mouth', the personal recommendation. Catherine continued:

> I can't tell you why my books have been so popular for so many years. I think it's because I write about human beings and their re-actions. A lot of people don't want sex, and they don't want four-letter words. They don't want salaciousness. And I give them a good story, I think, but the thing is, I *feel* what I write.

'So do you believe that if a writer expresses his or her feelings and emotions in their work, then their personality will emerge from the words?' I asked.

> I think so. Deep inside me, I talk about aloneness, as distinct from loneliness. Other people talk about aloneness, well I was using this sixty years ago, when no one else was ever using that term. It all started when I was rejected from that children's party [described fully in *Our Kate*]. I have this aloneness deep within me and I think this too comes over in my books. I understand . . . I have a deep feeling for people.

Her books have almost a cult quality about them, for they capture the period, the social environment, the poverty, cruelty and evil people, all the many facets of life in her home town and the surrounding countryside at the time of which she writes.

> I am a story-teller, and I still am a story-teller. I wrote my first six-teen books longhand, but I now use a tape recorder. I go over and over the dialogue, and I'm acting the parts of the characters I'm writing about. As I said earlier, I'm a frustrated actress.

She added that by dictating her stories she could see her characters acting and that through her voice, she could feel their emotions, their laughter, their humour, their sorrows and their joy. To her credit, Catherine always emphasizes that, though she never had any 'literary' help, it is her husband, Tom, who aids and abets her progress. His innate ability to spell any word, and his mastery of grammar, were of inestimable help to her; but Catherine holds a strong view about perfect English, adding, 'When I once tried to write one of my characters speaking perfect English, he might as well have been one of Madame Tussaud's figures. There is no life in them.'

Having a spouse who can help is surely an advantage, but for those who do not, what would she advise someone day-dreaming about writing their own first book to do?

> I used to say, at one time, that anybody could write, there's a story in everybody and anybody can write. That is quite wrong, because anybody can't write. Everybody has a story to tell but the thing is if they wrote it, who would want to read it? It's how it is put down. If I was talking to someone who wants to write, I would say: 'Read, read and keep reading.' To those who say, 'My grammar isn't right', or 'I know nothing about punctuation' and so on, I say again, 'Read, read and keep reading.'
>
> Write the story you want, then leave it for a while, if you can. Look at it again, and if you are going to be a writer this will be the test, all your mistakes will come out of the page and hit you.

Sound advice, and for Catherine this is a successful technique for over the years she has become one of the world's most outstanding authors, enjoying not only fame, but a substantial income, too; a good part of which is donated to needy causes and research.

Jilly Cooper

How To Stay Married, How to Survive From Nine to Five, Jolly Super, Men & Super Men, Riders, Rivals, Polo, The Man Who Made Husbands Jealous, Appassionata and twenty-eight others.

Among the myriad colourful books that can be seen on almost every bookseller's display stands are those of the prolific writers of romance. The mention of romantic novels will bring many authors' names to the minds of devoted readers of that genre. This is hardly surprising, since these books have such a wide appeal to all ages and classes. To many readers who are not 'switched on' to this type of novel, however, there seem to be far too many published along the same lines. Once an author or publishing house finds a successful formula, they tend to exploit it to the full. Who could blame them? One publishing house specialising in this category has, for many years, encouraged authors to write, if not to a set formula, then to a set of rules. In a sense, therefore, they have created a production line. Once an author is hooked into this market, he or she will write, or attempt to write, many more similar titles.

In the first place, it must be said, once you have read a few of these romances, it becomes easy to identify and predict the plot. And the inclusion of down-to-earth love scenes has, until recently, been almost taboo. When sex is mentioned, however, it is usually with very genteel phrases. Perhaps this is why these novels maintain a steady, if unspectacular, readership. On the other hand, a number of authors have made much by writing good, raunchy love scenes, creating what today are known as 'bonkbusters'. And Jilly Cooper must rank amongst the best-known.

She is one author who, even in her early career as a writer, was well-known to millions of readers. Jilly would be the first to admit that her fame was helped in the beginning by the wide audience, gained over the years from regular contributions to national newspapers, and from appearances on television. What is more, appearing on national television programmes ensured that her humour and repartee were appreciated by many more people than are regular book buyers; a rare ability in a writer. I was to learn that it was her witty conversation that originally led her to become a writer in the first place. So as I travelled to interview her at her country home in Bisley, Gloucestershire, I was also ready to be entertained.

She lives and works in what some might call a mansion, but which is in reality a house that was originally built, more than 700 years ago, as a place for monks to practise their chanting. From her drawing-room there are uninterrupted views across a small valley, carpeted with open fields. A peaceful environment which many would envy, and an ideal one in which to write; one step outside, and you are away from 'civilization' – and the telephone.

People tend to remember Jilly as a flirtatious blonde, often to be seen at parties with a glass in her hand and a gaggle of men around her. Don't be fooled. Despite that extrovert party image, she has been described as both 'insecure and ludicrously sensitive': characteristics of any successful creative writer. Jilly had the good fortune to have been born into an extremely happy upper middle class family who came from Yorkshire. After the last war, her father, Bill Sallitt, who had been one of the Army's youngest brigadiers, returned to Yorkshire, moving into a splendid Georgian house which was partly used as his office. It was the ideal setting, with seven acres of fields, ideal for her ponies, and not short of other amenities with a swimming pool, tennis and squash courts.

On arrival, I was warmly greeted by both Jilly and her dogs. Coffee was instantly provided, and we adjourned to the drawing-room, which seemed to double as a library. Books were everywhere, from floor to ceiling. My eyes searched the shelves for a copy of *Riders*, one of her better known novels, which I thought would be a good starting-point for our discussion. So it proved, for as I complimented her, she began to talk about the book with animated and bubbly enthusiasm.

> Soon after the book had been published in hardback, I had to go to speak at a literary dinner in Exeter. The guests included many paperback publishers, and élite members of the publishing world and booksellers. I noticed the long faces and dark mutterings, particularly from the women. I discovered afterwards that they had just seen the cover of the British paperback edition and were very far from happy about the design. They said it was far too sexy and sexist for their markets and that it demeaned women by having a man's hand on a woman's bottom. I myself was slightly startled to begin with by the cover, but I soon got used to it and now I think it is a great cover. Every other country has used it on their editions, except for the American edition.

Jilly then showed me the American paperback edition as it was finally published. The cover had a round hole cut into it and was somewhat reminiscent of *Dynasty* – certainly not the image that Jilly would have preferred. *Riders*, her twenty-seventh book, was published in 1985, but it took her over fifteen years to finish it. She says she is a slow writer, but not that slow! In fact the only copy of the first final manuscript was inadvertently left on a London bus, and was never seen again – an author's nightmare come true. Jilly had to write the book all over again; at the time she was living in London, with frequent parties and people dropping in – not an ideal situation.

> I wrote a lot at school, but never got beyond the third chapter. I used to also write romantic stories and plays, but most of all, I wanted to be a journalist. I used to see these men in macintoshes and hats, clustering around and interviewing beautiful film stars at airports, and I wanted to be one of the men in macintoshes.
>
> But I never could have written long books before I was married – because my love life was always getting in the way. I settled down after I was married, but life does tend to get in the way of writing, doesn't it? Actually, I find writing incredibly difficult, each article for *The Sunday Times* or *The Mail on Sunday* was re-drafted and drafted at least a dozen times, and *Riders* took at least seven drafts.

Jilly's bubbly, extrovert personality is in many ways the opposite of other writers I have met. After leaving school, she went through numerous jobs, from secretary to reporter, though she recounted her career with humour:

> I was sacked from twenty-two jobs. I was so incompetent as a temporary typist, the letters I did on Monday came back by Wednesday, and I was out that day. I've been a switchboard operator, advertising copywriter – that was a nightmare – but I eventually settled in a job with the *Middlesex Independent* when I was eighteen. I actually stayed with them for two years, but I nearly didn't last the first day. I reported a wedding and got the bride married to the best man!
>
> I always wanted to get to Fleet Street – there were riches to be had there – and with lots of boozy lunches.

But it was later, when she was working at Collins, the publishers, that the opportunity to start writing occurred. Each author's introduction into the world of writing is, of course, unique, but once they have got started, it is that intangible quality that singles one writer out for real fame and fortune which is so intriguing. If a common theme emerges, then it is for the reader to draw a conclusion – that could perhaps lead you down that difficult path to becoming an established and successful writer.

Jilly was working in the company's publicity department at the time, helping to entertain guests at all those parties held to promote books. This left her with time on her hands, and a friend at Odhams asked her if she would like to help edit a new teenage magazine. It was during this period that she realized that many of the stories submitted for publication were really very poor. In despair, she thought she could perhaps write better stories.

She succeeded surprisingly quickly, getting five stories published in other magazines, including *Woman's Own*. It was all very rewarding. She was living in Fulham with, at one time, twenty-two cats, and not being enamoured with the chores of housework, home was in a permanent state of delightful chaos. When she told a friend that she was thinking of writing a piece about housework, she received the cutting reply, 'But you don't do any!'

> I went to a dinner party and met Godfrey Smith, editor of *The Sunday Times* colour magazine, and started to talk about being a young wife and how awful it was, working all day, shopping all one's lunch hour, rushing home, cleaning the house, cooking one's husband's dinner, making love all night, getting up in the morning, going to work, shopping all lunch hour, getting home, doing the housework, cooking one's husband's dinner, making love all night, and after six months one collapsed from exhaustion. Godfrey thought this was so funny that he asked me to write a piece. I wrote it and *The Sunday Times* colour magazine accepted it and gave me £100. That week I was offered nine jobs and one of them was a column on *The Sunday Times*, another to write my first book.

Just what is it, apart from her skill as a writer, that singled her out for such huge success? I noticed that a number of her books carry her portrait, perhaps cashing in on her many appearances on television and contributions in national newspapers. She has earned what is called a 'high-profile' or 'public-relations' image, which is just one aspect of marketing books. Jilly has an immensely charming way of talking about so many varied subjects that it's no wonder that for some years she frequently appeared on television chat shows, or quiz games; perceptive enough to ask all the right questions, and witty enough to be remembered by the viewer long after the programme had been broadcast. She is very direct and her remarks can be very incisive. As a writer, she is also uninhibited in her attitude to sex. She believes that sex can be fun, and enjoys ribbing the stuffy English about their inhibitions.

In a curious way, as an author she is somewhat akin to Dick Francis, for they are both well-known to the public for talents other than writing novels. People were interested in Francis, firstly, as a jockey, so it wasn't too difficult to capture their interest with books related to horses and racing. So, I think, it is with Jilly: her press, and then her television appearances have undoubtedly helped her career as a novelist.

Nevertheless, none of her early romantic novels became out-and-out international blockbusters. Unlike writers such as Francis or Herriot, however, her work does embrace a number of literary fields. *Emily, Harriet, Octavia* and *Imogen* rank as romantic novels; *How to Survive From Nine To Five* and *Men and Super Men* - humour; *Class*, a send up of the English Class system - satire; *The Common Years* recounts life as she saw it; *Animals In War* is history; but her more recent titles, *Riders, Rivals, Polo, The Man Who Made Husbands Jealous*, and *Appassionata* have become the 'blockbusters' which both publishers and authors strive to achieve.

Rivals, based on life behind the television screen, has been published for some years now, so I can recount that when I met Jilly, she had just heard from an editor who had demanded a large number of changes which she regarded as trying to gentrify the book and which she flatly turned down. I found myself briefly involved as an adviser. A curious feeling, as I'm the last person she should listen to! In any event, Jilly has far many more contacts and advisors in the world of publishing than I, for her husband Leo is a publisher in his own right.

It is surprising how many successful authors have close links with the publishing world, but it is not essential; and becoming a journalist does not automatically result in becoming a writer of bestsellers. Strong and close links with publishers should increase an author's confidence, but she told me that her books have always been written with colossal despair and anguish; and she believed that each one was going to be a disaster until it was finished. This insecurity is a fear that other writers share, but there are social risks too.

> You can get very egotistical when you write books because you disappear into a shed at the bottom of the garden, as I do, and you live with these characters for twelve hours a day, seven days a week, so they tend to become more important, at least temporarily, than your family and this is very difficult to live with. Equally, when you meet people at parties, you lose the ability to listen.
>
> I think it is terrible the way the young writers come along to meet great writers and the great writers are often really dismissive. By all means revere great writers, but I don't think that because somebody is a great writer they are necessarily a very nice person. I have never forgotten at a party hearing some young writer going up to a female author and saying, 'Gosh, I so much admire your work,' and the author just turned her back on him and walked off. This struck me

as being very unkind and deeply stupid because he might turn into a reviewer and not be too nice about her books in the future.

I wondered how Jilly reacted to reviews of her books. Having been a journalist it seems that if they are very critical, she could exact revenge very easily.

> In the past I may have been treated lightly because I was a journalist and maybe there was a flicker at the back of their minds that if they were nasty, I would retaliate, but it is a long time since I have been a journalist that I don't think it worries them anymore, particularly bearing in mind some of the savage reviews when *Appassionata* first came out. But I think you should try and accept criticism and read reviews carefully because it is very possible they may be right and you may learn something from them.

She gets piles of mail, particularly when a book has been published. Many are from fans, but some of them are from the 'Mary Whitehouse' brigade, and are very caustic about the raunchy passages in her 'bonkbusters'. She recalled one riposte with obvious glee:

> One woman wrote to say that *Riders* was the most disgusting book she had ever read; and how could I, as a mother of children, write such filthy stuff as this? She'd put it in the dustbin only partly read.
>
> I replied that I was terribly glad that it was only partly read, because if she had got to the latter bits it would have really finished her off!
>
> Seriously though, I appreciate that to many people, simply writing a letter can be quite a frightening task, so I always take the trouble to answer them. You should always write back nicely, and I'm always pleased to get them.
>
> I just think it's terribly nice of people to write, but a few are extremely rude. *Riders* ought to have brought some horrors, but there were only half a dozen. Apart from the lady who threw the book into the dustbin, the others were signed but without any address to reply to. I wish they would [include an address] because I would write such funny replies. Normally I am polite but occasionally I get carried away.

Since then, she has received numerous letters from people in the world of television, polo and music. These letters come partly as a result of having had many more books published than most writers, so I was prompted to ask whether the rewards from her writing had made any real difference to her life.

The trouble for writers is they don't get taxed at source and so if you are given a great whack of money, you tend to spend it, or give it away to people who desperately need things and then the horror comes when you have to pay the tax. Equally, you may have a brilliant year when a book does terribly well, and then the next year you don't do nearly so well and you have to pay the tax on a brilliant year.

This was not the response I had expected, but if any author has fame and fortune suddenly thrust upon them, this is certainly a salutary warning.

I have asked everyone interviewed for this book what advice they would give to an aspiring author. Not that such advice should be taken literally, but it does in a way reflect what factors have helped, in the authors' own opinions, to make them successful. So what was Jilly's advice?

Without doubt, keep a diary. From the day you are born, keep a diary, because we all forget things so quickly. I didn't start until I was thirty and I missed so much.

When writing, keep your sentences short. Use colour as much as possible, and use the five senses as much as possible. Just try to explain what it was like to be there. Journalistic rules are very good. I think journalists write lousy English, but readable prose. I'd always rather write readable prose and lousy English. Except it can date you in twenty years or so.

I never went to a university. You learn to think logically there and write literary English, but you won't necessarily become a good writer.

I think if I wanted someone to learn to write, I'd send them to a newspaper for two years. No longer, because you become too hardened after that time. They are using computers now. I don't understand them, it would be difficult to use one here, the power goes off so often, I'd lose what I had typed. I'll tell you the other thing. All they do is turn in perfect typescripts and they won't be worth a penny in the future if they haven't got the writer's scribble all over them.

Our conversation digressed at this point, and we reminisced about her earlier titles, which prompted me to ask her, what, if she was starting her career as an author again, she would write about?

Without doubt, a novel about animals and war. I spent a terrible time writing a non-fiction book in 1982 about the way animals suffered in two world wars and how they helped us win the wars. We had just moved to Gloucestershire, and I was so moved by the subject, I sat here in floods of tears until the book was finished. Many people have written to me about vivisection and suggested that I ought to write a book about that. But, I can't. I don't think an entire book on vivisection would help. It would be too agonizing for people to read. But if I brought vivisection into a novel, just a few chapters, it would be much more powerful, and bring home the horrors.

This just goes to show that behind the façade of humour and wit, there is a serious and compassionate side to this very talented author.

Roald Dahl

Kiss Kiss, Switch Bitch, Tales of the Unexpected, Roald Dahl's Book of Ghost Stories, Going Solo, The Gremlins, James and the Giant Peach, Charlie and the Chocolate Factory, Danny, the Champion of the World, The BFG and forty-one others. Born in 1916, he died in 1990, his last book was *The Minpins*. This interview took place in June 1987.

Until I met him, whenever anyone mentioned the name of Roald Dahl my mind returned to those evenings I had spent, alone, watching on television his extremely well-written and very disturbing *Tales Of The Unexpected*. His stories had me absolutely transfixed and at times, I confess, scared. Anyway, those memories of mine came flooding back as I drove to his house in Buckinghamshire. I grew increasingly apprehensive, for surely he was going to be an awe-inspiring author to interview?

To get to his house I drove up a narrow dead-end road. Very apt, I thought. It seemed a most appropriate place for a mystery and thriller writer to live. It was midday. The front door was open, but no one seemed to be in earshot. 'Hello,' I called, to an empty hall. Then a voice boomed from the right, 'I'm in here, come in.' Dahl greeted me in his kitchen, where he was busy signing a huge pile of letters that his secretary had produced. 'Shan't be a minute,' he said, 'help yourself to a drink. It's all in the lounge.'

Roald Dahl was certainly an imposing man, even at seventy-two. Tall and still well-built, he had a voice that could have penetrated a heavy fog. During the preamble before I got down to the serious side of our meeting, I sat with him in his kitchen. Apart from the usual kitchen furniture, there was a large maroon-covered armchair at the end of the long pine table. Noticing that I was looking quizzically at this, he explained that the chair was essential, for he still suffered from back pain, the permanent legacy of a wartime accident and several subsequent operations. (His fans will know all about the background to this, but for those who do not, he was a fighter pilot during the Second World War, and crash-landed while serving in Libya.)

If you mention Dahl to older adults today, they'll almost certainly refer, like me, to that television series, *Tales of the Unexpected*, but younger adults and today's children know him better as the writer of some seventeen books for children. Contemporary biographies in reference books record that he wrote mainly in just the two fields, mystery and children's writing. As an opener, I asked him, just how he would wish to be remembered in years to come. He paused momentarily. 'After I'm dead, I'm sure that I'll be remembered more as a children's writer. It's what I would prefer.' 'So how did you get started as a writer?' I asked.

How he started as a writer is well covered in the tale *Lucky Break* (one of his stories in *The Wonderful World of Henry Sugar*), and he chided me for not having read that as well as the biographical entries. As it transpired, however, he went on to summarize much more than that chapter discloses. The accounts of his younger days are illuminating and should provide encouragement to every aspiring author.

Dahl was, unquestionably, a master wordsmith, but neither he nor his readers would have believed it from his school reports. From the age of fourteen, the annual comments about his ability in English Composition were consistently awful. There was nothing in any report to suggest the genius for prose that was within. They suggested that he could not put a sentence together, let alone write an acceptable essay.

His ability to express himself did not show itself until he started work, and even then he did not harbour any ambition to be a published writer. He left school at eighteen, preferring not to go on to university but to join the exciting world of big business instead. He also yearned to travel overseas, and secured himself a job with the eastern staff of the Shell Oil Company, though for the first few years he was based at their offices in London. He explained:

> Remember, these were the days of the great British Empire, and my boss, a man called Rowbottom, literally controlled what went on out in the far parts of the world, like South Africa. There, the local Shell Company had a manager, but he received direction and instructions by post from London. Within two months he had me writing his letters. He'd call me in and say 'Write to so-and-so, tell him his kerosene sales are lousy and he has got to do something about it.' And he'd give me the figures and I'd go away and write the letter. Sometimes the letters were quite frightening. But I was writing them all, totally.
>
> So I found it easy to put words on paper. But that is nothing to do with creativity. The trouble is, there are too many people who think that because they can put words on paper, they can write a book. We can all put words on paper, if we are educated; some can do it better than others. And some can have more clarity, and can state it briefly.

Dahl was in Africa when the war broke out, joining the RAF to become a fighter pilot. Dahl's real break came unexpectedly in 1942 when, as a twenty-six year-old veteran of the war, he was invalided home and then sent to Washington DC, as an Assistant Air Attaché. He was far from sure what he was supposed to be doing there, except that everyone was very keen to put Britain forward. There didn't seem much to do. America had by then joined the war, having been drawn into it after the Japanese attacked Pearl Harbor in December 1941. He hadn't been in Washington many days when he had an unexpected visitor to his office at the British Embassy, C. S. Forester. Dahl was impressed, for he knew of Forester, an author widely known, and destined to become yet more so, for those tales of seafaring derring-do featuring his hero, Horatio Hornblower. One author for whom Dahl had great admiration.

Forester explained that he was writing things about Britain for the American papers and magazines. He had a contract with the *Saturday Evening Post* which would publish any story that he wrote, and he believed that Dahl had a story about combat-flying to tell. How Forester had learned of the young pilot's exploits isn't known, but whoever tipped him off about Dahl can be said to have influenced the literary history of Britain.

They went for lunch in an upmarket French restaurant, and Dahl started to tell Forester about the time in Libya when he attempted to land his Gloster Gladiator in the desert, sustaining injuries and burns. He later flew Hurricanes and took part in fierce air-to-air combat in Greece where he claimed several victories.

Recounting the story, making notes and eating all at the same time proved rather difficult, so Dahl agreed to go away and write notes for Forester. That night, as Dahl sat alone in the house where he was staying, his mind strayed back to his battle days. He began to write, and as he did so, he became totally absorbed in describing the events. He was finding it easier than he had first thought and he wrote freely for the next five hours. The next day he had it typed out and sent off to Forester. Nothing happened for a week. Then he received a letter. As Dahl recalled, it said:

> [Dear RD,] You said you were going to send me notes . . . you have
> sent me a complete story. My agent, Harold Matson, has sent it to
> the *Saturday Evening Post* untouched, with my recommendation . . .
> and they accepted it at once. Their cheque is enclosed.

Dahl thought that this was easy. His story, called *A Piece of Cake*, was soon followed by others – after all, he had time on his hands. At first they were about his flying experiences, but soon he had to start making them up. All of them sold to national magazines, *Colliers*, *Lady's Home Journal*, *Atlantic* and *Harpers* – eleven in all. *A Piece of Cake*, only 5,000 words in length, earned him a thousand dollars, which was a great deal of money then. In fact, he received nine hundred, the agent's commission being ten percent. This may sound rather a high price to pay, but Dahl believed that getting an agent is the first major hurdle for any aspiring writer. His payment then, when converted into today's values, represents more than most authors receive as their first advance against royalties from sales of their book. Further earnings from other stories published, and from his first book, *Over To You: 10 Stories of Flyers and Flying* (published in 1946), helped establish Dahl as a full-time writer.

Clearly, it helps to know someone in the literary world. In Dahl's case, he was lucky to have been approached by such a well-known author. It is strange, too, that Forester's own good fortune was based on a chance meeting with a London publisher, Michael Joseph, who took him on when all his previous sales had been pretty mediocre. Forester had been affronted by the chairman of Heinemann, his publisher at the time, who had ignored him at their party. So, preferring to be a 'big fish in a small pond', he joined the then embryonic publishing company of Michael Joseph Limited. I mention this only to show how small events can influence literary history. If Forester hadn't been looking for another publisher; if he had failed to become a bestselling author with Michael Joseph; if he had not set out to meet Dahl; would Dahl have become an author of bestsellers? And, as events turned out, most of Dahl's adult books were published by Michael Joseph Limited. The world does seem to be very small at times.

> Had I not met Forester, I would never have dreamed of writing. I had read almost every classic by the age of fifteen and had become a lover of books. I used to wonder how anyone could write a 300-page book when it took me all day to write a two-page essay at school. What one forgets, of course, is that if you write a page a day for a year, you have your book. But it does mean that you have to keep your bum on the seat of the chair and get on with it.

If only all writers could have that sort of break – it is the substance of dreams. But Dahl told me that he never dreamed of becoming a bestselling author.

> No, emphatically no, but if I was dreaming about writing a bestseller today, I would say that a sex book is the answer, but it's humiliating to do so. I would never do so. I don't bring sex into any story except as a joke.

Early on in this period, during the war, Dahl turned his hand to writing a story for children, simply because he had run out of plots for short stories. From his imagination, he created a group of small people who lived on RAF fighter aircraft – it was they who caused the engine fires and crashes, not the Germans. It was published in *Cosmopolitan* before it was sold to Walt Disney. Disney was so impressed by the imaginative detail that his company agreed to make it into a full-length animated film. *The Gremlins* was destined to become world-famous, and as a result Dahl claimed to have passed the word into service slang, 'The gremlins have got into it' being the then buzz phrase for any unknown cause of malfunctioning equipment.

Dahl had his first book, a collection of his stories, published in the States, since his fame had started there. He remembered the day when the great New York publisher Alfred Knopf telephoned him. He was taking a bath in his little flat in New York. Bach was blaring from his gramophone when the bell rang – if it wasn't Bach then it was Beethoven (Dahl loved the great composers). He picked up the receiver, it was Knopf himself. 'I've just read your latest story in the *New Yorker*. If you've got enough for a collection, I will publish them.' He did, and the book *Someone Like You* was published in 1953. Dahl continued:

I never had a rejection, except of course the one time when the late Anthea Hastings of Michael Joseph Ltd, said 'no'. [I hadn't the courage to ask him which one that was – Anthea was my step-mother, and an extremely well-liked personality in publishing.] Anyway, it had already been published in the States.

Really, I am better known for my children's books than adult horror. There's over sixteen now, and in a recent trade journal I noted that seven out of the top ten children's books were mine. Lovely for me, but really rather horrid. I mean, what chance do the other authors have? In some parts of the world, Australia for example, the children don't want to read anything else.

So what have I got that other writers haven't? The intangible thing that you ask about. You know, I think it's unanswerable, and you'll get a lot of nebulous answers from others. I don't know why the others don't have it as well, but I think it has got to do with pace. I know that with children, you have got to hold their attention. Unlike adults' reading; to them you can say, 'Plough on through the first twenty pages or so, until you get into it.' With children, you've got to grip their minds straightaway. It's terrific, but much harder to write than adult fiction.

I've not lost my sense of fun either. I still shriek with laughter if anyone farts in the room and it's essential to retain this sort of humour when you grow older.

From other comments he made, I gathered that he thought most adult authors tend to underestimate children's powers of perception. They also misread their sense of humour, and find their cruelty incomprehensible. Not so Dahl. The young characters who populate his horror stories often delight in being rude, naughty, and rather nasty; they are sophisticated, yet enjoy the scatological. And his adult characters can be simply worse, revelling in being beastly to children.

Authors of children's books forget that youngsters feel things with a greater intensity than adults, and this makes them much more susceptible to the emotions of fear, happiness, disgust, hate or greed. So where did Dahl get his inspirations from for his sometimes emetic works? It's a question that many people put to him, and he had a quick answer.

Luck, you've got be lucky. I'm convinced you are born with it, though it's latent with many people for a long time. In my case, it wasn't until I had reached the age of twenty-six, and then I had this great bump on the head. But there's nothing very clever about the man himself in being able to perform these acts. Innovative plots are difficult to create, but good fiction demands good plots.

The bump on the head that he referred to was the legacy of that traumatic time when he crashed his Gladiator in the Libyan desert during the Second World War. It caught fire, too, but despite a smashed nose, and being badly burnt, he managed to crawl clear. This and his convalescence formed the turning-point in his life.

What Dahl did do, though, was to jot down the ideas that struck his imaginative mind. From these short cryptic notes, he would develop the marvellous stories that enthral readers all over the world. The message is clear: if you want to write similar stories then, like him, keep a small book and a pencil near you at all times!

I then turned to the subject of advertising. Why did he think his books had become so successful? Did advertising play an important part?

Well, I can only tell you about the children's books. Word-of-mouth recommendation plays an important part, but it can take some time to really become solid. Take, for example, *Charlie and the Chocolate Factory*. This was my second children's book. Sales of the first had probably been around 10,000 in the first year. Then came *Charlie* and sales for the first five years went roughly: 5,000, 15,000, 35,000, 80,000 and 100,000, all in hard covers; and *James and the Giant Peach*, the first book, took off on the back of *Charlie*.

More recently, the adult stories have been helped by the television series *Tales of the Unexpected*. But it's the children's books that I think will remain bestsellers. In my old age, I brood on this point, and I believe that twenty years after I'm dead, they will be very famous. Wildly famous, in fact.

Dahl did not feel inclined to disclose his global sales, but he had earned a fortune from his writing, and his books are still selling well. But which book had given him the most pleasure, I wondered?

By far the best, was *BFG*, then came *Danny, the Champion of the World*. Curiously, I don't get reviewed that often nowadays, and I don't worry. I'm doing quite well without them. But when my first books came out, one reviewer wrote 'and this man *can* write'.

Dahl, although far from being an ostentatious millionaire, was nevertheless quite a wealthy man. He employed a secretary who spent most of her time answering the mail. Unlike Catherine Cookson, who answers each letter, Dahl answered very few. He received much more mail than Cookson though, well in excess of 30,000 letters a year, mostly from children and teachers. Correspondence from schools and teachers was certain to get a reply; he emphasised that every school on his worldwide list was allowed one full reply a year. To spice the short replies, he would often include a little poem. He would change this verse every two months or so, and he recited the one he was using at the time I saw him:

> Dear children far across the sea,
> How nice of you to write to me;
> I love to hear the things you say,
> When you are miles and miles away.
> All children, and I think I'm right,
> Are nicer when they're out of sight.

This huge correspondence is a side of being a bestselling writer that is not often mentioned. It is a considerable responsibility; some take it seriously, others do not, but it strikes me that if I had written to an author, I would expect a reply. An efficient, and personal, correspondence routine seems to me to be important to the continuing success of such authors.

Those who know and love Dahl's work will recall that he did most of his writing in a small shed in his garden. I was lucky enough to be allowed through the famous yellow door and into his private domain.

It was not as I imagined. Only about twelve feet by twenty, the building was divided into two. Inside the door were a wood-burning stove, filing cabinets and golf clubs. The inner sanctum contained an ancient, and obviously very comfortable chair, with substantial arms across which Dahl laid his writing table. To his right, as he sat in the chair, was a filing cabinet and low table, with shelves to his left, and the floor was lino-covered. There was not much more room than that; definitely not enough room in which to swing the proverbial cat, I thought. The tall and narrow multi-paned window was covered with dusty polythene, casually hung, keeping bright sunshine out and, in winter, the heat in. But there was overwhelming evidence everywhere, of long hours spent ruminating over his plots. The walls and ceiling were covered with thick polystyrene sheets which had become yellowed from many hundreds of hours of cigarette smoke. His lair was far from tidy, and hanging from the ceiling over where he sat was an infra-red heating bar – clearly the room got very cold in winter. I could not see any evidence of modern technology either. So how did he write?

To my surprise, I discovered that he wrote in pencil. He would rub out single words, but start a new sheet if there were sentences that needed changing. His writing was quicker by then than it had been, taking him about a year to complete a book, but he told me that as he grew older he recognised good sentences more easily, and found dialogue very quick to put on to paper.

> You're bound to get more and more practised in saying what you want to say. Dialogue comes very easily. It's the easiest thing in the world compared to prose. That's why I don't have much time for the average playwright, apart from Ibsen and Shakespeare, that is. I really don't. I don't have much time for a playwright that can't write a book, because I don't think they can. A play is a piece of cake to write, if you can write dialogue, and you can write a plot. They get much lauded, everyone from Tennessee Williams to Pinter and Stoppard. I'd like to see them write a novel. They couldn't do it in my opinion.

* * *

Anyone who yearns to write fiction must wonder if there are any basic rules. Each author will of course have many and varying ideas as to what these should be. But Dahl, as a writer of fiction *par excellence*, set down seven basic qualities that any aspiring author should have.

1 You should have a lively imagination.
2 You should be able to write well. By that I mean you should be able to make a scene come alive in the reader's mind. Not everybody has this ability. It is a gift, and you either have it or you don't.
3 You must have stamina. In other words, you must be able to stick to what you are doing and never give up, for hour after hour, day after day, week after week and month after month.
4 You must be a perfectionist. That means you must never be satisfied with what you have written until you have rewritten it again and again, making it as good as you possibly can.
5 You must have strong self-discipline. You are working alone. No one is employing you. No one is around to give you the sack if you don't turn up for work, or to tick you off if you start slacking.
6 It helps a lot if you have a keen sense of humour. It is not essential when writing for grown-ups, but for children, it's vital.
7 You must a have a degree of humility. The writer who thinks that his work is marvellous is heading for trouble.

In addition to these tips I noted that Dahl worked to a strict timetable. He wrote for two hours in the morning. Then he would lunch, sleep for a while, and do two hours in the afternoon. Day after day after day. He had strong views on what to avoid, too, telling me:

> I'm quite sure that there are two enemies of fiction writing. The first is the intellectual, with which our universities – and the establishment in London – are filled.
>
> The other is pomposity; and I'm convinced that when a famous writer gets very famous, and grows a little older, pomposity sets in. That's why his work deteriorates as he gets older. I swear that fame breeds pomposity.
>
> One point you must include in your [that is, this] book, is that you should never meet your hero; in the arts it's a great mistake. When I first met Forester in America back in 1942, I was amazed. Here was the man who had written the best tales about the sea since Joseph Conrad. The tales about Hornblower were being avidly read the world over, but he appeared to me to be just an ordinary unpretentious and bespectacled man, in a plain suit, with nothing

that stood out stating that he was the world-famous writer. He was certainly not the character I imagined him to be.

Dahl had absolutely no time for writing schools. When I mentioned their role in the world of writers, he became quite agitated. In short, he despised them. He despised, too, those English writers who go over to the States and sit at some university, getting well paid and giving 'silly talks to eighteen year-olds'.

It is so hard to know who is going to be a writer and who isn't; and there's no way you can tell before the age of twenty, except for the facility with words. You can't tell about creativity. That's the technique.

So many people are taking up writing nowadays, it's just like those painters slaving away in attics. It's the same thing with books. The world seems full of people who write to me and say 'I want to be a writer'. They start doing this at the age of seven, and their teachers encourage them! If I write back, I say, 'Stop it. Learn a trade. If I was your age now, and in your position, I'd become a plumber, or an electrician, or a television repair-man. Then you can take up writing in your spare time; otherwise you will starve.'

Roald Dahl died in November 1990, at the age of seventy-four. His last book, *The Minpins*, a magical tale for children with an underlying 'green' theme, was published posthumously in 1991. It seems almost certain that his prediction will come true, and that he will be remembered – and admired – for his children's books for many years to come.

Paul Erdman

The Billion Dollar Sure Thing, The Silver Bears, The Crash of '79, The Panic of '89, The Last Days of America, The Palace, What Next? and others.

The American publishing company of Doubleday had sent me several contemporary press handouts about Paul Erdman, one of which proclaimed that 'Paul Erdman is one of America's most sought after economists'. Why I wondered? The handouts claimed that people actually take note of what he says and writes, that financial pundits take what he expounds very seriously. Clearly, he is an author of bestsellers with a difference.

He writes what he calls 'financial thrillers'; anyone who can accurately predict, as he did, a major crash in a nation's stockmarket, is almost bound to captivate the attention of financial 'experts'. For those not conversant with the money markets, he accurately predicted the colossal fall in share values in October 1987. Before the event, he made no secret of the fact that he was selling all his stockholdings. This public demonstration caused many more people than just the experts to sit up and take notice. Nowadays, people hang on his every word, and personal fortunes can often be made or lost from the very inflection of his voice.

To interview him, I travelled to San Francisco, where we lunched at one of the city's most prestigious hotels, the Huntingdon. Hitherto, I had held most of my interviews in the authors' homes, where they had felt relaxed and at ease. I need not have worried about this meeting either, for Paul knew almost everybody there.

Where, then, did he start his writing career? Born in Germany, he fled from there in the 1930's to Canada, where his schooling put him on the road to success. He explained:

> Yes, I was good at English, but I'll tell you what. I had been brought up in Great School, in Canada, and if you come from Canada at that time, then by definition you were better in English than anyone in the United States!
>
> I was also good at languages, I had six years of Ancient Greek, six years of Latin and was always rather adept at that. It's a game, languages, you know. I enjoyed playing that game . . .

I was also very good at mathematics, but that is another story. I remember when I sat the exams, you could walk out when you had finished, and I would finish a one hour paper after ten minutes!

Obviously then, he showed himself to be talented with figures, but did he ever believe that he would one day become a famous writer? Was he so good that he was encouraged by others to write?

No, no. I had no ambition whatsoever to be such, but I was, like, the editor of my Lutheran prep school newspaper, and editor of the Year Book. This was just because – I mean I was also Captain of the Debating Team. Perhaps that helped.

I also graduated *summa cum laude* from the University of Basle, where there was a certain, I guess you know, aura of qualification. Nevertheless I could have graduated the lowest qualification in that grading system, and if this 'professor' had insisted that it [his dissertation] would be published, it would have been published. I think, though, that this was not based on merit. It was a full doctorial dissertation, but it had to be condensed really for publication in this book form, because you have an awful lot of foot-noting . . . [It was entitled *Swiss-American Economic Relations*.]

I did get some flak on this, by the way. It was very interesting. The Federal Council, the seven-man council which runs the collective presidency of Switzerland, wanted to block the publication of this [the dissertation], or so I believe. Because there was certain elements of what they [the Swiss] had done in World War Two and subsequently, especially with the Americans trying to renege on deals, to cut with us. Most of which was not public knowledge and they certainly did not want it published – and my doctor father, to his great credit, said, 'I'll publish and you can be damned', which is what happened.

It sold out, but that does not mean much because they would only print two thousand, and one thousand nine hundred and ninety-nine would be bought by libraries, and my mother bought the other one!

No, I was never encouraged, in fact years later, after I had taken my degree in Georgetown, I decided to study in Europe. I went by sea, a ten-day voyage from New York to Le Havre; the North Atlantic weather was perfect. All you do is eat and drink all day.

On one occasion, I picked a good deck-chair, and the husband half of a couple next to me was a literary agent and so I thought, well, I mean, this is the time to peddle my memories . . .

He said, 'Wait until you are forty and know something, then write something', and he was absolutely right. That's almost the cliché, but that's the first time anybody had told me that, and I thought, what the hell, here I am, twenty-four, and on the marvellous liner, heading for Le Havre. I mean, there's a budding Hemingway here somewhere.

He smashed that daydream, and I think that's the only time I have ever, as they say in America these days, been verbalized.

Erdman's early career seems very different from those of other authors. For a start, he was adept at mathematics, a subject in which many writers are weak. Then, strangely, the publication of his dissertation did not encourage him immediately to start upon his first 'bestseller'. Most biographical accounts of Erdman record that his first foray into writing was with *The Billion Dollar Sure Thing*, but his first book hardly ever gets a mention.

One of my lasting impressions of this financial genius is that he displayed such a casual attitude to writing. He almost gives the impression that he is totally unaffected by all the fuss, and it is not until you read just how much he is earning from writing that you realize the size of his readership. In February 1987, the *Financial World* reported that he was earning anything from $500,000 to $1 million from each of his books. They even quoted him saying: 'I'm now making more than ever. This one, *The Panic of '89*, will earn me a minimum of $2 million.'

That may sound rather blasé, but then he has always talked in millions, no matter what the currency. Bibliographical sketches all mention his career in banking, so to talk in such terms seems quite natural. However, the amounts compare less favourably with the earnings of such authors as Barbara Taylor Bradford and Jeffrey Archer.

Erdman's own description of his career is remarkably candid:

I wrote a similar book, but in German and after that, I went on to the Stafford Research Institute out here [California] and used to write little essays on what your parents are going to look like in twenty years and stuff like that . . . Then I started my own bank in Switzerland and all that old story where I end up in gaol!

I'd better explain. In the fall of 1970, in Switzerland, where there is no habeaus corpus* (we Anglo Saxons enjoy that privilege, but there you don't), I was stuck there for a while – nine months, in fact. This was in 'investigative incarceration' and there was no way to get out at

---

* A writ of habeas corpus orders anyone who detains a person in custody to produce – literally 'have the body' – the accused in court. Thus habeas corpus prevents people being imprisoned on mere suspicion, or left in prison indefinitely without trial.

all. My embassy tried and my contact said, 'Look, Erdman, confess to something and we'll get you out. You are a young kid . . .'

Are you kidding? So there I was, and I thought to pass the time, I'd write something, such as I'd done earlier. These two books about economics but, of course, you don't have research facilities in gaol, even in Swiss gaols. So I gave that up.

Then I thought about some of those ideas which I had had in the economic realm; for example, as a result of the Vietnam War which we had just gone through, the inevitable outcome would have to be a decline in the dollar and a rise the price of gold. I took some of these themes which had never really been addressed in action and put them in a novel and that was precisely the origin of it. The motivation was simply boredom in gaol.

Only because of these peculiar circumstances, where you have literally nothing to lose, you can't make a fool of yourself, nobody is going to read it, I had a go. I would never have attempted to write a novel, because all of us grow up reading novels and you have enormous respect for people who do that.

I'm much too much of a realist, and I know that the odds on somebody like myself, in those circumstances, having a novel published are, I would say, a million to one. Maybe more than that. No, it was just a way to pass the time.

Without wishing to appear cynical, I wondered if the thought had ever struck him that it might have been quite difficult for him to return straightaway to the world of finance after having been imprisoned on suspicion of fraud, and that writing might therefore have been a welcome occupation and an alternative source of income. I also wondered how his incarceration in a seventeenth century dungeon in Basle ended? Was there a court case, or did the authorities give up their investigations?

Well, I subsequently got out of there with the help of some friends and governments, and a couple of years later, I was sentenced *in absentia* to nine years in gaol over there.

The charge was fraud, not fraud that I stole anything, but fraud that the balance sheets of my bank did not reflect reality. This was because my commodity and foreign-exchange dealers had suffered losses which they kept in the drawer and which were not reflected in the balance sheets. In essence, this amounts to deceiving the public of its money.

You know, because of the immense amounts that can be involved the penalty rises with the value. For 20,000 francs, you get like three months, if it's 50,000, you get half a year; if 50 million, the sky's the limit!

Life for him was anything but daunting. Paul went on to describe his experiences 'inside', which completely disabused me of my understanding of these institutions. His single cell had a bath, and he was allowed to have his typewriter so that he could write his 'scribblings'. He could order any meal from any restaurant and have it delivered, provided he paid for it, and he had wine from his cellar. He was also able to keep himself fully informed, for he had *The Times*, *Financial Times* and the *Herald Tribune* delivered, and he had television and radio as well; in fact, he could obtain anything that he needed, if he could pay for it.

* * *

When he finally got out of prison, presumably when the investigations were complete, he eventually moved to the United States of America, but what happened immediately after his return to freedom?

A friend of mine, one of the famous art dealers in Switzerland, had a marvellous villa on the hills overlooking Lugarno, and he said (and we never stay at people's homes, I don't like that), he said, 'Look, we have this place, we have servants and everything. Why don't you go down there and get over this thing?'

So down we went [Paul and his wife, Helly] and after a couple of weeks, we got a phone call down there from the head of the *Wall Street Journal* in Europe. I'd been feeding him material for years and he said, 'I'm headed for New York with my wife Margaret and I hear that you've been "scribbling away at something".'

I asked them to join us for dinner that Saturday up at this villa. There was some sort of village festival on that weekend; Italian type of thing, on the church square with lots of heavy wine and sometime during the early hours the subject turned to my 'scribblings' and he said, 'Well look, I'm going in to see Charlie Scribner [the New York publisher] shortly and whatever you have got, I'll throw the transcript at him.' So we xeroxed the thing the next morning and he took it to New York.

In the interim I moved to England, moved to Buckinghamshire and got a phone call one day from Scribner's in New York, who said they were interested but would like to see more.

They were very encouraging about this, so I did write more, and got this thing up to the halfway point and sent it over there. Then the President of Scribner's ends up on my doorstep three days later and said 'We'd like to buy this thing', and gave me a very minor advance of $5,000. So I finished this up, and then things started to happen.

That was in the spring of 1973. Then there was an agent in London called Molly Watters, she had heard about this and came to our house in Gerrards Cross, in Buckinghamshire.

She went away and flogged these rights to France, to *Paris Match*; to publishers in Germany and Italy, before it had come out anywhere. Then it came out in New York and hit the bestseller list within four weeks, and stayed on for quite a while. I forget how long, but it went to number one actually for a week, I think. It must have been on the list for twenty or thirty weeks. There we were and all thanks to Ray Vicar, the chief correspondent for the *Wall Street Journal*.

The reason why this book, *The Million Dollar Sure Thing*, grabbed so much attention at the time lay in the basis for the plot. Erdman's theme was international intrigue in the aftermath of the Vietnam War, and especially attempts to influence the price of gold and the value of the dollar. In reality, both had hit extremes of value in the year the book came out. The novel appeared to be very close to the truth and, in addition, timing, as other authors have established, is all-important to success.

As already mentioned, Paul's advance against the future royalties of *The Billion Dollar Sure Thing* had been only $5,000, but with the rights sales in Europe and the book's instant appearance on the bestseller lists, he would have recovered the advance and started earning more royalties very quickly. Whereas $5,000 would have been great news to most aspiring authors, it has to be remembered that Paul Erdman was one of Europe's highly paid executives. He told me that at the time he was earning something between 250,000 and 300,000 Swiss francs a year (about £115,000 to £140,000 nowadays).

Describing himself at that time, and perhaps in an attempt to justify such earnings, he reminded me that he had a PhD in economics, had founded a bank and had gained, for an American, an enormous amount of financial experience in Switzerland.

Now, though, he had suddenly become an established author and was, no doubt, tempted to write another book.

It was intended to be a one-shot deal that had been thrust on me by circumstances. As I said, I was doing it out of boredom and all of a sudden I was encouraged to finish the sucker and so, well, I thought, well, why not?

In fact, I only finished this thing because I was supposed to go on a long extended trip through the Middle and Far East and I remember how my wife Helly said, 'Look, if you do that, you'll never finish this thing. Right. Stay home and finish it.'

She helped me then, and helps me now. In two ways. Firstly, she reads it, and I trust her judgement; if she says it's good, I go on. If she says it's bad, I say 'What the hell do you know?' And go back and forget it.

Secondly, we did not have word processors then and I type, but not well. And so she would always retype it.

With *The Billion Dollar Sure Thing* a bestseller, was he asked to write another immediately?

Yeah. *Silver Bears* with Scribner's, but another publisher, Pocket Books, picked up the paperback rights on that one. I liked this book, and I thought it was funny, you know? And very light-hearted and amusing.

So, granted that, in the financial world, he was quite well-known, and with *The Billion Dollar Sure Thing* a success, did Scribner's have to promote him and *Silver Bears* – with television, radio interviews, book signings, and all the other activities of the bestselling author?

Well, Pocket Books was and is part of Simon and Schuster, and they were becoming the big boy on the block. Public relations and marketing are important and Scribner's being a small house, with a great literary tradition, has not got a great marketing tradition. Pocket Books fed them on the first book, I think, with 75,000 or 100,000 bucks, which was a lot of money then, just to market this thing. This impressed me and that's why subsequently I switched from Scribner's to Simon and Schuster.

*　*　*

I am always fascinated to find out whether authors who suddenly find fame and fortune (well, relatively speaking in Paul Erdman's case), bother to keep all the press cuttings and memorabilia?

No. I used to have a big cardboard box. Helly always used to ask, 'Why do you keep those things?' I really don't know. Everybody else keeps scrap-books, at least I can have a cardboard box. And about five years ago, we burned the box, because, I think, we needed the room. Now we never keeps reviews, we burn them.

Today we have computers which store all this stuff, so you don't need my box.

Reviews are important, depending on where they come from and who writes them. If it is somebody that you know, with some repute, you should pay attention. If it's good, I wouldn't pay too much attention, but if it's bad, or it includes some suggestions as to what you might consider doing next, you should listen to that. No doubt about it. Just to say that all reviewers are out to get you, are bad, is nonsense.

Other authors I have interviewed disregard reviews, though, if they are honest with themselves I am sure they would agree that this form of publicity can be very hurtful to the ego.

What are Erdman's views about other methods of promotion, then?

I think there are two phases of this; if one does not lead to the other then forget it. First, you do radio and television interviews, and that should promote word of mouth. I'm sure you've heard this a million times. If word of mouth does not pick up on that then forget it. You are flogging a dead horse.

But he started his writing career as a well-known banker, even if one forgets the 'fame' of having been in gaol. Surely that gave him a head start?

Absolutely. Especially, not only as a financial man, but in gaol. In Switzerland, it is a very sexy concept. It was a prime reason, but I don't know whether it's *the* prime reason.

I would be fibbing if I didn't agree that I had acquired a certain notoriety. And all . . . I remember this, though it was a long time ago. Financial people never went to gaol, you know, and this guy had not only ended up in a Swiss gaol, but had a bank, he must really know something.

I know my stuff in this field. It was like you have seen with Clancy [Tom Clancy - my interview with him is in Part 3]. He is a man who knows military hardware and his readers sensed this. And they said, 'Look, you've got to read this guy. He knows what he's talking about; knows his hardware.' And that is what has happened here.

Helly agreed. However, she added that reading about her husband's experiences in gaol had hurt. As to Paul being a full-time writer, rather than a financier, he thought:

> Being a writer was much easier. You don't have to be responsible for employees; you don't have to be responsible for other people's money either and you don't have to answer to a board of directors. As a writer, you answer only to yourself.
>
> If somebody screws up, it's only your fault! The only time you suffer, as a writer, is when you are too lazy to see that you do what you are supposed to do.
>
> I write, for example, when I'm in the mood and when I have a streak, and when the mood passes . . . I write about three or four pages a day, which is nine to twelve hundred words. This doesn't seem much but you have to rewrite the piece at least ten times!
>
> I don't know where I read this, but somebody said . . . 'you only have so many books in you', and he was suggesting twelve. I don't know who that was but I think there is something to that. You probably only have so many novels in you because your life experience only has been that broad and deep, or whatever, to allow you to write that many. I suspect a dozen is maximum. I would think that the total is closer to eight or nine. So I would suspect that I am getting close to that limit.

An interesting view, but as can be see elsewhere in this book, there are many authors who have produced more than ten top-selling novels. Each to our own aspirations, I thought. Our conversation then turned to that important, and often taxing question as to what title to give your work. Paul was very succinct:

> A bad title can hurt you, and a good title can help you somewhat. *The Crash of '79* was a uniquely good title. But titles do not good books make.

A large portion of Erdman's fame rests with the fact that he has succeeded in accurately foretelling developments on the stock market. I wondered if that was where he saw his future, leaving pure novels of financial adventure behind?

> Yeah. I think people expect mainstream Erdman. As my publishers, Doubleday, said, 'it's international, it's economic and it's financial.'

And it can or cannot be futuristic, but I think the futuristic element is not necessary.

For my next novel, I'm going to turn to the past; yes, it's going to be international, and yes, it's going to be on economics and finance, but it's going to deal with the latter years of World War Two.

It's a kind of financial Ludlum! [Robert Ludlum – my interview with him is in Part 3.] So I don't think it is going to be too useful, as my other books are. Universities use my books a lot, especially in the US. I suspect this book will be used a lot because I know this part of history extremely well, and very few people in the US have a clue about it.

Given that Paul is a man of finance, I thought he would, like Jeffrey Archer (see Part 3), know exactly how many copies of each book had been sold. But I was wrong:

Well, *The Crash of '79* was by far the most successful. If you take just the hardcover and paperback editions – worldwide, about five or six million. I have no idea just what the global sales are, though.

All my books have gone into German, French, Japanese, Portuguese, Spanish, Swedish, Turkish and Greek – twelve languages in all.

Each author has his or her favourite title, one that was easiest to write, or that secured gratifying reviews and subsequent sales, or that they just like the best. Paul is no exception, for he told me that out of seven or so thrillers, his favourite was *The Crash of '79*, and he enthused at length about the fun he derived from writing it. Nevertheless, he was remarkably vague about his successes and the numbers of books sold.

I would say that the sales outside the States, at least in volume terms, are greater than within, you know, sometimes they run to thirty or forty thousand in hard cover, and then the soft cover is pretty big too, especially in Germany and Italy – and in most of Latin America.

Silver Bears has been made into a film, yeah, and with Michael Caine in the lead. And I've got two 'in the works', with *The Billion Dollar Sure Thing*, and in Italy, *The Palace* is being optioned with a lot of foreign money here in the United States.

They did give me a lot of fun, of course; Michael Caine became a good pal and the producer of that one wants to get involved in *The Palace*. I was happy about most things, the casting was terrific, the plot was a little bit garbled but it doesn't matter, and good photo-graphy.

I didn't go to the première – I was doing something else in Europe and I was supposed to come to LA for it – not out of any pique, but it was just something that didn't quite work out.

If, as he said, he thoroughly enjoyed writing and the subsequent results, did he write what he wanted to, or what he believed the public, and the film moguls, might want?

No, I write what I want to write. I write what I think has 'legs'; in other words, a story which can end up as a full-fledged novel, so it has to have a story with sufficient strength of its own, with sufficient opportunity for sub-plots and so forth . . .

But in taking his story and developing it into a novel, was he aware of any weaknesses in writing, and if so, did he take these into account? He grinned:

Yeah. I have many weaknesses. I mean, God's gift to the literary world I am not. I think my primary weakness is character devel-opment; where there is a certain set of standards, I would say that one expects characters to be developed much more fully than mine are.

So when he planned his books, did he do so in great detail, or just take a theme and go for it?

Neither. I want to know where it starts, the beginning, the middle and end. A two-page memo to myself suffices for that, but then when I write, if I'm smart, instead of sitting down and waiting, like you're suggesting, the better way to do it is to take a shower and then get up, write yourself the outline for the day so you have your two-page memo, the beginning, middle and end, but also the sequences you outline.

This, I thought, sounded like advice to others.

I've never given advice to people. I usually say forget about it. That's sounds crass, but I'd forget about it. Unless somebody, someone with real brains and experience in the publishing field, suggests it, forget about it.

If somebody writes something, the first ten pages will tell you whether it's there or not. Don't you agree? If it isn't, don't push it, because you probably have not got it.

To write, I think you have to be gifted a bit. To write is not something you learn at Iowa State University, it is something you are able to do, but on top of that, increasingly, you have to know what you are writing about. The traditional American novel, about the professor in the small college in New England who, you know, starts to screw his secretary, that doesn't suffice any more.

I think it helps to have enough money because then you can write when you choose and you are not under the gun.

I think you have to produce these things at your leisure, but if you do that you'll write a book every hundred years, so there have to be incentives, but not just to make money. That might sound idealistic...

I believe that he is right, that authors must have the incentive to finish their work, but the reasons why people want to write in the first place are numerous. Other writers have suggested that what I next asked Paul is important for the would-be author: did he think that anyone who wants to write has to do something else for a living? Does that help?

No. I think that hinders. I think that if you want to write, you have to be able to get up in the morning, thinking full-time about that novel, in your mind's eye. You are seeing the scene developing. If you have a business on the side you can't do that. So I think that is an enormous disadvantage to have to be doing something else to make money.

So I posed my last question: what was the key to the success of his books? Was it perhaps the financial uncertainties of the future?

No. I think it's the way you tell the story that sells. And my stories are about a world which is very intriguing, a world of high finance, and a world of intrigue involving the names that they read about, say, in the newspapers every day, the Rockefellers, the Kissingers, the heads of these big banks; and in my case, they are told by a guy who knows these people.

Write what you know about. That is sound advice, but how does a science-fiction writer cope? How can he know? This was one question that I had in mind when I met the next author.

Alan Dean Foster

The Tar-Aiym Krang, Bloodhype, Icerigger, Splinter of The Mind's Eye, Nor Crystal Tears, Voyage To The City Of The Dead, and novelizations for *Star Trek Logs, Dark Star, Clash of The Titans, Krull, The Last Starfighter* and *Aliens*, as well as more than fifty-five other science-fiction novels. Worldwide sales in excess of ten million.

Alan Dean Foster lives in the USA, but in Arizona rather than amongst the jet-setters of Hollywood, Florida, or New York. Both he and his very attractive wife, JoAnn, like their privacy, which is one reason that they live in the small historic town of Prescott.

Their modern and spacious home is built from bricks salvaged from a turn-of-the-century brothel. He keeps an assortment of pets: three dogs, six cats and a salamander, suggesting that this master writer of scary science-fiction is no average soul. He clearly prefers the quiet life, for he told me that peace is essential to allow his imagination to run free, and so to create those ingenious and original stories. Judging by the long list of titles he has had published he is one of America's top science-fiction writers.

Unlike many of the other authors I have interviewed, however, he started writing at twenty-two, and has continued on steadily ever since. He was never destined to begin his career as a part-time writer, as most of the other authors have done.

With over eighty books published, he still does not claim to rank amongst the top contemporary bestsellers. Facts suggest otherwise. The majority of his titles average approximately 150,000 sales, and that's just in the USA. Nevertheless, he remains a very modest man, and eschews most of the trappings of stardom.

Alan and his wife were kind enough to make the two-hour drive all the way to the nearest large city, Phoenix, to meet me for lunch and, suitably refreshed, we began to talk about his enormously successful career and how he had become a writer. I also, of course, wanted to know just what made science-fiction his main choice as a subject. His formative years really did play a major part in shaping his career, and in choosing his subject, as he explained:

> If you think about childhood, a lot of things that happen then eventually make an appearance in your work one way or another,

and often in surprising ways. For example, I was a big dinosaur fan when I was a kid. Now dinosaurs have kind of come full circle, popularity-wise, and I suspect that my descriptions of alien creatures in alien worlds has to do with my fascination as a child with a world that once was.

Also, as a kid I was the proverbial skinny egg-head, yesterday's term for the more contemporary 'nerd'. As one of the underdogs, I always rooted for others like myself, whether they were human or otherwise. So when I began the series of books known as the *Universe of the Commonwealth*, I placed among a number of other intelligent alien races I invented, one patterned on oversized insects. These Thranx turn out to be our best friends, 'out there'. They are a reflection of one of my favourite literary devices, which involves turning the expected into the unexpected. Mankind has been warring with insects ever since we've been farming; giant bugs are a staple of cheapo Hollywood horror films, and so I thought it would be interesting if among all the intelligent species we might encounter, the one's it turns out that we get along with the best resemble our most persistent ancient enemies.

All that arises out of my being on the side of the underdog as a child.

Another childhood influence, and a particular powerful one, came from reading the works of the great American comic book writer and artist, Carl Barks. Barks created Uncle Scrooge, the only senior-citizen hero in the history of comic books (as opposed to the daily newspaper strips). While my adolescent contemporaries were eagerly devouring the superhero exploits of the likes of Superman and Batman and the Flash, I never saw the point in rooting for someone who already had super powers.

Scrooge McDuck, on the other hand, is a seventy year-old short person with feathers. His vision is short and so he has to wear glasses. He walks with a cane and suffers from a variety of old-age ailments, from bursitis to lumbago. Yet in spite of these handicaps, he travels all over the world looking after his assorted business interests, has marvellous adventures, and through the strength of his will and intelligence, always outwits (never outmuscles) the bad guys. Not only is he a hero who wins by using his brains, he's an *old* hero.

What I drew from this, was that old age is not to be feared – quite a lesson for a pre-adolescent. As a result, it strongly affected the portrayal of older characters in my own work. I like to think they're less stereotyped, more active, more involved in advancing the plot as opposed to standing around like antiquated window dressing.

That comment struck me as a powerful argument for letting children read as many comics as they can get their grubby little hands on. Other authors were not so candid about their experiences, but Alan, I am happy to report, still has many of those comics carefully stored away.

I'll give you another example, one that to my knowledge no one has ever done a paper or thesis on. In addition to Bark's work, I was also very fond of the *Tarzan* comic books that were beautifully drawn back in the fifties. In the back of each of these comics was an ongoing filler series called *Brothers of the Spear*. I don't know who created it, or drew it, or whatever, but it dealt with the lives of two brothers in ancient Africa. One brother was black and the other was white, a discrepancy my youthful self never questioned. They were entirely equal: both were married, and so forth.

I lived in and grew up in an all-white society, in the San Fernando Valley section of greater Los Angeles. As a young child I never had any idea that there was any difference between people just because they were of different colours, and I suspect that this comic book series was largely responsible for that. It was a quietly subversive comic epic. I often wonder how many offspring of bigoted families grew up unprejudiced, or at least with their parents' beliefs challenged, because as children they read that particular series.

As to the origins of my interest in science-fiction, my father and my uncle (the noted television producer Howie Horwitz) always read the stuff. The books were lying around the house. Their covers held an early fascination for me. Having read it from an early age, when I started trying my hand at fiction, it was one genre (though by no means all) that naturally attracted me. My early efforts were very imitative, and perhaps to a certain extent some of the work still is. It would depend on the critics you talk to.

All artists borrow, consciously or unconsciously, from their predecessors.

The first science-fiction book I remember reading was the Isaac Asimov short story collection *Nine Tomorrows*. The second was the juvenile *The Space Ship Under the Apple Tree*, at age eleven. And there were many, many others. I also remember A. E. van Vogt's *The World of Null A*, when I was eleven, and setting it aside as too complex to read.

Science-fiction novels and comics were not the only major influence during his childhood. He had the natural fears of most children, and he enjoyed going to the cinema, so films, too, made their mark – and one of them more than any other:

> Oh, yes, it's true that I used to fear such things as dark corners. My over-active imagination was always filling them up with childhood nasties. Interestingly, very little frightened me that I could see. So the one film that really terrified me and left me watching my bedroom window for months afterwards was one of the greatest science-fiction films of all times, MGM's 1956 production of *Forbidden Planet*. The monster in it, the 'monster from the id', is more not there than there. I feared, you understand, that which I couldn't see.
>
> Nowadays I enjoy walking about at night, and I'm not afraid of things that go bump in the dark. One other thing I don't care for are parasites: again, because you can't see them. That's why I worry about when I'm travelling in places like south-eastern Peru or Papua New Guinea – not jaguars and snakes and army ants, all of which I'm quite fond of. Exotic and alien, you see.

In an interview he gave to *Contemporary Authors* some years ago, he amplified the reasons for these views but with the benefit of hindsight, he added:

> There are a number of reasons why I write primarily (though not exclusively) science-fiction. Science-fiction is the only branch of contemporary literature that cares about and deals with what's going to happen tomorrow. It is also the only genre with absolutely no restrictions. The writer of speculative fiction can do anything, absolutely anything he or she wants. The only convention is that there are no conventions. Science-fiction doesn't attract writers; it seduces them. Total creative freedom, that's very seductive.

So what were the early signs that he was destined to become a writer? What gave him the confidence to start?

> I'm not sure that I was ever that confident. It was just that writing was something that I'd always been good at. When I was in High School, all the other kids preferred multiple choice or true/false tests. I was literally the only one I knew who preferred and even enjoyed essay testing.
>
> So we know there was something out of the ordinary right there. At university I had planned to become a lawyer, but in my senior

year at the University of California at Los Angeles [UCLA], I discovered their world-class film department. I found out that I could amass credits for watching movies. You go and watch Charlie Chaplin for four hours and they give you four credits.

At the same time, almost as a lark, I took some film and television writing courses because I'd always been good at writing and I thought they would offer a few more easy credits. They did. While other students laboured over the class assignments, I found them absurdly easy. While the others took a semester to write and refine thirty minutes of screenplay, I knocked it out in two weeks and took the rest of the time off. I can't explain this – it was just a natural ability I had, the way others are good at the high jump or working out difficult math problems.

I was also very adept at and interested in the natural sciences: anything that didn't involve too much math. Biology, zoology, and the like. Same for social studies, literature – anything that demanded a lot of reading and memory work. I was also good at public speaking, and sampled a lot of diverse subjects: everything from microbiology to fencing. I think you'll find that writers who favour science-fiction all tend to be, to a greater or lesser degree, polymaths. They're interested in everything. You have to be, if you're going to be skilled at inventing believable alternate worlds.

I was drawing pictures of rocket ships when I was seven years old and originally thought of becoming a rocket engineer. It was very disheartening to discover early on that in order to work in that field you need a certain, shall we say, minimal grounding in more than basic math.

I was also told from a very young age that I was a good writer. My work was often selected to be read aloud in class. But as to thoughts of actually basing a career on it, it never occurred to me that such a thing existed in the real world. Nor was I encouraged, beyond generalized classroom praise, to pursue the notion. All the scholastic aptitude tests that American children are required to take in school said I should become – you guessed it – a lawyer. My practical parents pointed me in that direction, and we even had lawyers in the family. Your choice was simple: doctor or lawyer. Since I didn't much care for the sight of blood, I decided to become a doctor.

Sorry – early and old joke!

I had already been admitted to the University of Southern California Law School as well as a couple of others, but I also, again almost as a lark, applied to the graduate film school at UCLA. No one was more surprised than I was, when I was granted admission. To this day I don't know why. I imagine someone saw something in my written application. If I hadn't been admitted, I would have gone on to law school and perhaps never have become a writer.

While churning out screen plays to satisfy the requirements for my Master's degree, I thought I'd have a little fun and try my hand at prose. So I did a handful of short stories and, lo and behold, the twelfth one sold. Meanwhile, none of the screenplays were attracting any professional interest. After graduating and losing my scholastic military deferment (this was during the Vietnam war when conscription was still in force), I joined the Army Active reserve. I figured that when I got out of my six months active duty I'd go to law school and that would be that.

But a funny thing intervened. I had written a novel, *The Tar-Aiym Krang*, and much to my surprise, it sold on its third submission, to no less than Ballantine Books. The book incorporates some wise suggestions from the editor of the first market I submitted it to. That would be John W. Campbell, the editor of the then premier SF magazine, *Analog*. Betty Ballantine, who finally bought it, published the manuscript pretty much as it stood. Meanwhile, I'm thinking to myself, 'Well, gee, I'm one for one at this, and I'm only twenty-two'.

So I thought, why not take a serious crack at this endeavour for a year and see what happens? I kind of muddled along for five or six years doing a book a year for advances running around $1,500 – 2,000 a book. Throw in a couple of short story sales, two years writing public relations, then a part-time teaching job at Los Angeles City College, and I survived pretty well. After that, everything kind of snowballed. So I wasn't an instant success in the sense that I had a lot of money right away, but I did sell right from the start.

Alan was extremely lucky in having his first book published, for he did not have an agent at the time. However, as he said, he did have one publishing contact, one of the more important editors of American science-fiction, John W. Campbell, and he had previously published one of Alan's short stories. While he had rejected Alan's book typescript, Campbell repeatedly encouraged him in subsequent letters, finally writing, 'You know, I can't buy this book because my inventory is full for the next two years, but I think you've got a pretty good yarn here. I definitely think it's saleable.'

Encouragement is so seldom given freely to those wishing to become professional writers, but when it is given it can be doubly effective. Coming from such a luminary of the science-fiction world, it made Alan feel most encouraged. He didn't have to rely on his own judgement, but an editor's. As Alan added: 'It's like with children, you know. Oftentimes, encouragement means so much more than criticism'.

His search for a publisher followed a very orthodox sequence, one which millions of would-be authors, without publishing contacts, follow.

> I got a copy of a magazine called *Writer's Digest* which suggested that I should put the typescript in a brown paper envelope together with a stamped self-addressed envelope, and submit it in that fashion. And that's exactly, perhaps naively, what I did. That's how I sold my first few stories and my first book.
>
> As I mentioned, I started writing screen and teleplays while at the UCLA film department, as a senior at university. That's what I wanted to do: write screenplays. Being naive, I thought, you simply write something good, and somebody buys it, and you go and make a movie. Needless to say, that's not quite how it works. To find out how it works, read William Goldman's *Adventures in the Screen Trade*, or John Gregory Dunne's recent *Monster*. But the world of film is a small one, and I'll tell you a story to illustrate just how small it is.
>
> The bulletin board at the film school was always full of hopeful notices and advertisements. One that caught my eye read 'Wanted – producer seeks writers to adapt property on spec [speculation – ie, no money]'. I knew nothing about the film business, but I did know that I was a prolific if untested writer, so I thought, sure! Why not? So I did a couple of spec screenplays, adaptations of a couple of Robert Bloch (of *Psycho* fame) short stories that this guy had somehow raised money to option. One of the screenplays nearly sold [to ABC Films], but when neither of them did, I forgot all about them, as well as the would-be young producer.
>
> Many years pass. I accept the job of doing the book version of a forthcoming film called *Alien*. And when I peruse the credits, whose name do I see listed as producer? Yup – the same young go-getter I did those ancient spec scripts for: Ronald Schusett.

Authors do not always have a happy time with the film world, as you can read elsewhere in this book. (See Joseph Wambaugh in Part 3.) Did Alan's affinity for film scripts lead to a good relationship with Hollywood?

> I did the treatment [the basic screen story] for the first *Star Trek* movie. It turned out to be an extremely discouraging and

disagreeable experience; it turned into the typical Hollywood writing-by-committee. The reason this is done is so that when the film becomes a success everybody, including the director's mother-in-law, can claim credit for it. But if it flops, eighty-three people can point their fingers at the poor, shivering writer and insist it was a bad script from the start and that they, with all their cumulative talent, couldn't save it. That's the Hollywood tradition. Writer's are considered a necessary evil, ranking somewhere between a tax audit and gall bladder surgery.

Unless you produce the film yourself (Joe Wambaugh knows only too well), you have no clout. Just as in any other business, only more so in films, those who sign the cheques have the power. Today, it's all investment bankers and accountants and dilettantes from other industries looking for fame, sex, and non-existent synergy.

I enjoyed teaching at LACC, but in teaching, you're always repeating yourself. There aren't many careers available where you have the choice of not repeating yourself. It's one of the greatest challenges in writing science-fiction. Many writers fail the challenge.

So I am always testing myself and trying new things, like my historical novel set in nineteenth-century New Zealand, *Maori*, or my as yet unsold novel set in contemporary Papua New Guinea, *The Last Paradise*. I firmly believe that writers who don't do this get bored and stale.

Returning again to beginnings: I had been writing stories and trying to sell them for months. At the time I was (and still am) a big fan of the writings of H. P. Lovecraft. So I wrote a long pseudo-story in the style of a Lovecraftian letter and sent it to August Derleth, the founder and editor of the small American publisher Arkham House. Sometime later I get back this odd letter that says, 'Read your story and would like very much to publish it in my next issue of the *Arkham Collector*.' This was his house's semi-annual literary magazine. This sent me rushing frantically to my files as I tried to remember what 'story' I had sent him. It was something I did purely for fun, and taught me a useful lesson. Everything I had been trying to write 'to the market' was going nowhere, while something I wrote out of love and personal interest sold immediately. It was published under the title *Some Notes Concerning a Green Box* and was actually my first sale, though a story I sold to Campbell at *Analog* appeared first.

Other stories appeared in journals, until he attempted that first novel. Alan was extremely fortunate, because with a firm base of several stories actually in print, he received an advance for his first book. Not much, even by the standards of the day, but $1,500 is always welcome and was worth more, of course, in 1971. *The Tar-Aiym Krang* was published in 1972 – the first of many.

Alan's big break did not occur immediately, which is hardly surprising. It did not happen, either, when his second book, *Bloodhype*, was published a year later. But his third effort was a different matter. In fact, he had a double stroke of good fortune:

> The first break, my big break, if you will, came with the publication of my third novel, *Icerigger*, which quickly sold something like a hundred and fifty thousand copies and made the genre's bestseller list. It surprised everybody including Judy-Lynn del Ray, who was then my editor at Ballantine Books (before the division was renamed Del Ray Books). It raised my credibility as a marketable writer much faster than it did my advances, as everybody ran around trying to figure out what had gone so right. A good deal of credit was given to the cover, by Dean Ellis. Eventually they reached the conclusion that maybe, just maybe, it was real good luck. For myself, I believe strongly in word of mouth among readers. No internet back then.
>
> Break number two came with the opportunity to do the novelizations (book versions) of the animated *Star Trek* TV series. These became the *Star Trek Logs*. Ten in all that made my name known to a much wider audience.

Star Trek spawned a cult following of ardent fans, and is if anything more popular today in its manifold incarnations than it was when the original series was on television.

The royalty payments for 'novelizations' are, however, very low, sometimes just half a percent of the cover price, so unless a writer is going to work on a project of the scale of *Star Wars*, or the *Alien* films, as Alan has, the chances of earning much are slim indeed.

> I've done spin-offs as well as straight novelizations. For George , I did the first *Star Wars* spin-off book, *Splinter of the Mind's Eye*. An original novel but set in the *Star Wars* universe. For that I received a higher royalty than I normally do for novelizations, because a great deal more original work was involved.

He had told me how he had struck lucky very quickly, by his own efforts, but surely, I asked, as soon as sales of his third book blossomed, he had a literary agent?

Actually, I obtained an agent on the basis of my first two book sales, before *Icerigger* appeared. I had two agencies for many years: one for media, another for print.

After I'd sold the first book, I thought it would be advantageous to get an agent, even though Betty Ballantine had already pre-bought my second. So I looked in the *Science-Fiction Writers of America Handbook*, found the agents who had the most clients within the field, and picked out the top two. One of them replied, we struck up a relationship, and she's been my agent ever since. In fact, it was something like seventeen years before we had any kind of written contract between us! That's Virginia Kidd. Through her, I obtained the media representation services of the Paul Kohner Agency in Hollywood. Today my media representation is through Matt Bailer of the William Morris Agency in New York.

Every writer needs help; agents certainly help by providing the contacts, but what help did he get from his wife JoAnn?

JoAnn gives me a great deal of help. She's even been directly responsible for a couple of stories (and was the genesis of the *Mad Amos* series). But her greatest assistance lies in providing me with the kind of support I need to be able to relax and write freely.

She does this by intercepting much of the outside world and taking care of the household as well as handling much general PR. Love and support is vital because, like so many writers, I'm not an easy person to live with. Very often, I'm not just living with my stories, but living in them. If I happen to be writing a comedy, like the recent *Jed the Dead*, then I can be joy to be around. But if I'm working on something like *Aliens*, then my moods can reflect that. She's very tolerant and understanding.

You know, the advantages of writing are obvious to most people, but the disadvantages are not. For example, you can never be free from what you are working on at the time, and you can never call in sick (who's going to replace you on the job?).

Surprisingly, JoAnn does not read any proofs, or even finished work. Maybe it's because, as she freely admitted, she is not a science-fiction buff. She quickly added though:

I read science-fiction a long, long time ago and I don't really read it at all now, but I do know what's going on with Alan's work. I mean, he tells me the things that are happening and sometimes he will just sit and talk to me, and say this is what's happening in the current story, is this what I'm going to do next. Sometimes I'm very opinionated and I say, no, I don't like that. He once suggested a gay unicorn as a character, which I didn't like, and said so. But he went ahead and used the idea anyway [in *The Day of the Dissonance*].

Without the help of another pair of eyes, I wondered how Alan coped with spelling. Authors, I said, often pass drafts over to their spouses for reading, and it is usually much easier for them to spot the obvious error. Alan interjected:

John Campbell once wrote saying that I was the most frustrating speller he'd ever encountered, because I will write so fast that sometimes I'd enter a word that was not misspelled, but which sounded similar yet meant something completely different in the context of the story. I drove him nuts. I can actually spell quite well, but not when I'm writing at full speed. Interestingly, this is one 'spelling' problem that contemporary computer spellcheckers can't solve.

Despite the fact that he was good at English at school, and later at university, had he felt the need to be taught the craft of writing once he had started to write novels?

Never. I never read one book on writing, nor did I take any courses beyond the screen and teleplay writing seminars at school. I never participated in any outside conferences or sessions, or belonged to any writing groups.

I taught writing for six years at college level, and the first thing I told my students when they came to class was that I could not teach them how to write. Sentence structure, grammar, elements of basic plotting, sure – but you can't teach *writing*.

That observation remained with me as I left Phoenix. In recording Alan's comments, I feel that they should go a long way towards encouraging other aspiring authors of science-fiction.

James Herriot

If Only They Could Talk, It Shouldn't Happen to a Vet, All Creatures Great and Small, Let Sleeping Vets Lie, All Things Bright and Beautiful, Vet In Harness, Vets Might Fly, Vet In A Spin, and others, including non-fiction such as *James Herriot's Yorkshire.* Over 60 million copies sold worldwide. Born in 1916, he died in 1995. This interview took place in 1987.

Back in England, Yorkshire was my next destination: the home of Britain's most famous veterinary surgeon, James Herriot. Our rendezvous, a hotel in Thirsk, seemed a long way off, and on my way I stopped in Scarborough on another errand. Once there, my errand done, a long cool beer seemed an attractive idea. The barman, being a chatty soul, asked me why I had driven up to Scarborough.

I muttered something about having to meet a vet. 'Oh,' he exclaimed before I had time to finish, 'you've come to see our Herriot. We *all* know him up here. He's done wonders for Yorkshire, and, thank goodness, the tourists are everywhere.' He continued without a pause for at least ten minutes, enthusing about Herriot's achievements. I hardly got a word in. Well, perhaps I should have known better.

The following morning, I set off early for Thirsk, for I have a poor reputation for keeping appointments and did not want to be late for this one. It was just as well that I did, for the route I had chosen turned out to be a very slow drive indeed. There were tourists everywhere – clearly the Herriot effect was in play.

Thirsk, when I eventually got there, was just as busy. James Herriot had suggested that we meet for lunch in one of the local hotels, the Three Tuns. The thought of lunch was very appealing, but I was a little apprehensive because such a famous writer would surely attract too much attention from tourists, and we could hardly have a sensible discussion whilst surrounded by an admiring audience.

How wrong I was. His arrival at the bar was ignored, and seemingly unnoticed by others; nevertheless we quickly adjourned to the restaurant, where a quiet corner table was found for us. As it turned out, I need not have worried about the curious.

He eschewed publicity, telling me with relish that he had turned down appearing on *The Parkinson Show*, not once, but twice. He also declined Terry Wogan's invitation, and prevented the recording of an edition of *This is Your Life* with the late Eamonn Andrews, having found out about the show before they approached him with that large 'Red Book'. Interestingly, too, he avoided interviews with the press; the exceptions seem to have been the *Chicago Tribune*, the *Yorkshire Post*, and more recently *The Sunday Telegraph*. There may have been others, but he claimed to have given very few interviews in his lifetime, having decided that once he didn't need them to help sell his books, he simply would not give them. He believed that in most interviews someone gets hurt, though, as he was quick to point out, interviewers had always been kind to him. He wanted, and he stressed the point, to continue enjoying his own unique lifestyle. His attitude will, no doubt, seem very strange and alien to many aspirant writers.

James Herriot had a good, if unspectacular, education; he went to Hillhead High School in Glasgow, and from there to the Glasgow Veterinary College. He chose to become a veterinary surgeon when, as a youngster of thirteen, he read a careers article describing a vet's life in *Meccano Magazine*. The description fired his imagination, and from that moment on he was determined to become an animal doctor.

He did not, however, strike me as one of those archetypal dedicated and determined men who set their sights on a goal and go all out for it. Very much the opposite: he was a most unpretentious man, so successful that he prized anonymity and privacy above almost everything. He revelled in his ability to walk about in public without being hounded by passers-by. He loved his work and even when he was in his early seventies, he continued as a veterinary surgeon – but for just two days a week, and then usually only at 'the surgery', where, apart from helping his son (also a vet)*, he dutifully 'signed' books. This can be quite a chore as, on occasions, up to forty or fifty people a day would ask for his autograph.

He needn't work at all, I thought. With, at that time, eleven major titles to his credit, and with translations in most European languages, as well as Russian and Japanese, he had achieved worldwide fame. The huge popularity of his stories had also resulted in a series of television programmes which have been, and are, shown repeatedly both here and in the USA. And there have been films made for the big screen, too. Why was it, then, I asked, that he had achieved so much success?

The one thing that I'm certain of is that I have had my share of luck.
Travelling on my rounds, from one farm to another, I used to listen

---

* Jimmy Wright is currently writing the official biography of his father.

to my car radio and to those excellent short stories broadcast by the BBC. They fascinated me. I often thought that I could write such stories, and mine would be just as interesting. I wanted to write, of course, like everyone else. And if I'd had one accepted, just one, of a few hundred words, I would have thrown my hat up in the air and claimed to be a writer. But it never happened.

To most people, writing letters is a tedious chore, but not to Herriot, I learned. In his younger days he wrote numerous letters home, and his father always enjoyed receiving them for their vivid descriptions of events and sights. Then one day his father suggested that since his letters were so good, he ought to think about writing a book.

Perhaps it was his father who sowed the seed. As Herriot explained, he thought he had to start somewhere, and writing short stories became his first goal. He was destined to write many adventure stories, aiming at getting them published in newspapers and magazines, or broadcast by the BBC.

They kept coming back with regular monotony and it's a terrible thing when you hear the postman pushing the rejected manuscript through the letterbox. It lands on the floor with such a sickening thud. Again, again and again, they were returned. I grew to hate that sound. And there wasn't one word of encouragement with any of them.

I realised that, though my style was improving, the subjects were wrong. So I returned to stories that I knew something about. When I rewrote them, and sent my first manuscript of a book off though, that was different. It wasn't immediately returned. Days passed; and the days became weeks, and still no rejection. I thought it must be under serious consideration, and I was delighted. But nothing of the sort. Eighteen months later, a reply came, 'Sorry, our lists are full, but we have sent it to our subsidiary.' Another six months went by, and then they, too, said their lists were full. Bitter, bitter disappointment. So I put the work back into my drawer and tried to forget all about it. I had tried to write and failed. As the months passed, my wife chided me to do as I had read and send it off to a literary agent. Well, eventually I did, and one week later, their memorable reply was, 'We'll have no trouble getting this published.' I had been lucky indeed, for my agent, Jacqueline Korn, had sent it to Michael Joseph Ltd.

An astute editor had spotted a similarity with Richard Gordon's *Doctor in the House*. There were similar anecdotal qualities but linked to animals, and books about animals always sold well. It was well written, too, and needed virtually no editing. He continued:

> When I reached fifty, I thought, being a veterinary surgeon is all very well. It's a decent living, but the hours are long, and it's a tough life. And not all farmers live up to their image of being very wealthy. It wasn't just the money earned by writing and the lack of money as a vet, but that came into it.

I suspected that, besides the long hours involved, the job was so physically exhausting at times that he didn't relish that sort of pressure for ever. And most people harbour the thought of doing something different at some stage in their lives. Perhaps, apart from the money, there were other motives for becoming a writer. He became nostalgic for a moment about his early days in practice:

> It was a funny time, you know. There were no antibiotics or modern procedures then. It was rather like black magic. I found it all very comical, and thought I ought to put it onto paper. I'm damned glad that I have, because those days have gone forever and will never come again. You know what's happened in the past. Surely we are all a bit apprehensive about the future? Not just for ourselves but for our families.

I soon realised that it was the past that fascinated him. He felt secure in thinking and writing about those times, which may explain why he once said:

> I wrote my books because of a compulsion to make some record of a fascinating era in veterinary practice. I wanted to tell people what it was like to be an animal doctor in those days before penicillin, and about the things that made me laugh on my daily rounds, working in conditions which now seem primitive. I suppose I started out with the intention of just writing a funny book, but as I progressed I found that there were so many other things that I wanted to say. I wanted to tell about the sad things too; about the splendid old characters among the animal owners of that time and about the magnificent Yorkshire countryside which at all times was the backdrop to my work.
>
> They say we should not live in the past and I have no reason to do so because I am still a practising veterinary surgeon, still enjoying life. But to me, my past is a sweet, safe place to be, and through the medium of these stories I shall spend a little time there now and then.

Many people are unaware, even today, that James Herriot is not the man's real name, he was born James Alfred Wight. Times have changed, but when he started to write, the ethics of the profession prevented veterinary surgeons from advertising their names. When he started to write short stories he used the surname Walsh, but in the list of registered veterinary surgeons he soon discovered many Walshes. Clearly, 'Walsh' was no good, but some time later, he happened to be watching a football game on television. Birmingham City were playing at home, one of the players was called Jim Herriot, which he thought sounded better as a *nom de plume*. On checking the list again, he found no such name – and so 'James Herriot' he became.

'How did your books start selling so well?' I asked. 'Your sales compare very favourably with those of Catherine Cookson, and Dick Francis.'

> Cookson. Ah, now there's a writer I admire and respect. But I couldn't write like her. She lives for writing. I do the exact opposite. When I was in full spate, I would arrive home late at night, probably from helping a cow to calve, sit down in front of the television [he worked with the set switched on; he liked to be with his family, not shut away in another room] and I squeezed my efforts into the last half hour each day. My job as a vet was an exhausting one; often twenty-four hours a day, seven days a week, with no Bank Holidays off, and often not Christmas Day, either. I have never written for more than half an hour in my life. Writing to me only occupies a teeny wee bit of my life. And to be truthful, I hate writing. I wouldn't like the idea of writing all day at all.

Like most successful authors, he read a lot, and in those early days he did read books on the art of writing. The best he recalled was *Sell Them a Story* by Jean Leroy which contained advice on the writing and marketing of short stories. (He has also been reported as having read other writers' handbooks though he didn't mention these when we met.) He told me he has little time for writing schools. The best advice he learned was to cut down on the adjectives and adverbs, advice which he followed in his first book; the one that lay languishing in the drawer for so long.

That book was *If Only They Could Talk*, published in 1970. It went on to sell millions. When it finally appeared Herriot was, of course, absolutely elated. He smiled broadly as he began to reminisce about those days. 'Nothing, but nothing, has ever equalled that time. It was a great thrill.'

With all the hype that there is in publishing today, it seems strange that there wasn't a launch party for his first book. No big celebrations: just the quiet publication of the work of a very modest vet. And he only got £200 as his first advance against royalties. Today it is very different, but at the time this was about average. Authors might then earn, on average, about £1,000 from a novel, which makes this sum look more realistic.

At first, sales of *If Only They Could Talk* were very modest. Michael Joseph had, in fact, only printed 3,000 copies; sales were slow, and it was touch and go as to whether the publisher would ever order a reprint. Months passed, then, as sales had improved, a reprint was ordered. Furthermore, the late Anthea Hastings, Herriot's editor, suggested that he should write another. In the meantime the publishers had sold the American rights to St. Martin's Press in America. They also believed the book to be a winner and, two years later, combined his second book, *It Shouldn't Happen to a Vet*, with the first to create *All Creatures Great and Small*. St. Martin's Press had, it seems, taken a gamble, sending the first chapter, bound up as a dummy book, to most of the important booksellers. Sales suddenly started to escalate: and what happens in America sooner or later happens here. In the next two years, greatly encouraged by the news of rapidly increasing sales, Herriot wrote *Let Sleeping Vets Lie* and *Vet In Harness*. Sales in this country started to rise too, and then all four books came out in paperback. It was like lighting the blue touch paper of a firework. Sales of all four books took off, and all of them began to appear in the bestseller lists. Herriot enthused:

> All down to the Americans, you see. That book sold millions, word for word, just as I had written it. The Americans are crazier about animals than we are, and anything that you write about animals is bound to sell. The sales are ten times better there than here, and the curious thing is that the short stories I had been writing, before I turned to books, were just that, stories.
>
> It wasn't until I had started to write about my job that my luck changed. There must be many potential books just languishing in drawers like mine.
>
> I'm not sure just how many sales have been achieved. Certainly they have been translated into every language you can think of; including Japanese, Russian and all the European languages. I have received a Golden Pan [an award from the paperback publishers, Pan Books, when one of their editions achieves 1 million copies sold] for each of the six titles, and since then, they have doubled their sales. So that makes 12 million; [plus] 500,000 for *The Best of James Herriot* and 800,000 for *James Herriot's Yorkshire* makes a healthy total. Then on top of these, there's the American sales.

After a moment's thought, he added 'Well, I suppose sales must have reached

20 to 30 million. Why don't you contact my agent?'

In all, he had eight humorous books published; three omnibuses and five children's books, *Moses the Kitten*, *Only One Woof* and *Bonny's Big Day* to name just three. These grew in popularity, with sales again rocketing in the States. Like most bestselling authors, his books are read all over the world, but when I pressed him about the total global sales, his response was very vague. I pointed out that as long ago as 1981 the national press had reported that his sales had exceeded 50 million copies. His vagueness was typical of such an unpretentious writer, but I was to learn from his agent, David Higham Associates, that world sales of his top-selling twelve books exceed 60 million copies, three-quarters of which have been sold in America.

Once the popularity of his books was established the film and television companies got to work, with the result that sales were further enhanced.

> The television series has been shown eight times round in the States, but when they were being made, I seldom got involved in the day-to-day filming, simply because I was too busy.
>
> I have one criticism of the films; they don't show Yorkshire in all its glory. Many of the scenes could have been taken just anywhere. Frankly, the first film could have been in the back streets of Halifax; even the actors asked the film crew to include the scenery. But it wasn't to be. The television series were much better, though – they showed the Yorkshire Dales as in my stories.

Is there, I wondered, a parallel here with actors who, when appearing with animals, often find that they are upstaged by them? Are the animals in Herriot's books better remembered than the author? I think not, for his books are not only funny, they are full of mistakes and disasters that beset the author and his human characters. The appeal to readers is vastly enhanced by the humorous, sometimes 'slapstick' descriptions of curing animals' ailments, but, as he said, 'there was an element of black magic in those early days' of veterinary surgery.

But on the subject of writing, he became more serious.

> You know, I timed my writing rather badly. The last Labour government [1974-9] cost me 83 percent of my income, which went in tax. [See James Herbert, in Part 3.] My accountant said at the end of it, 'You've written six books, five for the tax man.' He tried to get me to live overseas, and my wife and I even went over to Jersey for ten days. I had this awful claustrophobic feeling, but asked my wife 'How about it?' 'Give them the money,' she said. So I divided

everything by six and kept a sixth for myself, and forgot about the rest. That's stopped me from being very rich.

Given his income, I expected him to use some of the new technology for his writing. In fact, he used a typewriter. 'My handwriting is illegible,' he claimed. 'I'm totally non-mechanical, but everyone tells me that I should be using a word-processor. I could have done with one when I was writing full belt, but now I'm just doing a bit.'

All Herriot's fiction is based on his life and career, and is full of anecdotes about his experiences. But, as has happened to other authors, unless he changed his theme the public's reading taste may change and the demand fall away. Would he want to write about other subjects, I wondered?

No, I wouldn't like to write the pure pulp commercialism that is found on the bookstalls. That's not my style. I am writing another children's book, but they are really specially adapted stories, and they are selling extraordinarily well. And there may be others too.

* * *

Herriot admitted to having a terrible memory, at least in some respects. He could not recall what happened a week ago, but it was a very different matter when writing the past. He was able to recall all the roads, barns, cowsheds, and all the characters who worked on the farms, and as a writer he excelled at evoking people, places, events and atmosphere. He never needed to check which building was where, but perhaps this was fortuitous, since he did not believe in letting readers know, or even guess, the actual locations of his stories.

One aspect of Herriot, the writer, is that he very seldom did any research. All his best-known books are based on his own personal experiences and most of the stories are written exactly as they happened. However, in describing his characters he allowed himself a little licence in order to protect himself against any libel charge. Most of the colourful characters who feature briefly in the stories are dead, but there are always their descendants, who might be offended.

Local people were known, from time to time, to tease him by boasting that they knew who 'so-and-so' was or where 'such-and-such' a place lay, but he never admitted to any location or character. And, with a mischievous grin, he told me that he quite deliberately encouraged the locals to misdirect tourists. It was all part of the man's instinct for preserving his much-valued privacy, and the essence of his beloved Yorkshire.

Yorkshire will remain 'Herriot country' to very many people, but when our conversation returned to this subject, he became quite positive, if slightly rueful:

> The latest thing is a breakaway council; they want to call it the Herriot Council. When this became public, journalists rang me up to ask how I felt about this. 'What the hell do you think?' I replied, 'and don't put words into my mouth.' I spend most of my time trying to stop people cashing in on my name.

Despite the strength of his feelings, he has done much for Yorkshire. Many people, especially those in public office, say he has put the county onto the world scene. This was illustrated when, in April 1984, the Lord Mayor of Leeds awarded him the Yorkshire Salver 'for putting Yorkshire on the international map and bringing tourists, trade and employment as a result'. The list of awards doesn't stop there, however, and includes the OBE, to which, as J.A. Wight, he was appointed in 1979.

Herriot gained fame, money, official recognition, and above all else, great satisfaction from writing. But, I asked, if he had to sum up his success and provide tips for others, what would he say?

> There's a lot of luck in becoming a successful writer. I like a good read, and there are so many people who can write well. In those early days, I used to read Conan Doyle, Dickens and Hemingway with enthusiasm. I also enjoy reading theatre critics, for they write far better than I can. They express themselves so well. Above all, if someone wants to become a bestselling author, they must write, write, and keep writing.
>
> As I said earlier, I started writing short stories and at the time I was writing English like Macaulay's essays, with beautifully balanced sentences. I got that out of my system with the first book. I tried to develop a chatty, conversational style. Lightweight stuff. Once I got the hang of that, it just went.
>
> Don't use too many adjectives, that's important. And there's another little tip, which may not be the whole thing. Let the reader discover for himself. Don't describe too much. Don't say, 'He was a tall, fair-haired man', just say, 'he brushed his fair hair back off his forehead.' Corny, I know, but it illustrates the point. The reader likes to find the character out for himself.
>
> I had a classical education, which I think helped. It makes you reject the horrible things in your writing. But there have been a hell of a lot of writers who haven't been well educated. And it's better not

to be rich. A hungry writer is more likely to succeed.

You've got to want to write because no one has said before what you want to say; and only you have experienced it; and you believe that the stories are worth telling.

All of which is enough to give any writer, aspiring or otherwise, food for thought.

James Herbert

The Rats, The Fog, The Spear, The Dark, The Magic Cottage, Haunted, Creed, '48 and eleven more, with worldwide sales in excess of 38 million.

James Herbert is the British equivalent of Stephen King. Without a doubt, these two writers produce some of today's most widely read horror novels. Curiously, both had their first books published in the same year, 1974; King with *Carrie* and Herbert with *The Rats*. Of the two authors, King is more widely known in the UK, but Herbert currently outsells him here. Nevertheless, he is a good friend of King's, the two having met through sharing the same publisher.

When interviewing authors, I am frequently struck by their ability to imagine wholly original events and situations – writers of horror stories above all others. Those at the top of this genre possess incredible skills. Where do they get their weird and spine-chilling ideas from? Perhaps from nightmares, or unhappy childhood events; perhaps even from a sadistic streak buried deep in their subconscious minds. I doubt whether anyone, writer or reader, really knows.

As I drove down to Herbert's home near Brighton in Sussex, I had time to ponder on what it was that made him so proficient in the art of frightening people out of their wits. He rarely gives interviews, preferring instead to remain relatively anonymous. Would he be intensely overpowering, like Dahl, or would he make my flesh creep in surroundings reflecting his stories?

At the front door I was greeted by his wife, Eileen. I introduced myself, only to hear her reply, 'Oh dear, he's still at the funeral.' Instantly, thoughts of him researching another macabre story flashed through my mind, but as it turned out it was nothing of the sort. I had simply picked a bad day for my interview.

Herbert's first career was in advertising, mainly because at school he had developed a flair for drawing and painting. He was also good at English (like other authors I interviewed), an indication of latent skills. After a grammar school education he went to Hornsey College of Art, leaving at the age of twenty. The main attraction of a job in advertising was not only that it was well paid, but also that he could also practise what he liked doing best, art. Six years and many campaigns later, he had been promoted to Group Head, a status then unheard of for someone of only twenty-six. Usually people attained this level in their mid-thirties or forties, but he denies that he was any kind of 'whizz-kid'.

In those early days he promoted such diverse products as Chanel, Clairol, Harp lager and Van Heusen shirts, not to mention the service of more 'Establishment' clients such as clearing banks – Barclays and Midland in particular. His experience of writing was, up to then, very limited, and involved creative copy for captions, television commercials and comic strips – scarcely the kind of experience to lead one to write some of the best horror novels.

So how and why did he turn to writing at the age of twenty-eight, having had no such inclination before?

> Ego. Sheer ego. I had been very successful in advertising. I'd reached a pinnacle, and I told myself I could do anything. Yes, sure, there was always better work that you can do in advertising, and better positions, but it wasn't fulfilling me. I began looking for a new challenge.
>
> That's post-rationale, looking back, but it may not have been true at the time, you understand? I was very successful and I had been promoted at a very early stage – so I thought, what else is there to do? And I thought about writing books. Also, I had so much energy at the time, I needed another outlet that was both creative and challenging.
>
> It all sounds very glib now, but it seemed a good idea at the time.

These sounded like the views of a very ambitious man, but what became clear was that his role as a Group Head took him away from what he liked doing best, using his skills as an artist and creative copy writer. In his office, copy writers had often talked about their ambition to write a 'great novel', and this might have helped.

Did he make a clean break from advertising, or try, like other hopeful authors, to start writing in his spare moments?

> Oh yes. It was just evenings and weekends, which was crazy, because in advertising, it's pretty hairy. You often have to work into the evenings and at weekends as well. It was difficult, but I wrote in any free moment I had, which was bad news for my wife and daughters.
>
> Writing increased the pressure, you know. It certainly wasn't an antidote to pressures of work in advertising.
>
> I also opened a colour laboratory at the same time and I was there in the studio, painting, putting up partitions and arranging

cameras. I loved it, but both distracted me from advertising. One failed, the colour lab, thank God!

But where, I asked, did he get the ideas for his first book, *The Rats*?

Oh, way back. I lived in the East End of London, which was like five hundred yards from the City of London. Whitechapel and Aldgate were the scummy side of London. The part of London which you'd never wish to live in.

When I was a kid, I used to have a scooter; later, I bought a bike for ten bob [50p] in Brick Lane, and I used to escape and cycle, or scoot, all around the City which, on a Saturday or Sunday morning, would always be deserted; the whole atmosphere of those lovely buildings, always empty . . . Not slums, you understand, just open and free of people. It was a pervasive image that I have recreated in many of my novels.

Many of my childhood ideas are milling somewhere around in my memory. When I sit down to write they surface again.

There's a lot of truth in all the books I've written. In every one, there's something that's affected me, the good things and the bad.

That is why in *The Rats*, I had London empty and, in *The Fog*, London gone berserk.

Childhood memories of places and sights remain with us for the rest of our lives. Herbert still vividly recalls the devastation of the bomb-sites left over from the last war, places where children used to play during the day, and rats at night. There were still a good many bomb-sites and at night, unlit, they presented a stark and forbidding background (again, recalled in Herbert's eighteenth novel, *'48*).

He also remembered seeing Bela Lugosi as Dracula. In one scene, thousands of rats appear, and their myriad eyes appeared to stare out at him as he watched. At this point Jim (as he likes to be called) echoed the advice of so many other writers: 'You're supposed to write about something you know, so it seemed an obvious choice. I was very familiar with the scary sight of rats scampering around in the East End, so why not write about them?'

When the manuscript of *The Rats* was finished, he sent copies out to six different publishers at the same time. Hardly adhering to convention − many publishers still frown on 'multiple submissions', especially from first-time authors − but as he had no contacts in the book publishing world, it seemed to him a logical thing to do. To me this is a sign of an eager author determined to get someone to publish his work. What happened to the typescripts, and who gave him the break, I asked?

Well, one went to Gollancz and one to Michael Joseph. Both turned me down. Eventually New English Library accepted it and we went on from there. The other three also rejected it, even though they knew NEL was interested. One, at least, hadn't even bothered to read the manuscript.

Sending copies of typescripts to several publishers at the same time is no sure way to get a first book accepted, but his case was an exception. Having taken him on, New English Library only paid Herbert £150 as an advance against future royalties – he probably earns that tenfold each day now. But despite his worldwide fame, and his huge earnings, he still hates reading bad reviews of his books, especially from those who haven't read them. And that really does happen, as Barbara Taylor Bradford, and others, will angrily confirm. When it happens, the hurt sears deep into an author's pride.

* * *

This led me to ask him how the sight of his work actually in print affected him. Being in advertising, and having written copy for countless advertisements, he was used to seeing his words in print. Perhaps he was less excited than other first-time writers when the book came out?

Oh no. In the first place, I was ecstatic when I received a letter saying that it was going to be published.

Then I got a great kick like every other author when it was finally published, but I was soon brought down to earth. I remember it well. They always publish on a Thursday, why, I don't know.* And I went into W. H. Smith in Cheapside, where, over the years, because my agency was nearby, I frequently bought books. Sometimes I bought three, four or five at a time. Sometimes I think I kept them going!

I went in and looked for *The Rats* in hardback, and didn't see it anywhere. I mean, that's how naive I was. I expected to see it. I saw the manageress and said, 'Um, have you got a book, called *The Rats* from New English Library?' I was too embarrassed to say my own name: 'by James Herbert'.

She said, 'No. And we are not likely to have that sort of book.'

That was a choker for me. On my big day, too. But it was a good lesson to learn, though it did spoil the day for me.

---

* In those days, most books pages in the national daily newspapers appeared on a Thursday. Publication on that day also gave the national Sunday newspapers time to get a review in three days later; as close to the publication date as possible. Some publishers still keep to this practice.

Even if the publishers had failed to ensure that the author's local bookshops had his work (read Jeffrey Archer's views on this topic in Part 3), it was not unreasonable for Jim to expect to see a few copies. After all, New English Library had an initial print run of 100,000 copies, a huge order suggesting that mass circulation was planned. The publishers ran out of stock after three weeks, however, and since then there have been at least thirty-three reprints.

Then came the reviews, or so Jim hoped. The following weekend found him rushing down to his local newsagents to buy all the 'Sundays'. There was absolutely nothing in any of them. This put a further dampener on the heady joys of becoming an author – as it does for so many other writers. Then *The Observer* finally published a review. It was terrible, and condensed, ran: 'this is rubbish, deserves to be tossed into the dustbin.'

> I said to my wife, Eileen, well, it's obvious I'm not a writer. I mean I was truly crushed. You spend a year working evenings and weekends, doing something you really believe in. And you've got to remember that *The Rats* wasn't just a horror story for me, it was a comment on the East End as I knew it; the way it had been neglected by governments over the years since the war. I was really incensed. How could they say it was rubbish? I was ready to give it all up, and I nearly did.
>
> The very next weekend, *The Sunday Times* carried a very different review. They said it was brilliant. My confidence was immediately restored. So I learned the lesson that everybody is entitled to their views . . .
>
> In the end, I realised that you can't listen to anybody. It was neither brilliant nor rubbish.

Today, eighteen books later and, more than 38 million copies sold worldwide, he still gets critics who carp. 'Usually', he says, 'they come from those within the horror genre, [writers] who are thoroughly envious of my success.' He is also a very private person, and does not attend conventions and authors' meetings. Naturally, this invites people to think that he is aloof or stand-offish, which, emphatically, he is not. He added, 'I'm just not a "clique" man. I prefer to go my own way.'

After *The Rats*, was he commissioned by his publishers to write another?

> Yes, they asked me to do another book, and I wouldn't accept it. I wouldn't be commissioned.
>
> It's a very funny story. I did *The Rats*, then they said, 'Can we have all your other manuscripts? We would be interested in anything

you've written before.' I said, 'No. No. I promise you that is it.' They tried again, and said they would like to commission me.

But I said, 'No, I'm in advertising. I've got a great job and it's good money. I don't know whether the book was a flash in the pan or not. I don't even know if I can write another one.' I said I would certainly try. 'I enjoy the process. If I manage to write another, then we can talk.'

So I wrote *The Fog* and they took me out to lunch. They actually tried to get me drunk, so that I would say, yes, OK, they can have it, but that's a very bad mistake to make with me. Within forty-five minutes the editor was literally under the table. He kept popping his head up and repeating, 'Jim, I shink you shud come with ush . . .' I said, 'No way'. It was very funny, really. Very, very few can out-drink me!

At that time, I didn't know much about publishing, and I figured the publishers had a good deal with the first one. I decided to get an agent and find out a bit more about the business, and what they should be paying. That's what I did in the end.

His first agent, David Higham, put him on the right road, but over the years he has had several others. Agents are clearly very important, as other writers have found out; certainly they can – and should – ensure that an author gets a fair deal. I wondered, though, what sort of editorial help he had received, either from agents or publishers.

Yes, I have an editor, but I'm my own best editor. Things like punctuation, grammar and spelling, that's instinctive with me. I'm not a great academic, although I've been to a grammar school and art college. If in doubt, I'll look it up. I won't trust to luck, or trust my editor.

And I've never read anything on how to write books; if you have got to do that then you can't write.

That is a strong statement, though I wonder what the owners of writing schools would say.

* * *

It was an innocent event at work that gave Herbert the idea for *The Fog*. He was in his office, and sitting at his desk, when a rather boring visitor got up and walked over to the open window. Jim's mind began to wander a little. What if he were to jump out, he thought? What if the population of London began to jump out of windows? What could make them do it? A poisonous gas, perhaps? From these fleeting moments of imagination sprang the concept for *The Fog*.

I had read this book, and when I commented on it, he exclaimed, with some feeling, that all interviewers who came to see him had only read *The Fog* or *The Rats*, though he had written many other and better books. He felt that I should read *The Magic Cottage*. When, later, I did so, I found it an equally good read though totally different. I was also struck by the design and presentation of the book and its jacket, but then I should have been – Jim was the designer. The jacket had great visual appeal, the endpapers were decorated, and the text was illustrated; he even chose the typeface. Few authors are lucky enough to be able to design their own books.

After the success of each of his novels, had he ever considered what it was that made them so popular? Did he believe, for example, that he was writing novels that the public wanted, or was he writing to suit himself?

I used to say in interviews that I just happened to tune in to public taste; what they wanted at the time. Then I realised, looking more deeply in to it, that I didn't tune in to anybody, but the public tuned in to me. There were lots of horror writers around, but none had made the big breakthrough. I – and Stephen King – happened to offer something different, in the way that Presley, and then the Beatles, did in music.

To an extent, my personality shows in my writing. Mine comes through in the humour. That's more me than the supernatural, though there's obviously some corner in my mind that drags out all this horror and the bizarre. I'm not going to say nastiness, because that's a label I despise.

It's directed towards that certain aspect, of life and death, if you like. That comes out, but there is a lot of humour in the idealism. Call me a cynical idealist, because there's a lot of cynicism in my books, but always, in the end, they're optimistic. They always have that bit of hope at the end. And again, that's in my nature.

And I know that the public's taste varies over the years. A lot of kids write to me to say they loved *The Rats*, loved it, the blood and the gore, but I'm not into that any more. If it happens in a story that there is a piece of blood and a piece of ghoul, then fine, but I'm not writing solely for that. I know that a few other horror writers are out to exploit that, but I like to be moving on.

Each of my books is little different from the others and I carry most of my old readers with me and collect new ones on the way. I think, for my sake, I have to do something different each time. If you read *Magic Cottage*, and then read *Sepulchre*, you'd think that they were written by two different people, and then if you read *Haunted*, you'd think that they were by three different authors. *Fluke* isn't even a horror story.

But there are certain people – who shall be nameless – who write the same thing time and time again. That's fine, if they want to do it, and the readers still buy it, [but] eventually the public will find you out, and ultimately reject your work. I also think you're damaging your own creative ability by writing to format.

In this respect, Herbert makes a significant and powerful point: he has quite deliberately chosen to vary his subjects and storylines. His first two titles, *The Rats* and *The Fog*, depict large groups of the population at the mercy of terrible forces; his next, *The Survivor*, is based on the supernatural; *The Spear* has an anti-fascist slant; and *Fluke* is a humorous story concerning a man reincarnated as a dog.

When he handed the manuscript of *Fluke* over to his publishers, they were aghast because it was so different from earlier novels, not what they had expected at all. They wanted to make major changes, but he told them that they could publish it only as it was, and that there would be no changes. If they did not agree, he was happy for it not to be published at all; he still had a good job in advertising. These are the actions of a principled writer.

Usually, once a winning formula has been established, authors stick with it, while publishers, for commercial reasons, are very reluctant to change. Given what Herbert had achieved, it is interesting to reflect on the contrast he makes with authors who have followed the same theme, like Dick Francis, Clive Cussler, James Herriot or Barbara Cartland; or who have continued a saga, like Dora Saint. Yet the market for their work has not dried up. Any aspiring writer should give this point more than just a passing thought. Established authors will confirm, it is a subject they debate 'ad infinitum'.

So, if Herbert varies the books each time, how does he assess the importance of the ingredients: the plot, characters, subject, and storyline?

If you tried to pin it down to the ingredients, I don't think the separate ingredients are the answer. You can't say, because they're devious, because they're sexy, because they're humorous, or because they have a *grande* theme, they will be successful. It's just the way the story is told, which is why I say that there is something indefinable, a kind of magic, about putting words on to paper.

Every ingredient you mention is important, but it is the alchemy that brings it all together. You can't just define it, because if you could, then everyone would be doing it. If everybody knew the secret, there would be several thousand bestselling authors.

It doesn't have to be high literature, but it has to be literate. And you have to tell a good story.

And I will write a sex scene if it's called for. If the story warrants a sex scene, I'll usually write it in detail. If one can write about horror in detail, why should I not write about sex in detail? And sex is a wonderful thing to describe, but it has got to be of value to the story. It sounds a cliché, but it's true.

I was once asked, in the form of an accusation, why all my stories contain vivid sexual encounters. Well, look again. They don't. Such scenes are never portrayed if they're blatantly unnecessary.

Whatever opinions are held about this aspect, and authors have many differing views, his sales seem not have been adversely affected; certainly it has not prevented his novels being translated into thirty-three languages. With his worldwide sales in excess of 38 million, and given his unusual break into writing, I wondered whether his advice to would-be writers would be significantly different from that of other successful authors.

In the first place, it's no good asking for advice and just talking about it [i.e. writing a book]! You've just got to sit down and endure . . . But there *are* practical things.

I always tell them to get *The Writers' and Artists' Yearbook*, just so that they can see how to set out a manuscript.

Research your subject, and jot down one line ideas. And always plan your book.

Although amazingly, he confessed that he never plans his books – a case of do what I say, not do what I do (which is not, perhaps, so strange coming from an ex-advertising man).

His first four books were written in his spare time while continuing in advertising, and yet Jeffrey Archer believes that you cannot write a successful novel part-time. Even so, in this respect Herbert is in full accord with James Herriot and many others.

There is more than one reason why I continued to work as an art director; the first being that I loved my job. It was busy, exciting, very social, and satisfying. Another, more profound reason was because of my background, I was insecure and I wasn't prepared to give up such a well-paid and enjoyable profession. Ultimately it was the Tax Man who helped me decide. I was working seven days a week, day and night, and paying the government 83 percent of my earnings and 98 percent of my savings for the privilege. I was also becoming a little exhausted, so I had to make the choice: advertising or publishing. I realised I could do much more with the written word, and that was the clincher for me.

The case for taking up writing as a second career is well made. Success in the world of advertising requires a creative mind. There must be others with creative minds similar to James Herbert's, just waiting for that big break.

James A. Michener

Tales of the South Pacific, Caravans, The Source, Centennial, The Covenant, Space, Texas, Legacy, Alaska, Caribbean and twenty-eight others.

Now in his nineties, and the author of thirty-eight books, James Michener might be expected to be quietly resting on his laurels. When we met, however, he was quick to tell me that he still works as hard as ever, and plans to keep on writing.

Though his worldwide sales have earned him a real fortune, he remains extremely modest and unassuming. He likes to live, as he told me, 'just to get through the day', and has always been like that, living for the day, or the week, or month. It is the same with his writing. His books are huge, heavily researched and fascinating, and not only tell a good story, but are crammed with interesting facts. That is Michener's style.

But why such large books? A paperback edition of *Space* exceeds 800 pages, and *Texas* more than 1,000. This feature alone sets him apart from other authors. As he explained:

> I have been abroad a great deal, not by design, just the way life worked out. I was not here when television made its appearance, but when I did see it, I saw with absolute clarity that a lot of the work consisted of forty-eight minutes and twelve minutes of advertising and breaks. I said, people aren't going to go for this and there's going to be a revulsion against it.
>
> I thought to myself, they will want longer books; and they will want this unconsciously. Not that I felt that this was an invitation to do it, but that it was justification for doing what I already wanted to do.

James Albert Michener (he seldom uses his middle name) was born in New York City on 3 February 1907. Sadly, he never knew his real parents, for he was taken as an orphan to Doylestown, Pennsylvania, where he was adopted by a Quaker couple, Edwin and Mabel Michener. He is modest about his ancestry, telling *The Guardian* in 1972:

I never felt in a position to reject anybody, I could be Jewish, part negro, probably not oriental, but almost anything else. This has loomed large in my thoughts. Raised in a poor house, I missed a whole cycle of childhood, but I've never used it as a device for self-pity.

I interviewed him when he was living in a house lent to him by the University of Miami, writing not in the luxurious surroundings that many contemporary authors enjoy, but in a converted bedroom at the back of the house. The room was cramped, and the atmosphere, with books and papers piled around us, rather academic. As will become clear, this was not, perhaps, altogether surprising.

He is an author who eschews the luxuries of life; there were no noticeable signs of wealth (though admittedly such possessions might not be displayed in a temporary home). But wealthy he most certainly is. Equally, there were few signs that he had adapted to the new technology. No word-processor for him (he uses a conventional typewriter), although I noticed that he had a modern hi-fi system in the room where he worked. I was to learn that he is a great fan of opera and had a large collection of recordings.

As he began to reminisce, I noticed that he seemed quite nervous, for he wrung and twisted his hands during most of our meeting.

I am different from anybody you'll talk with. I had an extremely hard childhood, and my only concern was survival. I never dreamed about being a writer, or a policeman, or even a business tycoon. My only concern was to get through Friday afternoon. I was a guy just slogging along.

The first fourteen years of my life were a constant injustice – very severe, and no money. I lived in a poorhouse quite often, but I was surrounded by a lot of love. I was really well protected by affection, and nothing else. Maybe that's the best deal you can make. One or the other, but it's best to have that psychological security.

My adoptive mother, by the time I was aged about five, was reading Dickens aloud to us at nights. I grew up in a family with a lot of foundling children, and there were always six or seven around.

I've grown up with books, ever since I was a child. They opened a new library in our home town when I was about six or seven and the first two people to sign up were Margaret Mead* the great anthropologist, and me. I love books. I've published some fine ones, and I take it all very seriously. I am a book man and have survived because of books.

* 1901-1978 – she is best known for her studies of tribal customs among primitive people.

At school, none of the teachers encouraged me to write, but I did go to this very fine college which is entirely different from the average American college. Swarthmore [in Pennsylvania] is probably one of the highest, academically, in America. In my last two years there I never attended a course with more than four or five students in it. Classes lasted for two and a half hours, and when you went in, you knew you were going to be called upon. You might fool the professor, but you couldn't fool your fellow students, who were, by and large, just as bright as you were. I grew up under a very unusual regime. I wrote long papers almost every week, about four or five thousand words. Maybe longer. Life was competitive.

People say I'm compulsive and ambitious, but . . . I don't think of myself as either. But the record of that constant series of big books, all of which have been widely received all around the world, must show some motive.

Whether he is compulsive or ambitious may be irrelevant to his career as a writer, but it is significant that, at fifteen, he was for a short time the editor of the Doylestown High School magazine. He cannot recall what attracted him to the job, since no one encouraged him to start, and he took no active part in the college magazine when he went to Swarthmore. But if his editing experience appears to have been very ephemeral, it does at least show that, by his teens, he was already interested in writing.

While at Doylestown he had showed himself to be good at tennis, baseball and basketball, and it was the combination of sporting ability with his interest in writing that helped him to win a scholarship to Swarthmore. He wasn't altogether the model student, for he was suspended twice, became a bit of a drifter, and developed quite radical attitudes. But the one subject he was good at was English, and it was his English teachers who encouraged him to continue studying.

As he had said, his childhood experiences had a profound effect on him. Life as a member of the kindly and loving Michener family was not always easy, and records show that on at least three occasions there was simply not enough money to make ends meet, and he was forced to live in the Bucks County Poorhouse for periods of eight to fourteen weeks. His mother worked hard to help him get through college, even taking in laundry and sewing to earn a little extra cash. His adventures as a restless youth took him hitch-hiking and riding across America in railway boxcars. The people he met and the sights he saw made a singularly important impact on his mind. He travelled much by these methods, and by the time he was twenty, he had visited forty-five States (there were then forty-eight, fifty nowadays).

Through the encouragement of his teachers and, doubtless, with some hard work, he graduated *summa cum laude*. He clearly liked the academic world, for no sooner had he obtained his degree than a nearby preparatory school accepted him as a teacher. That was in 1930, but he could not settle down and, a year later, armed with a grant from Swarthmore, set out to see Europe. He spent a winter in the Outer Hebrides and, as a graduate student at the University of St. Andrews in Scotland, visited Spain and the Mediterranean.

On his return to Pennsylvania, he took up an academic career again, teaching English at the George School, Newtown. Three years later, in 1936, he became a professor at the Colorado State College of Education, where he continued to excel as an academic, becoming more interested in history as time passed. This interest led Michener to take up a post at Harvard University's School of Education where he was a visiting professor of history. His environment created the right atmosphere in which to pen scholarly articles about education, and reference books show that his first noteworthy publication was *The Unit in the Social Studies*, published in 1940. Such works were, however, hardly an indication of what was to come.

Though he never dreamed of becoming a professional, full-time author, Michener's early experiences in education led him to concentrate on writing. He revelled in providing explanations, and his wide research, detailed analysis, and assimilation of information for the reader are the chief characteristics of his work. He is never satisfied until he has explored every avenue, considered every possibility, which is why he has earned himself the reputation of being a difficult man – some say a martinet, even.

He says he's a very *different* writer. That is particularly true in one important respect. Most writers do their work at home, or in some quiet place central to their normal life. Not so Michener: he goes to the location of the book he's working on. When he set out to write what resulted in *Centennial*, he devoted a year to travelling over 25,000 miles through fourteen States. When I met him he was in Miami, where he was to spend two years working on a vast novel about the Caribbean (which is easily reached from Florida).

* * *

Michener's big break came while he was serving in the US Navy during the Second World War, but it was not obvious at the time. Lieutenant Michener was sent by sea to a small island in the Pacific, Espiritu Santo in the New Hebrides. His was not a front-line posting but a support role in keeping records of navy aircraft maintenance. The voyage, lasting some four weeks, is described in Michener's autobiography, *The World Is My Home*, and was significant for the marked contrast between the hardship endured by naval personnel and the well-fed and well-paid civilian crew. At the end of the voyage, he and two close friends, Bill Collins and Jay Hammen, were relaxing in the absent captain's cabin. Collins discovered a blank form for assignments of naval personnel amongst the papers on the desk. Michener had often talked about his travels, so Collins decided to create an order for Michener to travel on missions around the military war zones of the South Pacific. He even signed it 'Admiral Collins'!

Keeping maintenance records allowed him to fly from base to base around the area. Nevertheless, the document created by Collins was sufficient for Michener to embark on his exploration of the South Pacific, though it was backed up later by properly authorised orders. Naval records had alerted his superiors to the fact that he was a trained historian; thus he was given the task of recording events and the history of the US Navy in the region. His travels and investigations were also to provide the raw material for his entry into the Hall of Fame.

Months later, after a particularly tricky landing at dusk, he unwound the tensions built up during the flight back to base by walking alone on the airstrip. It was a soul searching time and a momentous moment in his life.

Before the war he had worked for Macmillan, the New York publishers, and with time on his hands his thoughts returned to the world of books. He decided to start writing an account of life on Espiritu Santo and on neigbouring islands, which was eventually to become world famous as *Tales of the South Pacific*. The first draft was created in most unusual circumstances for an aspiring writer. After his military duties had ended for the day, he would set to his task in a Quonset hut (the US equivalent of the British Nissen hut), fighting off mosquitoes and typing by the light of a lantern. Little did he know that his work was destined to become one of the best-known and most successful musicals of all time.

However, Michener knew that Macmillan, like many other publishing houses, would not publish a book by one of their own employees, so he submitted his typescript under an assumed name.

> It seemed a devious trick, but it wasn't really because theoretically I wasn't under their employ at the time. I was in the Navy and I had my relationship with Macmillan fractured, but it was assumed that I would go back. Everybody recognised it at the time for what it was. It wasn't deception, it was just that I didn't want to raise the issue at that time.
>
> I was lucky, in the Navy, in Macmillan and everything else. The good thing about that book of mine was that it was done in such a low key. If you ever saw an original edition of *Tales of the South Pacific*, you would be appalled. It was published at the end of the war when

paper-saving devices were still in. They start a new chapter four lines from the bottom of a verso [left-hand page]. They just slapped it together, even the paper had two different surfaces. Toilet paper really.

I don't think they had any hopes for it really. I certainly didn't. I wanted it to be on the record.

He was forty when he wrote *Tales of the South Pacific*. His motivation had been boredom, though he thought that an honest record of what had actually happened would be of value, as he put it, to 'a few people'. Macmillan not only accepted the typescript but allowed Michener's name to appear as the author.

The experience he had gained as a publisher at Macmillan, where he had been employed in the Education Division, was considerable. He had been lucky just to get the job.

They needed somebody about thirty-five years old. There were many, many enquiries. Only three of us turned up. I was the third on the list. The first man, in the meantime, got a much better job, I think it was president of a university; the second had also got a job, so I was left. It turned out that I was infinitely worse than the other two and certainly not their first choice.

I didn't even know I was under consideration, and when they offered me the job . . . It's been my record all along.

After the war, he returned to Macmillan. Reflecting on his aptitude as a writer for handling exacting material, it is not surprising that his forte turned out to be in the detailed costing and pricing of books. To be effective at such work, he had to understand every aspect of publishing, including, as he said, 'buying the plates, paying the editors, paper costs and advertising.' These are experiences and abilities which most authors, if they were to be honest, would agree are major advantages. It gave Michener a head start.

However, his book did not immediately leap into the bestseller lists, though it was published just at the right moment, as far as Michener was concerned. That year there was a dearth of good books published in America, and the publishers submitted *Tales of the South Pacific* for the annual Pulitzer Prize. This was an overtly nice gesture, and is one that many publishers make, partly out of a desire for the author to win, and partly because if he or she does, it means greater profits. And Michener *did* win the 1948 Pulitzer Prize for fiction.

There were other books in contention, but they never say what they are, but you don't have to be very bright to decide which ones they probably were. The year before I got the prize, there was a blockbuster, *All The Kings Men*, by Robert Penn Warren. I never would have been in competition with it.

The year after I got the prize, there was a wonderful book by James Gould Cozzens, *Guard of Honor*, which just swept the field. I would have been terribly small potatoes that year.

It was fortune beyond what one had the right to expect. There was no way that my book would have been on the shortlist the year before, or the year after.

It was a great stepping-stone, for immediately afterwards I had a letter from the well-known agent, Jacques Chambrun. I think he wrote the following morning.

It is no wonder that Michener was singularly impressed by winning the award with his second ever book. Penn Warren had had no fewer than twelve books published before he won, and Cozzens had also produced a number of highly regarded novels.

The prize brought Michener not only Jacques Chambrun's attention, but also that of the public. Chambrun, however, for all his fame, was an agent of somewhat questionable reputation in the publishing world, mainly because on occasions he had been known not to pass on all the earnings due to authors. His main claim to fame was that he 'represented' Somerset Maugham, and he used this connection when sending glowing letters to any author whose name appeared in the press suggesting a successful future. Michener, however, did not succumb to Chambrun's attention, but he did sign up a literary agent immediately afterwards.

Michener's new agent, one of America's best, took on his second novel, *The Fires of Spring*. His work required many changes and if these were made, his agent told him, he would submit it for a major Hollywood prize worth $100,000. Michener had a full-time job at the time, so he rose early each morning to get the work done.

It is not surprising that Michener does not name this agent in his autobiography. Having completed the revisions and submitted the typescript, his agent wrote to sever their agreement on the grounds that, even after the numerous changes, Michener's work was never going to be good enough to be published. Then came the news that Michener had won the Pulitzer Prize.

In Hollywood the ex-actor, Kenneth McKenna, was employed by Metro-Goldwyn-Mayer to purchase novels for the studio. He read the book but it was turned down by his bosses. Then he alerted his half-brother who worked in a New York theatre. Jo Mielziner was more than impressed by its possibilities and took it to Richard Rogers. The rest is history, but it shows how luck and personal contacts can help authors.

Michener's book was the basis for the now world-famous Rodgers and Hammerstein's musical *South Pacific*, a show which has run and run since its opening at the Majestic Theatre on 7 April 1949. Broadway then saw 1,925 performances over the next five years, grossing $9 million, and this was followed by two and a half years in London. The film version grossed over $16 million in the States alone, and huge additional sums were earned through sales of sheet music, long-playing records, franchised cosmetics, dresses and lingerie. When the musical opened, Michener was given a share of the business in the form of a royalty which, together with the royalties due to him from sales of the book, provided a steady income. More importantly, the combined income was sufficient to allow Michener to go on writing without worrying about money; something that an author's first book seldom confers.

* * *

Centennial, Space, Texas, Caribbean: the titles of James Michener's books are straightforward, sometimes evocative, usually attention-grabbing. Choosing the right title can make or break a novel, as many publishers will testify. Michener shares with other writers the problems of finding suitable titles.

> I usually allow the New York office to title the books. Of course, I send in six or seven acceptable titles. Then they kick them around. If I had a strong feeling – I might on this book I'm working on now [which eventually appeared as *Caribbean*] – I'd send it up as the first suggestion, and a strong one, but I haven't ever done that.

If he works hard to get the title right, James also works hard at getting his text right, often going to six or seven drafts. As has been said, he uses a conventional typewriter, so his methodical mind has come up with a colour-coded system for the various stages of a typescript. The first draft is typed on white paper, the second on yellow, the third on blue. Then sections are cut and pasted onto the first draft, with the result that the latter stages are multi-coloured. He finds this method essential, for it lets him tell at a glance just which draft the amendments have come from, so enabling him to backtrack if need be. It takes up much of his time, of course, time which other authors have saved by using word-processors.

A problem that he also shares with other bestselling writers is that of coping with the plethora of incoming telephone calls, correspondence, and requests for interviews. The fame and fortunes of this fraternity are tainted by the publicity they attract. Authors' experiences vary enormously but, as anyone will appreciate, any interruption breaks their concentration. In Michener's case, all these problems were in the capable hands of John Kings. They met because James Michener needed professional help when he set out to research *Centennial*. John's background was extensively editorial, but he had six years' experience as a rancher in Wyoming. It was this combination that prompted Hobart Lewis, Editor-in-Chief of *Readers' Digest*, to arrange the introduction. Kings accepted the challenge, knowing that Michener had a reputation as a hard taskmaster.

Writers must, of necessity, cut themselves off from other people whilst they are actually writing, and if they become highly successful, they need to have someone to look after the more mundane chores of life. Michener is no exception. His wife, Mari, takes care of all their financial affairs. 'A typical American situation,' he said; 'I have not been inside a bank for the last ten years except for signing or notarizing documents.' Meanwhile, he can concentrate on his current novel, always a vast tome, crammed full of accurate detail about matters from the historical to the scientific. But why the wide range of subjects?

> I write about just what I want to write about. Supposing, some years ago, you had gathered together all the bright people in publishing and said to them that you wanted to bring out a book that will knock them dead; that will stay at the top of the bestseller list for over a year; and that everybody will want to get a copy of?
>
> Do you think that the group would have said, what the world really yearns for is a book about an archeological dig in the Holy Land? Going back 5,000 years? No way. No way.
>
> Or, a few years later, about a rabbit travelling through the north of England?
>
> No, books are written by writers. And writers are people with insights and imagination. With courage and crazy ideas, and some of them pay off.

One little known fact about the books he has written emerged from his autobiography. With the huge success of *Tales of the South Pacific* behind him, it emerges that he wrote five books on Japanese art; mainly because he loves the subject. Most publishers he approached turned them down, so to ensure publication he invested some of his own money to ensure they were produced. Crazy he was not, for many were later reprinted and first editions have become collector's items. Self publishing is nothing new.

After *Tales of the South Pacific* came *The Fires of Spring*, *Voice of Asia*, *Return to Paradise*, and *The Bridges of Toko-ri*, which was filmed under the same title.

It would be invidious to single out any one novel as being better than others, but some stand higher in the public's estimation, notably *Hawaii*,

Caravans, The Source, Centennial, The Covenant, Space, Texas and *Chesapeake. Texas* is a good example of Michener's standing. He was formally invited to write about Texas by no less a person than its Governor, William Clements. One report I read stated that he was offered staff to help him, and a room at the University of Texas. He spent two years of his time and about $100,000 of his own money in visiting all the people and places needed for his research.

The finished book runs to over 1,000 pages, but Random House's initial print-run was in excess of 750,000 copies, and the American Broadcasting Company bought the television rights before the book was published. Michener has come a long way from his early days.

As has been said, all his books are very long, and he takes a correspondingly long time over the writing; *Hawaii*, the longest, took seven years to write. By then Michener had another eleven books besides *Tales of the South Pacific* to his credit which, with the success of his first novel and of *South Pacific*, allowed him the sort of financial security most authors can never attain. This, above all, is what makes him a 'different' author.

Michener's books cover a very wide variety of locations and subjects. He does not put this down to timing, but he has, all his life, been determined to travel as much as possible. His books encompass Alaska, Hawaii, Texas, the Holy Land and, when I interviewed him, the Caribbean.

> I'm terribly sad about the ones I didn't write, that I should have written. I am one of the few people you will meet who has lived in all the Muslim countries, except [Saudi] Arabia, and I wanted to do a book about that part of the world, but I didn't. How valuable that would have been. The same with South America.
>
> You think of all those Spanish colonies, all have failed, even today, to find a stable form of government; and the damned old British colonies just slog along and everything works. When they leave, there's a cadre there to carry on. What a difference.

As we have seen, his approach to writing is indeed different from that of other bestselling writers. So how, I asked, did he organise his time?

> You know, you write your first three books at four o'clock in the morning, and you have a full day's job. Then you want a little exercise, or a little recreation. Go to bed early, and that alarm goes again at four. You'd better get up again. If you can't, I don't think you'll make it.
>
> It can also be at eleven o'clock at night, but there has to be a time

for you to prosecute your dream, while you're doing something else to live.

And the bulk of us do that, and if that terrifies you, or you feel you don't have the sticking quality, or if your wife can't visualize the long apprenticeship, then don't start.

This advice differs from that of Jeffrey Archer (see Part 3), who believes that writers must cut themselves off from everything else and write all the hours they can. Each to his own, but the point is surely that a writer must have the drive and stamina to continue writing, at no matter what time of day or night.

Authors often live lonely lives, and one consequence of their sometimes myopic interest in a single subject, is a lack of general knowledge of others in the book world. So it is with Michener, who told me the revealing tale of how he came to hear of Barbara Cartland.

There was no way I would hear of her. I was working on a commission that supervises NASA, on the peninsula, and in search of reading material and some old almanacs, I went to this marvellous bookstore nearby out in the country. The owner had acres of books on display.

'Oh yes, we don't get too many of your books. We get rid of them pretty fast when we do get them.'

He took me to the back where he had, maybe, six or seven, which was rather gratifying to see. Six different ones.

Then for some reason, I looked at a bookcase, which was about forty inches wide and eight shelves high. I said, 'What's that? There's a similarity about those books.'

'Well, that's our Barbara Cartland section.' I said, '*What?*' I'd never heard of her name. I looked again, and dammit, the whole thing was Cartland.

While I was in the store, a woman came in with three or four Barbara Cartlands in her bag, and she was bringing them back for exchange. I think she paid ten cents for each book and you get a new one. She selected a clutch of new ones, then asked the owner, 'Have I read these?' He said, 'I think you've read that one but these are all right.'

It told me all I wanted to know. It was awesome!

I agreed with him: Barbara Cartland's sales have topped 650,000 million worldwide; many more than any other contemporary author (see Part 2).

Nevertheless, sales of Michener's books are not insignificant, even when ranked against those of other current writers who are considered to be the world's top sellers.

A few years ago, his total world sales were estimated at 150 million, but this is not something that ranks very highly in Michener's mind. *Hawaii* or possibly *The Source* have been the most popular, and *Texas* achieved sales of at least 1.3 million, but he does not understand why his books are so popular.

> It's a total mystery to me. They are long. They are difficult. The opening chapters are very uncongenial. When they reprinted *Hawaii*, they reprinted the opening chapters in italics. The intimation was, if you really wanted to get into the story, you could skip that part. They didn't say that, but that's what they meant.
>
> I didn't react, because I've been so lucky with my books.

If, somewhere, there sits a young 'would-be' author contemplating the idea of emulating James Michener, what should he or she be doing? What is this famous author's advice to others?

> I've said two things about that. One, unless you wear bifocals by the age of twenty-two, you'll never make it. You haven't read enough. I don't know how you get a feeling of what a great book is, or what fine people have done in your generation, unless you read something. I don't think it can be done by osmosis. So maybe I'm stressing my own education too strongly, but I still believe it.
>
> The other is, if you do get your first book published, be sure that Rodgers and Hammerstein read it!
>
> I tell young writers – and I meet quite a few of them – the great thing is to get the books on the shelf. Don't worry about contracts, don't worry about possible movie sales. Get them on the shelves and then they are eligible for amazing things.

The chances of other authors finding a contemporary equivalent of Rodgers and Hammerstein (the former died in 1979, the latter in 1960) are very remote, but the idea is a logical one. Shows, films, television series, radio: all can promote even obscure or old books to the bestseller lists.

Michener addicts need not worry that his books will run out. There will be plenty to read for, as he told me, once he had finished *Caribbean* he had plans for at least another thirty...

How did he imagine his readers? Were they mostly academically minded?

I get four pictures [of readers]. If you read this batch of fifty or so letters, typical of all those I receive, you will find letters from very learned people wanting to know about things and checking my errors.

You will find extremely well-written and sophisticated letters of appreciation with some interplay of ideas.

You will find quite a few letters from people who have never read very much, or have stopped reading and then picked up with my books and read them all.

Then you would get a fourth group, moderately limited, who have never had an idea of what a good book is, and are 'snowed' by the fact that a writer can do these things.

There have been one or two surveys on this subject by major magazines. One asked the chiefs of the 'Fortune 500'* companies what they read for leisure. The majority said, quite honestly, they're so busy that they can't do much reading. Those that did read said, by an 'overwhelming majority', that they tend to pick up something by me because they were sure it wouldn't waste their time. They might not like it, but at least it was worth wrestling with. Now these are not literary people presumably, but they are not dumb people either.

James Michener has always impressed his readers, and indeed everybody that he meets. Compared with many other writers, he has had a fascinating and absorbing life. He has also, during his fifty writing years, given literally millions of readers immense enjoyment.

With all those 'solid successes' under his belt, earning him riches beyond most of our imaginations, what does he do with his wealth?

I write nothing for free. I demand . . . and I'm very serious about this, I'm a professional writer, and I take it terribly seriously. It's one of the greatest professions in the world and I'm going to get paid for it.

But having been paid for it, I give it all away.

We have given a lot of scholarships to colleges and universities, but I think the finest thing I've done with the money I've made, is to give a very large share of it for the care of elderly writers who are down on their luck. It's all administered by the Writers' Guild of New York.

---

* A list regularly published by the American magazine *Fortune* of the 500 richest companies in the world.

It is also believed that he has given away $2 million to Swarthmore College, and endowed the University of Iowa to the tune of $500,000. That generosity must surely make James Michener unique amongst this group of authors.

PART TWO

SEX, SAGAS AND ROMANCE

Barbara Taylor Bradford

A Woman of Substance, Voice of The Heart, Hold That Dream, Act of Will, To Be The Best, The Women in His Life, Remember, Angel, Everything to Gain, Dangerous To Know, Love In Another Town, A Secret Affair, Her Own Rules and *Power of A Woman.* Over 58 million copies sold worldwide.

'Someone once asked me what a novel is and I said: It's a monumental lie that has to have the absolute ring of truth if it is to succeed.' So Barbara Taylor Bradford wrote in a feature article aptly titled, 'So You Want to Write a Bestseller?'

This pearl of wisdom, reiterated at our meeting, first appeared in the 1988 edition of the American *Writer's Handbook*, and she was well qualified to make it, having published eight bestselling novels by then. A useful work of reference, the *Handbook* is equivalent to the British publication, *The Writers' and Artists' Yearbook*; however, the *Handbook*, not to be confused with the similar title published by Macmillan, sadly has not always been readily available here. As my interview with Barbara progressed, many of the points made were not only reiterated but, more importantly, amplified.

To illustrate how far her writing career had progressed during eighteen years as one of the world's top writers of fiction, a British newspaper published an article which carried a headline: 'I want £3 million before I write a single word.' A touch melodramatic and a statement that Barbara Taylor Bradford denies ever making, but it serves to illustrate how the media hypes the huge sums top writers can command.

She would be justified in making such statements, however; in one week, as long ago as June 1986, she had two of her titles at the top of the UK's bestselling lists at the same time: *Act of Will* in the hardback list and *Hold That Dream* in the paperback. With these and two other novels, her total sales of just the English language editions were reported in late 1989 to have exceeded 30 million copies. (Today, these exceed 58 million copies; more, if the thirty-eight foreign language editions are taken into account.) Someone, one day, will top that, but for the time being such sales establish her as being unique even amongst her peers.

People from Yorkshire are known for their bluntness and for their single-mindedness in pursuing what they seek. The origin of Barbara's confident directness and determination can be traced to her early life. Her upbringing must take much of the credit; it is a period which is still very clear in her mind today, as she wrote in her article in the *Writer's Handbook*:

> When I was ten, my father bought me a second-hand typewriter and I typed out these little tales and stitched them in a folder with a hand-painted title.
>
> When I was twelve I submitted one – about a little horse, I think – to something called *The Children's Magazine* and it was actually published. I got ten-and-six for it. I have never stopped writing since.

For the record, Barbara told me that the fee was not 'ten-and-six', but seven-and-sixpence (respectively, 52.5 pence or about 84 cents, and 37.5 pence or about 60 cents), though such a sum was, of course, worth much more in 1945. That was a lot of pocket money to a small child, and it certainly made a big impression on her. It was, too, the first time she saw her name in print, which added to the impact. Put the two together and one can understand why Barbara, with the benefit of hindsight, proclaims, 'My destiny was sealed that day I saw my name in print'.

Her background provides more than a clue as to why she chose to become an author. Unlike many other writers, her emergence as an author of bestselling fiction was no 'second-career decision', but a conscious ambition from a very early age. Her mother, Freda, a former children's nurse and nanny, was an insatiable reader, and introduced Barbara to books when she was four. By the time she was twelve she had read all of Dickens's novels and those of the Brontë sisters (not, she admits, that she fully understood them all). Once hooked on the habit, she read avidly at all hours, even by torchlight under the bedclothes at night.

Her mother supported Barbara in other ways, too. For example, she introduced her to classical music and ballet at the Theatre Royal in Leeds, and encouraged her to believe that, provided she worked hard enough, she could achieve anything she wanted. Barbara is full of admiration and gratitude for her parents' help, to which she owes so much. Although naturally gifted, she has always been very ready to acknowledge their support, saying of her mother:

> She really did make me feel rather special. And I do believe the whole thing of Freud's, which is 'give me the child till the age of seven, and I will give you the man, or woman.'

Barbara attended Christ Church Elementary School and then Northcote Private School for Girls in Leeds, where she studied shorthand and typing. She excelled at English literature, however, and in this respect she shares a common link with other authors like Dora Saint and Penny Jordan (see Part 2), or Craig Thomas and Frederick Forsyth (see Part 3). She was awarded several certificates for her English, and this doubtless helped get her first job with the *Yorkshire Evening Post* in 1948.

* * *

Her meteoric rise to bestsellerdom has been recounted many times, but these articles or programmes usually follow the basic details from the biographical notes handed out by her publicists. These are necessarily brief, and omit the background that lies behind the bland statements of success. In particular, they usually leave out the events that led up to an author's break into writing.

Although she had always dreamed of becoming a writer from childhood, it was when she became a cub reporter that her life really changed. This, as her millions of fans will know, began with her local paper, the *Yorkshire Evening Post*, as she told me:

> I started work at my local paper's office as a junior typist, typing letters for the advertising people. I used to make lots of mistakes on their expensive stationery, and my pile of waste daily grew steadily higher, so out of embarrassment I took some waste sheets into the ladies' room and set fire to them over the toilet, but I took much more home to burn in my mother's grate. I always had problems reading my shorthand book. This went on for weeks, but towards the end of the first three months, the lady who ran the typing pool put me in the telephonists' room.
>
> There, you sat at a little desk with earphones on, and a typewriter in front of you. Whenever a reporter phoned in saying 'I want to dictate a story . . .' you began typing. One of those reporters was Keith Waterhouse and I remember he once phoned to dictate a story and it went, 'Today, a fire broke out in the Queen's Hotel and nine people were killed . . .' [The story was big news at the time and she and Waterhouse became great friends afterwards. Years later, he went on to become famous in his own right, as a novelist – he wrote *Billy Liar*, among others – journalist and playwright. At the time, they both realized that of all those they knew at the newspaper, they were the only two determined to get on in life.]
>
> With a cup of machine-made coffee in my hand, I regularly used to take this sort of thing down to the sub-editors' room. This was a

big room with desks and people everywhere. Some got to know me, and it was there that I met a reporter, Arthur Brittenden, but he worked for the *Yorkshire Post*. [He went on to become editor of the *News Chronicle*.] I made it known to him, and to another girl who also worked for the *Yorkshire Post* and who had become a great friend of mine, Jean Stead, that I wanted to become a reporter. She said, 'The only way you'll become a reporter is to move out of the typing pool and start writing things.' 'For the *Yorkshire Post* or *Evening Post*?' I asked. 'The *Evening Post*, of course. Maybe you could do a little feature or something.'

Then I quite coincidentally stumbled onto one [i.e. a subject for a feature article]. There was an old woman who lived in Armley, and I remember, as a child, that everyone called her 'the old witch'. Polly was just like the old woman who lived in a shoe, except that she didn't have any children. She was very poor, and a sort of menace in many ways; she had all these cats and dogs, and would often wave her stick at everybody passing. People were always complaining about 'Old Polly'.

Well, it turned out that she was the sister of one of the wealthiest men in Leeds. My story was about Polly Legard, or 'Old Polly', the woman who lived in a shoe but had a brother who owned all these buses . . . and Jean helped me put it together. I quickly learnt how long a piece should be, and when I had finished it, I just dumped it anonymously on a sub-editor's desk, a usual thing for me to do, and it got printed as a little feature.

I kept on doing little features like this, and dumping them on the subs' desks. They usually got published.

Like any workaholic, she was known to stay on late at work, writi something, anything, just to get it in the paper. For Barbara, getting publish was a case of hard work and Yorkshire grit.

Then one day I was sitting typing letters and looking at my shorthand book, wondering, as usual, what a squiggle was, when the lady who ran the pool, an ogre by the name of Miss Worfolk, came up to me and said accusingly, 'What have you done? The editor wants to see you.'

At sixteen, I was still a little fearless; anyway, I knew who the editor was, and off I went. But it was very unusual for the editor to ask to see a junior.

Outside his office, his secretary gave me an odd look, a bit of a scowl, and said, 'Go in.' And into the inner sanctum I went. Barry Horniblow worked in a very large and imposing room. There he sat, behind his large desk. 'Sit down,' he said – it was more of a command really – so I did, facing him, full of awe, across his desk. What had I done? What had I done? Our conversation went something like this:

'So you're Barbara Taylor.'

'Yes.'

'Are you the Barbara Taylor who wrote these stories?' he asked, as he brought out a bunch of press clippings. Four little things they were, [each] 700 words or so, written over a period of two months.

'Yes, why? They must have been alright, as they were published.'

I was nervous, so much so that I managed to lose my shoe under the desk. He went, on unaware of my predicament.

'Well, we have to pay you. When the accounts tried to pay Barbara Taylor, they thought it was a stringer from somewhere in Knaresborough or Doncaster. No one could find a person of that name. Eventually, they found that it was you here in the typing pool.'

'Oh sir,' I said, 'you want to pay me? Is that what you wanted me for?'

'Yes. But tell me, why did you write these pieces? Do you want to be a reporter, then?'

'Oh, I don't want to be, sir. I'm going to be,' was my reply. Talk about fools rushing in where angels fear to tread!

'Did you write them all yourself?' he asked.

'Yes, well, Jean showed me a little bit.'

'Jean who?'

'Jean Stead.'

'And how do you know her?'

'Well, she sometimes lets me go with her on Saturdays,' He laughed at this. 'You do the leg work for someone on the *Yorkshire Post*?'

But I didn't mind, as I was learning. Then I told him, flushed with enthusiasm, that I had done other pieces for the local papers. 'Do you keep clippings?' 'Oh yes', I replied, 'I've got a clippings book.' 'Well, sometime, let me see them, and we'll see what we can do.'

I left his office, returned to the pool and finished the letter. But instead of going to the canteen for lunch, I set off home to get the clippings book. I took the tram back to Upper Armley. My mother was very surprised to see me; she thought I'd been given the sack, and was quick to say so. She was praying for me to get the sack because then I could go back to my schooling and, later, on to Leeds University to finish my education. I grabbed my clippings book, ran all the way back up the street and just caught the tram back. I made it to the office, I think, within the allotted hour off for lunch, but it was very close!

There was no one outside Mr Horniblow's office. His secretary must have gone for lunch, so I knocked, and on hearing the phone being put down, entered.

'I've got my clippings book', I said. 'But how did you get that? – you didn't have it at ten o'clock this morning.' I told him how I had rushed home. 'Had any lunch? No? Well, come in and sit down.' He picked up the phone and asked his secretary, who had by then returned from lunch, for a sandwich for me and one for him, and a glass of milk. He was very sweet. He talked to me and we ate our sandwiches together and from that moment on, she hated me.

I gave him the clippings, glued in a school exercise book, and told him that they were mostly from the *Armley and Wortley News*. He must have been impressed, for after a long silence he said, 'When we get a new women's page editor, I'll probably move you into the reporters' room. Until then, keep writing.'

Three months later, I moved.

To seventeen year-old Barbara, Barry Horniblow thereafter became more than an editor, more even just an employer; he became her hero, someone to emulate. When he left for a job in Fleet Street, joining the *Daily Sketch*, he set a goal for her: to work as a journalist in London's Fleet Street.

* * *

These lively reminiscences illustrate what I meant when I wrote earlier that most accounts of how authors broke into writing are glossed over in a few sentences; certainly they don't compare to Barbara's own recollection. Nor do they give any aspirant author a chance to discover what it is that singles one writer out for fame and fortune, yet not others.

If there is a formula, it varies with each individual, but there is, without doubt, an element of magic in people's reactions to each other. Was Barbara just plain lucky, or did she engineer her good fortune? And if she did engineer it, was it through brazen confidence that she would do what she wanted to do?

Perhaps her friendships with Jean Stead and Keith Waterhouse helped shape her career more than she realized at the time, but life was not always easy. She achieved her first ambition by starting work as a cub reporter in the newsroom. It was an environment in which she learned all about society's problems: the rich pattern of daily-enacted dramas; the coroner's courts, the crimes committed, and the problems the local police encountered. Above all, she witnessed the emotions of the people involved in all these events. Any reporter will testify that the pressures of working in a newsroom can be horrific. The newsroom at the *Yorkshire Evening Post* was no exception and, as press deadlines approached, tension rose. Junior staff got the worst of it, as usual, and Barbara suffered like the rest. On one particularly bad day, the editor, Horniblow's successor, bawled at her across the newsroom for misspelling a name, a serious error. The venom behind his criticism was just too much for Barbara, for whom nothing was going right that day, and as faces turned her way the embarrassed young reporter simply melted into tears.

Afterwards, Keith Waterhouse took her off to the local café and, over a soothing cup of coffee, sympathized with her. He had become not only a good friend, but her mentor, too. She recalls him saying, in an effort to comfort her, 'Oh luv, you mustn't cry in the newsroom, you know, go to t'ladies' room. Newspapermen don't cry.'

* * *

To Barbara, working as a reporter on a newspaper was only a step along the path of her ambition to be writer. Certainly the number of successful authors who started in journalism suggests that it is an excellent beginning. Barbara Cartland, Sarah Harrison, Jilly Cooper, Frederick Forsyth and Arthur Hailey will readily testify to this, but becoming a journalist is not an automatic passport to fame and fortune as a writer of bestsellers. However, the wide range of subject matter, and the discipline required, provide not only the confidence to write, but also that other vital ingredient, experience.

However, once assigned to the promised post on the women's page, she was overwhelmed by opportunities of a different kind. More genteel subjects became the order of the day, such as trends in fashion, or local social events. The pages editor, Madeline McCloughlin, persuaded her parents to allow Barbara to go with her on a special trip to Paris for a major fashion show. To Barbara at that time it seemed like the trip of a lifetime, and it meant travelling through London. This was a heaven-sent opportunity to call in at the *Daily Sketch* to visit the man who had given her a golden opportunity, Barry Horniblow. Arranging a meeting with him herself would have been too embarrassing, but she was delighted when she extracted a promise from

Madeline to fix the meeting. Moreover, her parents had to be persuaded to pay the expenses, which they duly did. It was not all plain sailing, however:

> Madeline had never made that appointment. When we called, they said, 'He's busy, and in a meeting so he can't be disturbed.'
>
> 'That's not fair,' I carped at Madeline. 'We've been to Paris, and I only wanted to go because you'd said we'd go and see Barry. You never made the appointment, did you?' I was very accusatory.
>
> 'Don't worry, we'll get in.' We skirted round the building and went in through the press room and made our way upstairs, and just our luck, we ran into him in a corridor.
>
> 'Oh, if it isn't my Barbara! What are you doing here?'
>
> Before I could speak, Madeline said, 'How are you?' Explaining the trip to Paris, she went on, 'You don't know the time I've had with Barbara,' and blamed our surprise visit on to me. I went scarlet with embarrassment, but nevertheless he invited us to stay for tea and, as usual, was very charming.
>
> 'How can I give you a job in Fleet Street?' he said, 'Your mother would never let you leave home.'

The trip to Paris encouraged Barbara to start what she thought was to be her first full-length novel, about an unhappy Parisian ballet dancer, Vivienne Ramage, who lived in great poverty. The story was to be full of drama, but she had scarcely started writing, however, when she stopped, thinking that the plot reminded her of another book. Her novel, she realised, was far too similar to *La Dame aux Camélias* by Alexandre Dumas *fils*.

> I thought, I've read that before. Somewhere. I can't do that. And that is where it ended. And that reminds me, years later, when I was writing about Emma Harte as a child in *A Woman of Substance*, I had this marvellous line – 'the strongest steel goes through the hottest fire' – two days later, I remembered it came from *David Copperfield*.

She struck out the line, as she abandoned her first 'novel'. All of which does show how easy it is to retain in the memory passages read over the years, and thus innocently to plagiarize another writer's work.

* * *

Back at the *Yorkshire Evening Post*, exceedingly hard work and a certain amount of luck brought dividends. She became, aged only eighteen, the editor of their women's page. Two years later, an opportunity occurred to join *Woman's Own* in London. It was an exciting move, for not only did it mean leaving home, it meant that she would be much nearer the world of the Fleet Street newspapers. As the fashion editor, she had to concentrate on publishing requirements, and she gave little indication of the world-beating novelist lying dormant within her. (Incidentally, *Woman's Own* can boast of sponsoring at least two top authors: eighteen years later, Sarah Harrison also worked there.)

Once in London, Barbara was tempted by other work. After a year at *Woman's Own* she joined the *London Evening News* as a feature writer, then became a feature writer on *Today* magazine, and was for a time an executive editor of the *London American*.

Naturally, her work brought her into contact with many successful and self-motivated people – businessmen, actors, film stars and, of course, politicians – characters whose experiences and emotions would be stored away in her mind for future novels. She little suspected that she was herself destined to marry a Hollywood movie producer, or that she would reach the pinnacle of fame as a self-motivated achiever in her own right.

In 1963 she married Robert Bradford, and moved to the States. One could easily imagine that, having attained so much in such a short career, and with the advantages of being the wife of a successful film producer, she would now relax and enjoy married life. The fact that she continued her career, first in journalism, then as a compiler and editor of books, demonstrates just how much determination the would-be novelist needs.

After a while Barbara returned to her literary work in earnest. Her first edited book, like the second, was for the young, *Children's Stories of the Bible from the Old Testament*. Compared with so many other aspiring authors, it was relatively easy for her, given her background and experience, to write publishable material. From a publisher's standpoint, she was already an established writer, editor and journalist; a far cry from all those people struggling to become writers while working at other jobs.

Her experience as a fashion editor not only gave Barbara a discerning eye for good clothes, it also channelled her thoughts towards the world of interior design and decorating. (Incidentally, clothes and fashion feature largely in all her novels. And when she appears on television, she takes care to heed her parents' advice, 'always to look one's best for special occasions', and will ensure that she wears exactly the right dress. Aware too, that television cameras can make people look chubby, she insists that studio professionals prepare her make-up, rather than trusting to her own ability.) Her new lifestyle doubtless gave her ideas, and she set about writing what became *The Complete Encyclopedia of Homemaking Ideas*, which was published by Meredith Press in 1968. The choice of subject, publication and promotion were all well timed and sales took off, but it was not a book likely to catch the eyes of fiction reviewers. Three years – and two other titles later – she produced a second 'homemaking' book, *Easy Steps To Successful Decorating*. This sold over 165,000 copies – a bestseller for sure, though not one for which she is remembered.

For the vast majority of authors, sales of this magnitude would be fulfilling enough. They would, too, suggest that the writer had found a niche, and few would be tempted to change direction and turn to fiction. Barbara is, therefore, a marked contrast to Catherine Cookson, Dora Saint, Penny Jordan, Dick Francis, and Clive Cussler, who have all stuck to their original themes.

Easy Steps to Successful Decorating led Barbara to even greater success. The book, published in 1971, again by Meredith, attracted the attention of *Newsday*'s syndication department, who asked her to write a regular column for them. She readily agreed and, under the by-line 'Designing Woman', wrote three articles a week which appeared initially in eighty to a hundred newspapers. Barbara was a little vague about the number, but added, 'after I had been doing it for twelve years, it appeared in 183 papers across America! That's quite a number and a major achievement.'

Why, I wonder, do the majority of newspaper and magazine articles about Barbara Taylor Bradford omit any mention of these very successful titles? Do editors or reporters believe that they will not interest readers of her novels? According to Barbara, many interviewers simply fail to ask about them, though they are listed in her official press notes. Curiously, even Barbara herself avoided this aspect of her writing history when interviewed by Paul Kelly for the television programme *The Write Stuff*. Perhaps her comments were edited out.

While all this was going on, she still hankered to become a novelist. She admits to starting four books which she never managed to finish, and these remain safely stored away today. Despite the intervening years, she still says they are 'not too bad', so perhaps they will eventually appear on booksellers' shelves.

> I don't know why I stopped. I think I was in the wrong genre. They were more the Helen MacInnes suspense-type of thrillers. In fact, the last one I started reached 125 pages . . . [But] one Monday morning, I suddenly stopped. I looked at it and thought, this is another one I'm bored with. If I'm bored with it, then the reader will be bored.
>
> I sat there, and I literally asked myself a lot of questions. I've got to decide why I keep starting a novel and getting so far. Some were 300 pages long. What's wrong? I asked myself, what do I really want to write about?

These semi-suspense novels weren't working for me. My God, what do you want to write about, Barbara? I thought, I'm nearly forty. If I don't do it now, I never will.

I thought long and hard. In the end, I decided that I wanted to write a saga, perhaps a family saga, but certainly a saga. I wanted to write about England, more specifically, Yorkshire. I wanted it to be one of those long, traditional, old-fashioned novels, about a woman who makes it in a man's world, at a time when women weren't expected to do that. I wanted to write about a woman of substance . . . I wrote that down in longhand, and that's how my first real novel started. And the phrase stuck too, becoming the title.

I have never written what I thought the public wanted to read, ever. I wrote what I wanted, and I never set out to write a bestseller, and make lots of money. I just wanted to tell this story and I think that's why the books work. They come from the heart, not from the head.

Perhaps it was her homesickness for Yorkshire that sparked it all off. Anyone who has suffered it knows just how strong this yearning can become, and how unsettling, too. Unconsciously, Barbara had discovered the missing ingredient: as her readers know, expressing emotions is one of her writing strengths.

Once her idea was on paper, she realized that she did not know what Leeds was like in 1904, nor all sorts of other historical details. So she flew to England to research the facts, to view the setting, and to interview her relatives, at the same time assuaging her homesickness. Armed with the information she needed, she finished the book in just eighteen months.

When *A Woman of Substance* was published in the USA in 1979 (and 1980 in the UK), it hit the jackpot. It became an instant bestseller, running far ahead of any of her dreams; when the first paperback edition went to press, the first print-run reached 1.4 million copies. Sales reached 3.5 million in the first year of publication – and now about 18 million copies worldwide. To most of her readers, and to the media, for that matter, this was her first successful book. It is certainly the one most talked about. Yet she had had ten books published before *A Woman of Substance* saw the light of day, none of which bore any similarity to this first novel. To the trade, however, she was already well known and not surprisingly an agent soon sought her out.

Through a friend, Carolyn Blakemore (then of Doubleday) telephoned me, inviting me to meet her for a drink. She had heard about me from my column; would I bring the outline of the novel I'd started [i.e. *A Woman of Substance*] to our meeting, as she thought it sounded like the kind of book they were looking for?

Over that drink, I explained I was still finishing a book for Simon and Schuster on decorating, and my current agent in New York might like to know about this, though I had only written the outline.

All agents are persistent, and she was no exception, asking me if he had any call on the fiction, any fiction, that I write. 'No, but,' I said, 'it might be unethical to give it straight to you.' I telephoned the agent, explaining the position, and he said I couldn't let them have it. 'There's nothing in any of my contracts about this,' I said. 'Anyway, why don't you show it to Michael Korda at Simon and Schuster? I was going to send it there anyway.' On this basis, he agreed I could let Carolyn see it too. One hour after receiving the first 192 pages, she telephoned me. It was the first working week in September, a Thursday, just after Labor Day. It was the best she'd read from any author, bar none. 'It's got a great sense of time and place, the dialogue is wonderful, characterization . . .' and on the following Monday they [Doubleday] made me an offer. In the meantime my agent, who had insisted I send it to Simon and Schuster, had heard that their editor didn't particularly like it, but Michael Korda was on vacation and the editor simply wouldn't make a decision. Well, Doubleday put the pressure on me and asked for a decision. They got it. Michael Korda has never forgotten.

A Woman of Substance did not get the major hype treatment, as is the case with so many authors' first novels. Doubleday, Barbara thought, had initially only devoted about $25,000 to promoting the hardback edition, a small sum. Nevertheless, the book made the bestseller lists for several weeks, reaching number seven in the *New York Times*. She feels very strongly that it was the book itself that made her success, rather than any publicity or hype.

The storyline centres on a strong-minded Yorkshire woman, Emma Harte, who is determined to become a successful business leader. But before she can achieve her ambition she has to confront and overcome many personal handicaps – from a humble start in life, inadequate education, to the customs and prejudices of the day. This sounds a little like Barbara Cartland (see next chapter), except that their approaches differ. Cartland concentrates on the aristocracy and on virginal heroines, whereas Barbara Taylor Bradford's heroines seek material power, success, and a release from poverty. This would seem to emphasize authors' frequent advice to would-be writers: write what you know about.

Sales really accelerated when Avon Books brought out the paperback edition. They promoted *A Woman Of Substance* in magazines, and produced a television commercial which appeared during popular talk shows. To all this was added that other ingredient, the personal recommendation. Word soon spread, and the result was huge sales. By 1988, this book alone has sold over 12 million copies.

One consequence of her original career was that, having worked in journalism and publishers, she had the advantage over other authors of understanding how publishing worked. Furthermore, she recognized the benefits of literary agents, having been helped first by Paul Gitlin and then by Morton Janklow, whom she praised enthusiastically. She also knew what to look out for in the small print of authors' contracts. She insisted that the foreign language and dramatic rights remained with her. The American publishers, Doubleday, only secured the rights to publish a hard-cover edition in the US and Canada, with relevant rights for paperback, serialization and book clubs.

Writers of Barbara's standing can command unbelievably large advances. She was paid something 'in the region of 10 million dollars' for her next three titles.' I was still absorbing this when she added:

> It was actually more than that, when you consider this was for US and Canadian hardback and paperback rights only. Oh, and I still retain the rights for the rest of the world.

Evidently, to reach this level of success you have to be more than just a talented writer. An acute business mind helps too.

* * *

During our interview Barbara touched on that famous writers' dichotomy: whether to write what they believe the public wants, or to write what they themselves want. Like many, she prefers to write what she wants, but was she, I wondered, in choosing her stories and characters, affected by reviews, be they good or bad?

> I certainly had some strange reviews of *A Woman of Substance*, especially in America. They don't read the entire book, which is rather unfair, so I pay as much attention to the good reviews as I pay to the bad reviews – which is none.
>
> My books are not written to any formula. Each has been very different, but they have all touched, moved, entertained and

enlightened my readers. And I think I'm giving the reader quite a lot of the things that involve them, particularly identification with my characters.

No, I write what I want to write, whether the books are about interior design or a good story.

I think I taught myself to be a novelist. I don't believe writing can be taught, but you can learn it. You can teach yourself by trial and error. I think all that writing schools can do is to teach you how to use grammar properly, how to put a sentence together so that it makes sense, that it has clarity.

But how can a writing school teach you to have imagination? Or give you an insight into people? Because those are two of the things that you've got to have, if you are going to be a reasonably good novelist. I am wary of these schools. They take money away from people and sometimes it's a scam.

Reading helps. I like Robert Ludlum's spy books [see Part 3], James Clavell and Wilbur Smith, especially when he is writing about Africa. I constantly read biographies, but not a lot of women's fiction because I'm still afraid of accidentally echoing phrases like 'the strongest steel goes through the hottest fire'.

The only books about writing that she has read were borrowed from the local library, but this was early on in her career, when she was training to become a journalist.

Barbara clearly believes that there is no one who can teach you to become a novelist. You have to teach yourself, but she is ready to pass on some tips:

Basic writing ability is still not enough. A would-be novelist must also observe what I call the five 'Ds'.

D for desire – the desire to want to write that novel more than do anything else.

D for drive – the drive to get started.

D for determination – the will to continue whatever the stumbling blocks and difficulties encountered on the way.

D for discipline – the discipline to write every day, whatever your mood.

D for dedication to the project until the very last page is finished.

Finally, there is a sixth D – to avoid! This is for distractions – perhaps the most important D of all, the enemy of all writers, whether would-be or proven.

If writing novels is the hardest work she has ever done, then answering the many letters from readers is a pleasure. She receives about 800 to 900 a year, but does not answer them all personally.

> If they just write and say that they loved the book, I acknowledge that in a standard letter and say thank you, and I'm so glad you took the time and trouble. Most of which are done at [her husband] Bob's office in New York.
>
> But if they ask questions then I have to write something out in hand, but they are all replied to, though it may take a while.

Unlike Catherine Cookson, Barbara Taylor Bradford does not subscribe to the idea that answering readers' letters is the most important way of maintaining future readers. Bestselling authors seem to have very different ways of treating readers' letters, but they are an important responsibility, and some writers say that they are ignored at the author's peril.

Barbara Cartland

Known worldwide for romantic novels, but also writes or has
written biographies, verse and books on sociology, history, health,
etiquette and cookery. Over 651 titles and more than 650 million
copies sold.

In any discussion about romantic writers, it is a fair bet that the name Barbara
Cartland will be mentioned in the first few minutes. It does not matter
whether one loves or hates her work, one cannot ignore her. After all, unlike
Barbara Taylor Bradford, she has written a phenomenal number of books,
mainly Regency-style historical novels which have remained popular for over
seventy years. She is an ardent moralist, believing in the strength of the family
unit, and whenever she is given the opportunity, she speaks with passionate
intensity on this and other wide-ranging subjects. With frequent appearances
on television and articles about her in the national press, it is hardly surprising
that she is a household name the world over. Add her non-fiction titles to the
long list of novels and her total exceeds 651 published books, which is more
than some authors' sales of a single title. By the time this book appears, the
total will doubtless have exceeded this figure.

Surprisingly, this prodigious output does not make her unique. A quick
look in the record books shows that other authors have achieved similar
figures, certainly in terms of number of titles. To put her extraordinary output
into perspective, Józef Ignacy Kraszewski, a Polish author, wrote over 600
novels; others include Kathleen Lindsay (Mrs Mary Faulkner) who wrote
904 novels (involving the use of two other married names and eight pen
names); John Creasey achieved 564 (using about twenty-five pseudonyms);
Ursula Bloom 560; and Enid Blyton 600.

The sales of Barbara Cartland's novels (which typically portray the
aristocratic hero wooing a pretty young virgin, yet always behaving
impeccably) have reached dizzy heights, exceeding 650 million copies
worldwide. Despite this unprecedented success (she says 'because of it'), which
makes her the highest-selling writer in the world, she still keeps writing. 'The
Pink Lady', as she is affectionately known because of her love for things pink,
has been known to average twenty-three titles per year. These are just a few of
the reasons why she has become a legend in her own lifetime, something very

few authors, even the élite bestselling authors, can ever claim. Without doubt, she has earned herself a permanent place in literary history.

The public-relations side of her career underlined this when I went to see her, for I was not only sent detailed printed directions on how to drive to her house, but also a twenty-page booklet outlining her achievements – printed, I need hardly add, in black and pink. She is clearly a practised and well-organised interviewee.

At the assigned hour I rang the bell at her large mansion, in Hertfordshire. Built in 1867 by Edmund Potter, great-grandfather of Beatrix Potter, it seemed a fitting home for such a renowned character. I was welcomed by one of her secretaries, and some friendly but very noisy dogs. 'Mrs Cartland is still with a television researcher,' the secretary told me. 'She's on tomorrow night, so would you mind waiting in the library?' Barbara Cartland is clearly very popular with the media, as well as her public. But where and how did she start on this high road to fame and fortune?

Those who read her romantic novels will know that her writing is unique. Not for her the raunchy bodice-ripping yarn, nor couples leaping into bed in every chapter; neither do sexy illustrations adorn the covers of her books. As she told me when we met, she has *her* standards, and she will not deviate from them. Perhaps this is why she has remained so popular for so long, but if so, why are other authors like Jackie Collins, Jilly Cooper and, in her day, Molly Parkin, so well liked and widely read? Is it because they write about the very aspects of life and love that Barbara omits?

Much has been written about Barbara Cartland – even her entry in *Who's Who* is the longest in that book, almost a full page (though mainly, it has to be said, because it lists all her titles). She also keeps huge archives of press cuttings and other memorabilia at her home. Every author keeps some, if not all, of his or her press cuttings, but in Barbara's case everything is on a grand scale. Her son, Ian McCorquodale, maintains the files with a view to the fact that one day they will be needed for an 'official' biography. But, even given the mass of words written about her, what were the origins of her flair for writing? And what was it that singled her out for such astonishing success?

Like other writers I interviewed, she had experienced poverty and hardship earlier in life, something which often tends to strengthen character. Born in July 1901, she grew up to enjoy the famous 'good times' of the 1920's. Her family had had to endure two periods of austerity, however; first, and most seriously, when her grandfather was forced to return a large bank loan at a time of slump. Unable to face the humiliation of trying to find £250,000 (about £6 million today), he shot himself. The collapse of the business meant that Barbara's parents, Bertram and Mary Cartland, were forced to sell their house. How Bertie and Polly, as they were affectionately known, came to terms with this situation is evocatively described in her volumes of autobiography (of which, incidentally, there are four). Then, in 1918, when she was seventeen, her father was killed in Flanders, leaving the family without a main source of income. Again they moved house, this time to London, and here Barbara's writing career really started. Her interest in reading, and later, writing, naturally began with the attention her mother gave to the subject.

Her mother had read many fairy stories to Barbara, which stimulated thoughts of imaginary princes and princesses struggling through evil, eventually to live 'happily ever after'. She received a solid education, at Malvern Girls' School and Netley Abbey in Hampshire, reading no more than most girls at the time, though in her later teens she would sometimes read up to three library novels a day. 'So where did your interest in books start?' I asked.

> I discovered that libraries would lend books out for twopence. Of course, I borrowed Bertha Ruck, Elinor Glyn, E. M. Hull and Ethel M. Dell; and I read every love story, you know. It wasn't until I was about twenty-three that my brother, who was much older, said, 'God, you're badly educated . . .'
>
> So I sat down and read . . . Jane Austen and Trollope; these led me to read books about history. These really did fascinate me, and nowadays all I want to read is history.
>
> And from that moment on, I thought, now this is me. I love history and I'll never read anything but history. And I read between twenty and thirty of these books for every novel I write. And that is why they read true, because they *are* true. The background is always completely true, do you see?

One feature of 1920's English society was the notion of 'propriety'; society had its 'dos' and 'don'ts', as well as its parties, its 'at homes' and *thé dansants*. For a young girl in society, it was *de rigueur* to be a débutante. Barbara had been presented at Court some years after her mother's mourning for her husband had ended, and had worn a dress designed as an advertisement by a then young Norman Hartnell. However, many of her clothes were bought second-hand, which at least enabled her to attend the numerous functions held by her friends, although it wasn't easy at first:

> I came to London really knowing nobody at all. In fact I borrowed a boyfriend from a girl I'd been at school with, to go out to my first dance. I was very pretty then and Randolph Churchill said I was

the prettiest girl he had ever seen. Very pretty, very bouncy and full of excitement. I gradually collected many young men as friends, mostly from the Guards. Most, too, had little money and didn't take you out to dinner. You weren't allowed to dine alone with a man. Men took you out after dinner; those were the rules made by mothers, so we used to go along to the Berkeley and dance all night for ten shillings [50 pence today, though a great deal more in real terms].

Barbara's books tend to be either adored by readers, or ridiculed. Those who ridicule them do so because her romantic novels all follow very much the same formula, and for the most part there is little salacious activity. Such sex as there is, is left until the last page, and is then expressed in emotional terms, and only when the hero has married his loved one.

One wonders why she embarked on this high road of morality. The evidence is that it stems from those early days in London. After the fun of *thé dansants*, she told me, girls and their escorts would often go for rides in taxis and, while the driver went for his coffee break at a taxi stand, would then be able to whisper 'sweet nothings' in the back. One of these stolen moments was to play a role in forming her writing style. At one time, she was secretly engaged to Dick Usher, a young Guards officer. She took her engagement seriously, but grew concerned because, somewhere in a borrowed book, she had read the inference that passionate kissing can lead to having children. So after one evening's sojourn in a taxi she asked Polly how did one become pregnant? Her mother's factual answer came as a major shock; so much so, in fact, that she called off the engagement.

Barbara told me that she received forty-nine proposals before finally getting married. After one of these unfulfilled engagements, Polly, who had more to worry about than Barbara's engagements and parties, suggested that she should find something 'useful to do'. Just what was not clear, but at one of the *thé dansants* Barbara had met Richard Viner, who worked on the *Daily Express*, then owned by Lord Beaverbrook. Richard, aware that Barbara was a frequent party-goer, suggested that she write little reports of these events. This proved to be an ideal pastime, though the pieces had to be unsigned, otherwise her friends would ostracize her. The best part, however, was that she received five shillings (25 pence) for each effort.

Encouraged by her success as an anonymous contributor, she wrote a few articles with the headline 'Flaming Youth', again for the *Daily Express*. These were seen, of course, by Beaverbrook. He must have been quite impressed, for he suggested that she brought these annonymous reports to his suite at the Hyde Park Hotel. He appreciated her efforts but they lacked the journalistic style required and he set about editing them before sending them in for publication. It was the beginning of a long friendship, and it was through invitations to his parties that she met many other notable people.

The relentless round of partying finally exhausted her mother's patience. The only obvious work for Barbara, if 'work' was the right word for something a society girl might do to earn a little money, was to write. Having had many short pieces published, as well as several articles, she found the confidence to start upon a novel. 'You'll never finish it,' her brothers taunted, but Polly never stopped encouraging her. Besides, Barbara hated being told that she wouldn't finish it, and the taunting only made her more doggedly determined to continue. She put her heart and soul into the challenge, writing, she admitted: 'in bed, in the mornings, after late nights, at odd moments when I was waiting for an escort to arrive to take me out to dance, or as I dressed for dinner in the evening.' And finish it she did.

Then, at a party (whether one of Beaverbrook's parties is not certain), Barbara was introduced to a talented literary agent, Raymond Savage. He agreed to help her and took her work to Thomas Balston, a partner in Duckworth, the publishers. They published her first effort, *Jigsaw*, in 1923. It caused a minor sensation, mainly because the author was 'in society' – someone who, in those days, normally did not have a 'job' at all. It does show, yet again, how an agent can successfully start an author off on a major writing career.

The fact that she was well known in social circles, and was someone who had actually done something noteworthy, must have helped her sales, at least initially. It seems to me that she had some of the same advantages that Barbara Taylor Bradford, Jilly Cooper, Jeffrey Archer and Dick Francis all had when their first novels were published – they were all relatively well-known people. Her friends – Max Beaverbrook, Richard Viner and the historian Sir Arthur Bryant among them – may also have helped, but nevertheless the book had to be readable, and clearly it was popular reading at the time. *Jigsaw* has been described as 'Mayfair with the lid off', and is the story of Mona, who survives the corruption and immorality of life in the Mayfair of the day, to end up married to the heir to a dukedom. The book ran to six editions and was translated into five languages, making Barbara the princely sum of £165 – quite a start for a writer at that time.

The book did have one consequence which Barbara had not anticipated, though. 'On page 200, I wrote that the heroine kissed the hero, and my great-aunts never spoke to me again. They said it must be from personal experience, but I didn't know a single duke in those days.' Even Polly, concerned about the novel's effect on readers, warned her that she should be more careful in future. Barbara heeded the advice, and all her books still carry a moral message. This prompts me to wonder what the outcome would have been had she included bedroom scenes of the kind often written today.

On this subject, she has written:

> I never specifically describe the sex act because it's such a bore laid bare. It makes readers wonder if they're normal if they don't have sex upside down, swinging from a chandelier. So I'm their escape, their fairy tale. I give them the glamour and the beautiful clothes and the marvellous attentive men they are starved of.

After the success of her first novel, Barbara turned her hand to writing plays. At twenty-four she wrote *The Mayfair Revue*, which was performed by a group of her society peers. For her friends, taking part in a revue written by this much-talked-about society girl was a great social attraction, but it was also put on to raise funds for charity. The stage gowns merited comments in the press, for they were again created by Norman Hartnell, then an undergraduate at Cambridge. This success was quickly followed by *Blood Money*, staged in London during 1925. Whether this was a huge success isn't clear, but Barbara preferred writing novels and several more quickly followed: *Sawdust* in 1926 and *If a Tree Is Saved* in 1929, both published by Duckworth. At this point she decided to dictate her work, which she found much easier than laboriously writing in longhand.

A number of authors have suggested that aspiring writers should read as many books as they can lay their hands on. It helps, they say, to gain a better understanding of grammar, syntax and spelling. Barbara told me, however, that she never looked at any 'how to write' books at all and readily admits that even now, despite the many books she reads, her syntax and spelling are very poor.

> Oh yes, I spell terribly badly – I can't spell at all. It was Godfrey Wynne who said to me, 'Barbara, if you are writing for entertainment, dictate.'
>
> So I started to dictate and while my secretaries were always saying that I am inhuman, and walking out, I got along quite well with one. Do you see? – because it was the thing to do to get it done as quickly as I could, because I could then go out and dance and enjoy myself.
>
> Now, do you see? I have two Oxford dons who 'do' my books – the spelling and punctuation. I punctuate in a funny way . . . I cut everything, and my paragraphs are very short, not more than two to four lines if possible. So it's awfully easy to read.

More has been written about Barbara Cartland than any of the other authors I have met. Throughout my research, and my interview with her, I naturally hoped to find something new. My luck held, for I discovered I knew one of the two dons she had mentioned, although she did not identify him by name at our meeting. I went to see him.

His unsung work checking Barbara's typescripts is, of course, no more than that which any self-respecting publishing house carries out on an author's work. (All books receive a degree of editorial treatment, some much more than others.) Barbara takes pride in her work, and prefers to have the editing done herself, thus making it easier for the publisher. The 'Oxford don' (I will not give his name, because he told me that he preferred to remain anonymous and since my writing this book, he has sadly died) had been helping her for the last thirty years or so. When he originally agreed to read her work, she was only writing about four books a year, a relatively light workload for him, though he did find it hard to cope with the twenty-five she wrote in one year! Many full-time publishers' editors would jib at having to handle that number of typescripts in a year.

For many years, he had been a housemaster at one of the United Kingdom's élite public schools. When I interviewed him, he had retired from academic life and had lots of time to devote to her output, although he only read her fiction – her other books went elsewhere. As most of her novels follow a similar plot, I asked him if he ever became bored.

> Not at all. They are interesting and they amuse me, partly because I'm a pedagogue and enjoy using red ink! A hangover, of course, from my days as a schoolmaster – and it's a bit of a challenge to eliminate any possible errors.
>
> Her secretaries do provide her work in a pretty good shape except, perhaps, when Barbara is talking in French. The secretaries are not always good on vocabulary, though. I mean, they occasionally get a word or phrase wrong, but I can generally guess what it is that Barbara had said.
>
> On one occasion, she involved a man and a girl who were in such close rapport that each knew, when they were separated, what the other was thinking. One of them was in London and the other in New York. In the story, something happened that was rather important to the man, and the girl knew about it at the same time of day. Well, of course, she had forgotten the time difference. And she sometimes misjudges time and distances for journeys by stage-coach or private carriage, but all these things are a normal part of editing.

I did once say to her, about one of her books, that 'I've made an awful lot of corrections, I'm afraid', and her reply was very comforting because she said she 'always accepted everything I put'. But I never see the book again until, about a year later, it comes out.

She is a really a remarkable lady, unique amongst the authors you have met.

There is one rather curious aspect of her books which was raised during my meeting with her 'Oxford don'. He remarked that it was strange that none of her heroines had a mother alive. They had always died – sometimes without a detailed explanation being given in the novel – there would be, though, a living grandmother who was always very understanding. Her young innocent virgins, very often orphans, are also remarkably independent and often cleverer than the hero.

I think it would have complicated her plots: if there had been a mother, she would have stopped the girl from doing something damn silly. But it always turns out alright in the end. The girls are nearly always eighteen, or sweet seventeen and never been kissed, and when the Marquis does kiss one for the first time, it is always the first time she's ever been kissed and she realizes that this is the real love she's been looking for.

I'm sure that if there had been a mother, a lot of the plots would not have been possible.

'You've now had so many novels published, but has a publisher ever turned you down?' I asked Barbara.

Oh yes, once. I was asked if I thought anybody could write a book and have it published. I can't remember what it was, but I think it was called *Wings of Love*. I finished it, and sent it in under a false name, and with false details about myself, to a publisher [name deleted to spare their blushes]. They returned the manuscript, saying that I ought to go on writing and perhaps I would have a chance in the future. I then changed the author's name back to mine, and sent it to my usual publisher, and it sold enormously well, like all the others.

It just goes to show that the whole thing is hocus-pocus.

'What is it, then, that drives you to keep on writing?' I asked.

In the papers, there is all this nonsense that I have 10 million pounds. I wish I had. You see, the papers today – they say, I have

160 acres and 10 million pounds. I've absolutely nothing of the sort, except an enormous overdraft. They count the house, which isn't mine; and they count the estate, which isn't mine, it belongs to the children. It sounds an awful lot, but there's simply no cash-flow.

'So you write to keep the cash flowing. But having written so many books, what advice do you give to the hopeful writer?' I asked her.

My dear, there are far too many authors today, and too many titles. My advice to any aspiring author is, don't.

They write to me every day. The whole point is that you have got to write about something you know. I wrote about love because I know everybody's in love with me and I know a lot about love, but, don't you see?, it's no good writing about gold-digging in Australia if you have never been there. That's why I travel so much.

It's terribly difficult to get a book done if you are an ordinary author. People write to me all the time, asking for advice; how they ought to paragraph and so on. They have long lumping paragraphs and they obviously don't take the trouble. They are frightfully casual about it all.

I'm terribly fussy and send things in beautifully typed and beautifully done. Everything must be in absolutely perfect order.

In all her romantic novels, then, is it the plot, the characters, the narrative, or the background which assume the greatest importance for her? And where does she get all her ideas for plots?

Sometimes, I say a little prayer, and I know you won't believe this, but a plot comes, just like that. Then I know I have to read about twenty or thirty historical books. I do like to get the background right.

Every day, I have lunch, then retire to the library, lie on the sofa, and start telling the story, usually a chapter at a time. I talk very quickly, so it helps to record it all on tape.

My secretary is typing the first part now, as we talk, and she will have the rest done tomorrow morning, in time for me to read before I start the next chapter. I have five secretaries to cope, and I know it is jolly hard work because there is so much coming and going all the time.

I was taught, you remember, to write like a journalist. I write between 6,000 and 7,000 words every day that I am at home. That's about a chapter. Each book is about 50,000 words, just enough to tell the story and get the hero married and into the bedroom on the last page.

Each of these sessions lasts about two hours, which means that she dictates at about sixty words a minute! No one is allowed to interrupt these sessions and, at the end she always asks, 'How many words have I done?' The text and ideas for her novels just seem to flow out, as though from a story-teller of earlier times. Her non-fiction books, though, often need more research and so take longer to complete.

There is only one notable person who has ever provided ideas for her novels, and to whom she really listened, and that was her very close friend of fifty years, Lord Mountbatten. Before his murder in Ireland in 1979, he used to telephone Barbara regularly, as well as corresponding with her.

> He was always giving me ideas for books. Some were rather improper, so I'd say, 'No, Dickie. I stand for purity.'
>
> He thought he had caught me out once and told everyone that one of my virgins had gone to bed with the hero before the end of the book. It was my fifth book, and in fact she had been raped. He never let me forget that!

Given all the typing that has to be done, surely she must use a word-processor?

> Yes, we do have one, but they [the secretaries] mainly use typewriters. We receive 25,000 letters a year on health and a further 25,000 fan letters. All get answered. I've dictated most of the letters on to the word-processor, so it is all my own work, though all they have to do is to press the right button and the answer to someone's problem or question comes out.

This illustrates a dilemma that confronts all bestselling authors. Do you make your home address available to readers; or do you hide behind your publishers, agent, or a PO Box number? Barbara took the first of these options many years ago, but she pays a heavy price. She answers all her calls and letters, she told me; however, every letter answered encourages the writer to purchase another Cartland title. In this respect, she, Catherine Cookson and Jeffrey Archer share the same outlook.

'Surely you have more than one secretary to cope with all this work?' I asked. 'Oh yes, between the five, they cope. 50,000 letters a year is a huge amount of mail. 'And I suppose they are mostly from women?'

Yes, nearly all. And I'll tell you what's interesting. Practically all of them have headed writing paper so you know what sort of class they are. An awful lot from America and Mexico; an enormous amount from South Africa; and quite a lot from Sri Lanka and India.

'Surely you must get many from Europe?'

Yes, a fair amount from France. Germany, at the moment is the worst. They are all men, and all want autographs. I have no idea why.

Looking through her long list of published titles highlights an interesting aspect of her career. It was not until the 1970s that her output, at the tender age of sixty-nine, really accelerated. At this age most people are thinking of slowing down, so perhaps she is right in actively encouraging people to keep themselves busy as they grow older. The practice, she claims, leads to a longer life span. For the next fourteen years she averaged twenty books a year, and then the rate increased even further.

Barbara Cartland has boundless energy. Apart from time spent writing, she periodically launches herself into campaigns to help the underprivileged, as her biographical notes record. She has more drive and energy than most people have in their fifties. Everything about her is on a grand scale. Whatever she turns her attention to is treated with intense passion, and her unrelenting energy ensures that the maximum publicity is achieved for whatever cause she has espoused. She has a knack of persuading people who make the decisions to react in the way she wants them to.

Since she has such an assured view on most subjects, I wondered if she thought that there was such a thing as a typical reader. Receiving so much mail, she must surely have a visual image of her readers?

They are mainly those people who crave for real love and an attentive husband. Mostly women, single and married, but also doctors, lawyers, and of course, so many people read my books who are in hospital, and need something cheerful to read about. That's the thing, do you see? All my books have happy endings and everyone knows that there is nothing nasty in them.

Barbara is very intense about the importance of true love. That may have been one reason why she attacked Jackie Collins when they appeared together on *The Terry Wogan Show*. She rebuked Ms Collins for including so many sex scenes in her 'shocking literature', and reminded her that books by well-known authors really can influence the reading public. Her outburst touched a nerve in a huge number of listeners. In the following weeks her postbag included hundreds of supportive letters.

Nowadays her eyesight is, sadly, not quite as good as it was; she likes large-print books to read, and she has also become a little hard of hearing. One is tempted, however ungallantly, to wonder how much longer this energetic and talented lady can continue. One thing is certain, however: she will not easily yield to the constraints of anno domini.

Sarah Harrison

The Flowers of the Field, A Flower That's Free, Hot Breath, An Imperfect Lady, Cold Feet, Forests of the Night, Foreign Parts, Be An Angel, Both Your Houses and *Life After Lunch.*

Sarah Harrison will readily agree that she is not as well-known as Barbara Cartland or, for that matter, Barbara Taylor Bradford. This is hardly surprising, for her success is comparatively recent, but who knows what the future holds if she continues to write?

Her chance to achieve her ambition of becoming a novelist did not come about in any conventional way. Not for her the endless submissions and rejections; instead, she was plucked from among the millions of aspiring novelists by the paperback publishing house, Futura, and it was their backing that helped her to the fame she now enjoys.

Best known as an author of family sagas, she has also written humorous fiction; as I found out, she has a great sense of humour. One has only to read her book *Hot Breath* to understand her appreciation of the funnier side of life, especially the life of a lonely author. So I was intrigued to find out more about how she started, since I felt sure that having become a writer in an such an enviable way, and still being a relatively recent recruit to the ranks of bestselling authors, she would have vivid memories of how it all began.

Sarah is now well established in her second career, but like others, her first was in the allied field of journalism, where, for a time, she was a trainee editor with *Woman's Own*. She is, though, manifestly clear as to why she's now a novelist and not a journalist.

> I can actually remember being a scribbler as far back as a young child of seven, but it wasn't until I was at boarding-school that I really had these fantasies of becoming a writer.
>
> My father was in the Army, so I was packed off to boarding-school . . . I used to scribble these sort of historical fantasies; and out-and-out fantasies they really were, because I had no real facts to go upon. I got most of my ideas from the term's lessons – Roman centurions and the invasion of Britain. Some of the stories, though, were really quite steamy. But best of all, I had captive audiences in the dormitories and classes.

My efforts were mostly very short fantasies, but one I recall, written I think when I was eight, ran to at least three exercise books. It was heavily facetious, but writing was easy for me, and I found it very easy to come top in English.

Oh yes, I certainly daydreamed of becoming a famous author.

If she was good at English, surely her teachers encouraged her to take up this career?

Oh, no. It was always a case – if you were a high-flyer – of going on to a university, or taking teaching, nursing or secretarial courses. I think they saw me as a nuisance, really.

I told my parents about my ambitions, of course, but their attitude, and I think quite rightly, was: 'Well, that's all right, but nobody makes a living out of writing books, so it would be better to get a grounding in something else.' Much the sort of thing I'd say to my own daughter. You wouldn't actually recommend that you cut your traces and went off to write books and nothing else.

Very few of the authors I've interviewed have done just that. Catherine Cookson is one who springs immediately to mind, but did the schoolgirl Sarah ever believe that she was destined to have her work published?

Funnily enough, I think I did, actually. I certainly remember once entering for a Poetry Society competition. I got a fairly smart brush-off, though, but it was the thought of winning some prize money and getting my poems published that attracted me.

There wasn't a school magazine [in which] to have your story published then, but I do remember that I won essay competitions with relentless regularity. There weren't many outlets, really.

. . . I remember seeing the film *The Singer Not The Song* with Dirk Bogarde in it. I remember him riding around in a Mexican western, and at the time the film made a great impression on me. I was terribly struck by the idea, and set out to write a saga based on the film, without, of course, really having any true facts to go on.

I think I was slightly stage-struck then and it was always in my mind, if unconsciously, that I had deliberately set out to entertain. Even in those days, as far as I was concerned, this was a branch of show business.

It took a long time for those childhood dreams to become reality, however. After she left school, Sarah went on to London University, where she read

English, which effectively precluded her from writing creative fiction. After she obtained her degree, a full-time job became a necessity because, like most people, she had to earn a living. Writing a novel, though much more appealing, was not a practical option at the time.

The prospect of a job in the provinces, either as a journalist or in publishing, was naturally less attractive than working in London, mainly because of the greater opportunities there. Besides, London was where the action was. Sarah soon found out that the International Publishing Corporation (often referred to as I.P.C.) offered a training scheme for journalists on one of its titles, *Woman's Own*. Working there would mean that she could live in London and be employed by a well-known national magazine. In addition, the idea appealed to her vision of herself as a magazine journalist. Her spell on *Woman's Own* was to play a significant part in shaping her career.

Disenchantment set in quickly, however, when she discovered that she could not immediately join the team of fiction writers, but had instead to do the normal round working in each department in turn. But while with the features department she did have time to meet one of their fiction editors, the late Lesley Saxby, who proved to be most helpful. So Sarah started to write her own stories covertly and, whenever she needed advice, all she had to do was to pop down the corridor to Lesley's office and get all the help she needed. Whatever Lesley suggested was clearly put to good use, and it was not too long before Sarah had several of her stories published. To have that degree of free editorial advice on tap is just the sort of help that writers dream of, but very seldom get.

One interview Sarah remembers doing for the magazine was with that doyenne of romance writers, Barbara Cartland. Barbara was not prepared to give the interview over the telephone, and insisted that Sarah went to her home in Hertfordshire. It was a meeting Sarah recalls well, though it took place many years ago.

> The first thing that happened when I got to her large and impressive manor house was that I laddered my tights – and it was the very first thing she noticed. I was wearing a mini-skirt but, I mean, it wasn't my fault. Then we sat down to lunch. I was at one end of the table, she at the other. It was just like *Little Lord Fauntleroy*, with four empty places between us on either side. Lunch, of pheasant and game chips, was served by an immaculate butler.
>
> Then she showed me her bedroom, and, as they say, it *is* all pink and satin.
>
> I found her an extremely irritating woman, but at the same time, I do feel a great admiration for her. I think she's so remarkable and she's a self-made woman.

While working at *Woman's Own*, Sarah married Jeremy Harrison, whom she had first met at university. Marriage naturally brought many changes to her way of life and, after four years, the appeal of a career in journalism waned a little.

> My heart wasn't in *Woman's Own*. As a journalist, I was terrible [she grimaced to emphasize the point]. Really terrible. Being a general dogsbody and trainee didn't help either, but I met lots of people I liked and it was tremendous fun, and I enjoyed being there.

A lifelong career with I.P.C. no longer seemed a good choice and she decided to leave, hoping to make her way as a freelance writer. She confided in Lesley Saxby, who strongly advised her to find an agent. Sarah found Carol Smith, who had been working as a secretary at A. P. Watt, the literary agents. Carol had just seized the opportunity of becoming an agent herself, and consequently was actively looking for new authors. The timing could not have been better. Sarah badly needed an agent, and Carol needed writers of real ambition although Sarah admitted that, at the time, she had little evidence of her writing ability.

Her aspirations then suffered a temporary set-back, however, when she spent what was, in her own words, 'an ill-fated sojourn at the North East London Polytechnic.'

> I edited their staff magazine which was an absolute farce. I was so bored to death that I left and went freelance.
>
> I wrote several short stories with reasonable success. One, I remember, was published in *Honey*. My success rate improved, with something like twenty or so published in women's magazines. I edited a children's annual for Ed Stewart; you know, the disc jockey. That was fun and very satisfying. My agent then suggested I tried writing novels. I did two. One, a romantic novel, a sort of Mills and Boon, was a failure because I broke all the rules – I included a gay dinner-party. Both were rejected everywhere, and I was getting terribly depressed.

Not only had Sarah included a gay dinner-party, but she had vividly described, in the first fifty pages, how the heroine thoroughly enjoyed having sex on the hearth-rug with a man who was not even her fiancé. Scarcely Mills and Boon, I thought.

> Then Carol introduced me to Rosemary de Courcy, an editor at the paperback publishers, Futura. She was looking for books to

commission for their Troubadour imprint, which was Futura's new line in 'hot historicals'.

At Carol's office and over lunch we discussed numerous ideas for their Troubadour imprint and these were finally whittled down to three. The only trouble was that they were all for historical novels, and history is not something I'm good at. Rosie was looking for someone to write about the First World War, but from a woman's point of view. That's the one I decided to work on and when I sent in my thirty-page synopsis, I was still doubtful whether it would be good enough. They accepted it and agreed on their standard advance: £2,000.

That was probably very good, but to me it was riches, it was the most money I'd seen. I got £1,000 on signature and £1,000 on delivery.

That was the good side: the other was that I had to write 100,000 to 150,000 words, anything less was not worth publishing!

Aspiring writers do not always realize that publishers do occasionally commission novels, even from relatively inexperienced authors. This is where literary agents can help. Sarah's experience is, however, a rare one, for it is a fact that fiction is seldom commissioned. Most novelists write what they want, rather than what a publisher has asked them to do.

Rosemary de Courcy was actually looking for an author to follow the popular 'bodice-ripping' successes of 'hot' historical sagas. She and Futura's managing director, Anthony Cheetham, saw this new genre of fiction not only as a potential moneyspinner but, if they could find a bestseller in this new field, as something that would establish Futura as a market leader. Sarah seemed just the right author for them.

As it turned out, the novel took some eighteen months to write – all 250,000 words of it. (This compares, incidentally, with the average novel extent of 80,000 words, and the average Mills and Boon of 50,000.) It is worth emphasizing that there were then, and there are still today, publishers who look around for people to write what they, the publishers, want, in order to meet what they think the public's reading tastes will be in two or three years' time. It takes an extremely talented publisher – or agent, for that matter – to choose the right subject, and the right author for it.

It was at about this time that Sarah had another real break, when she again entered a literary competition. This time it was for a children's book, and was sponsored by *The Sunday Times*. The winning entry would be illustrated by Nicola Bayley, and would be published. Despite the realization that there were likely to be some 60,000 entrants, Sarah thought she would have a go.

I never really stood a chance, you know, with all those entries, but I spent the best part of half a day on it, and of course I didn't win. It's very hard to get a children's book right. Then it sat on my agent's desk for many weeks afterwards while she wondered what to do with it. Then quite by chance an impecunious illustrator from the Hornsey College of Art came to her office asking if there was anything he could demonstrate his talents on. She said, 'Well, I've got this. Why not take this away?' Two days later he returned with the most wonderful pictures. They were absolutely beautiful and then we sold *In Granny's Garden* to Jonathan Cape within a week. The illustrator was Mike Wilks. He's a very successful man now. He did *The Ultimate Alphabet Book*, which was in the bestseller list for weeks. Now he lives in the south of France and you almost can't get to talk to him now without an appointment.

I was over the moon when the book was actually published, first in America, then here. But it never sold very well. Just seeing the book was just like a Christmas present and so unexpected. It really was.

Just after *In Granny's Garden* was published, Sarah finished the novel contracted by Futura. *The Flowers of the Field* was published in April 1980, receiving a great deal of notice, though it must be said that the publishers advertised it widely. To Sarah, it was probably one of the best years of her life, with two books in the bookshops. The 666-page book is a family saga set at the time of the First World War, a story centred upon a monied family, the Tennants of Kent. The novel and its sequel, *A Flower That's Free*, describe how the war affects the family, both 'upstairs' and 'downstairs'.

I was very lucky really. My grandfather, a major-general in the First World War, left me a huge collection of postcards, regimental histories and albums. They provided the background and helped get the facts right.

The hardback edition was well received, though there were few reviews. Sales began to soar. What followed will make any hopeful author, hungry for money, instantly sit down and begin writing...

The paperback rights were quickly sold to an American publisher for $175,000, and an American book club paid a further $70,000. In England, *Woman's Realm* bought the serialization rights for what was then a record sum of £5,000. Overseas rights sold included deals with publishers in Australia ($600), Finland ($5,000) and Holland ($10,000). An author usually gets around 50 percent of the money paid for these rights (and 50 percent of subsequent royalties once the initial sum has been recovered), but Sarah got a good deal more, demonstrating how much depends on the negotiating skills of an author's agent. In addition, the initial hardback print-run was 20,000, but the advance orders were so good that the novel was reprinted on publication. Heady stuff, especially given that the average print-run for a first novel is nowadays less than 2,000 copies.

What was it, then, that made *The Flowers of the Field* such a hit with the public? Certainly it was energetically promoted by the publishers, who spent over £20,000 on publicity and promotion, many times the amount then normally allocated to a first novel. The process of raising the public's interest in the novel began months before it was actually published. Futura, with an eye on profits from volume paperback sales (the hardback was published by their sister company, MacDonald), committed themselves to a number of unusual promotional ruses. For example, during the previous autumn they had printed 1,000 proof copies and sent them as Christmas presents to major booksellers. This was followed by a heavy, if conventional, advertising campaign, firstly in the book trade papers, then in women's magazines and national and provincial newspapers. Booksellers were supplied with dumpbins – 'bins' (in fact, specially printed cardboard boxes) in which books are piled high for customers to pick from – colourful posters, and window stickers, all designed to promote the novel and its author. The theme used in Futura's press releases was that of 'a housewife's journey from rags to riches', emphasizing that this novel was bound to be widely read. One consequence of all the press notice was that Sarah had to travel around the country giving interviews on radio shows and to newspapers and magazines, all of which may sound very good for the ego, but is in fact an extremely tiring and often a lonely occupation. Finally, the BBC invited Futura to feature the story of how the novel and its author had been promoted. The result was a forty-minute film for BBC TV's *The Risk Business* programme.

'Looking back at all those events now,' I asked Sarah, 'what would you think was the largest single factor that made *The Flowers of the Field* such a success?'

I would be absolutely naive to say that I wasn't extremely fortunate that the publishers homed in on it, and spent all that money publicizing it, though it didn't get many reviews. There's no doubt that the hype was a help, of course. The other thing was the whole story of the hype was made into this TV programme. That generated an awful lot of interest. But I have to say that I think word-of-mouth recommendation was most important.

She went on to compare her novel with another, *The Four Hundred* by Stephen Sheppard, which was published at about the same time. Sheppard was then, like Sarah, relatively unknown, and a similar amount in publicity and promotion was spent on him and his novel. However, in spite of the sale of hardback rights to Secker and Warburg and of paperback rights to Penguin, bulk paperback sales simply failed to materialize. Reviewers did not like *The Four Hundred*, and shops were unable to sell it. Film rights were sold, fetching, reportedly, $1 million, but even that failed to help the book's sales.

Sarah's own novel, she said, had taken some seventeen months to write, so I asked her whether in all that time she had become depressed, had wondered whether it was all worthwhile?

> Yes, I got *very* depressed at times, but I was getting positive encouragement from Futura because I was sending in chunks as I went along. They enthused madly over it so I knew they liked it very much. And when it was only half-finished they managed to sell it to America. That helped immensely, but it doesn't all just happen.
>
> You have got to keep driving yourself to put words on paper. It's the point I'm making to these would-be writers I'm talking to at the moment. Writers say they often find it difficult to achieve 'flow' so I genuinely think covering the paper is the most important thing, because if you make yourself write a page, then suddenly, halfway down the second page, you find that you've written a couple of paragraphs that *do* flow, and you did not notice it happen.
>
> I have barren wastes though, and when I find it difficult to maintain the momentum, I give everybody here at home real hell! So I'm not smug about it at all.

The Flowers of the Field had been written in extremely difficult conditions. With three young children playing noisily in the house, Sarah elected to write in the corner of a bedroom, and then mostly during school hours, which limited her writing time especially during the school holidays.

I was interested to learn that she had sent in 'chunks' of copy – usually three chapters – as she went along. This practice goes against the advice of Jilly Cooper, who believes that the submitted typescript should be the complete finished work, something the publisher can either like, or lump. In this instance, the editor and Sarah's agent wanted to see how the novel was progressing, since Futura had invested quite heavily in an unproven author. Another advantage was that having material in advance allowed them to offer the book for overseas rights well ahead of publication.

I wondered what, with her first novel behind her and having then written the sequel, *A Flower That's Free*, had made her switch subjects to write *Hot Breath*?

Well, both *The Flowers of the Field* and its sequel are enormously long books. Probably the equivalent to three or four average-sized books, and I badly needed a change. Since I started to write *A Flower That's Free*, it had been in the back of my mind to try to write something lighter and more contemporary. I wanted a rest from all the research and complications.

I had the feeling that my publisher would not welcome this idea with open arms, so I thought I would nip off and do it. So during the long period waiting for *A Flower* to be published – which was about a year – I wrote *Hot Breath*. It was a very therapeutic exercise and fun to do, and it led to all sorts of other things. It is extraordinary how doing something different, and showing yourself in a different light, opens up a completely different readership and a different sort of attention. It actually did get a few reviews, so perhaps I'll write another before I'm too much older. [*Cold Feet* was to be her next title.]

For any would-be writer, preferably one with a broad sense of humour, *Hot Breath* makes very good reading, particularly for the reader who is determined to assume that, like some authors, Sarah based the book on her own experiences.

I quote part of the copy from the back cover:

What has transformed Harriet Blair, contented wife and mother and bestselling author of torrid hot historicals into a rampant vamp?

Could it be the arrival in sleepy Basset Parva of Constantine Ghikas, blond Greek god and latest addition to the local medical practice?

With husband George safely marooned in the Middle East, Harriet feels the Fates have conspired to throw a real-life romantic hero into her path. But her carefully staged seduction scenes are thwarted by the unwitting sabotage of family and friends, not to mention the demands of her publishers, panting for the new masterpiece . . .

The chairman of the fictitious publishers in *Hot Breath* bore a vague resemblance to her real publisher's chairman, the late Robert Maxwell

(Macdonald and Futura were among the publishing companies he owned). Most readers would not have spotted any likeness, but when the manuscript arrived at Macdonald, the supposed resemblance gave one or two executives a fright – they feared for their jobs if the book was published in unexpurgated form. Sarah rewrote the character to be less like Maxwell, and all was well.

Hot Breath sold very well, and there was even a German edition which had not been the case with her first novel. 'Long books,' she said, 'do suffer from this problem that they are terribly expensive to translate.'

Would she like to change subjects again, I asked, and write something entirely different? (Though most authors I have met seem to keep to the formula that has brought them success.)

> You know, the people who make money want to write serious well-reviewed books, and people who write serious well-reviewed books want to make money. I would just like to write a life-enhancing novel, but I do not know what the hell it would be. Usually when people say that, it means that they feel that they're not fulfilling their potential, or they are not doing what they could. Whereas I have a nasty suspicion that I have.

Sarah does seem to be achieving her ambitions, for her fourth novel, *An Imperfect Lady*, is not like any of the first three. I was, therefore, curious to learn if she was able to change subjects without undergoing many rewrites. Some authors have admitted that they rewrite their work several times before they are happy with it, whereas Dora Saint, for one, simply writes her stories without making any corrections or amendments.

> I've written my books in many different ways. For *The Flowers of the Field* I did a chapter at a time and then rewrote it once and that was it. Extraordinary, really, for it to be cast in concrete, but that's how I did it. And the sequel was done the same way, I think. *Hot Breath*, though, was written through to the finish, then I went back and rewrote it all. And I did *An Imperfect Lady* the same way, but it is another very long novel of some 700 pages. I had to do three drafts, which took me nearly two and a half years to finish . . .
>
> Funnily enough, with *Imperfect Lady* it was different. I decided to change the ending with four weeks to go before handing it all over. I actually sat down and wrote it all longhand on a ruled notepad. I can't say why. It was more sympathetic somehow. It seemed to relieve the stress, and then I went back and typed it all out.

My advice to any aspiring author is, I think, not to stop writing. I think people put their all into one short thing and send it off and wait for the result, instead of immediately writing something else. I know it sounds terribly banal, but if you keep the muscle working, it's better.

It seems obvious that it pays a writer to have an agent, although her success did, however, initially incorporate a large element of luck: not many authors find publisher actively looking for someone to start a new line in fiction.

So just what has success brought Sarah? Money, certainly, though she would be the first to say that it has not made her rich. And fame? – yes, that too. And yet another consequence of her burgeoning success is that, like many authors, she is often invited to speak at dinners and writers' conferences.

If Sarah practices what she preaches and her luck continues, it seems likely that we will be reading much more of this talented writer.

Penny Jordan

Falcon's Prey and over one hundred Mills and Boon titles, achieving sales of over 50 million copies worldwide.

Mentioning the British publishers Mills and Boon, will usually – like mentioning Barbara Cartland – guarantee an immediate reaction. Opinions amongst women seem to be divided between one of smug cynicism that states that such novels are trash or pap, and its opposite, which say they 'make a very good read'. Most people will admit to having read a Harlequin Mills and Boon title at some time or other, though few, I have found, enthuse wildly about them. Nevertheless, the publishers are very successful.

To the majority of readers – and it is irrelevant whether they like or dislike the Mills and Boon novelette – this is the one publisher whose name epitomises romance. Since it was founded in 1908, this unusual publishing company has carved a unique place for itself in literary history. Today the company of Harlequin Mills and Boon, part of Harlequin Enterprises, claims to sell over 180 million books a year. The imprint of Mills and Boon has become a cult name among readers of romantic novels.

Unlike writers published by other companies mentioned in this book, Mills and Boon authors rarely get the same degree of high-profile publicity as that enjoyed by, say, Barbara Taylor Bradford. A few have been promoted, people like Sally Beauman, Charlotte Lamb, Anne Weale, Marjorie Lewty, Elizabeth Power and Dana James, but most authors who contribute to M and B's output are relatively unknown. Many prefer it that way. In all, the company averages some thirty-two novels a month, which at least suggests that there is scope for new authors.

Penny Jordan, one of Mills and Boon's more successful authors, is certainly one who eschews publicity. The publisher's press release provided me with some background notes about her, but I was amazed to discover that she had actually published over one hundred books. It seems clear that, where Mills and Boon romances are concerned, it is the publisher's imprint that is important, rather than the individual author.

Penny, as I have said, avoids publicity, but this does not seem to have affected her sales.

I've done the odd newspaper interview and a few radio discussions.

But I'm terribly anti all publicity. I know it sells books, and I know it's the new way, but I still hate it. I'm sure I'm not the only writer who has told you that.

She was right on that point. James Herriot had similarly strong views – perhaps this is a characteristic of people who live in the north of England. Penny also lives in the north, but Cheshire rather than Yorkshire. Her home is also probably as difficult to find as his, set high on a hill with impressive views of the surrounding countryside, although it is only a few miles from Macclesfield. The fourteenth century Yeoman's Hall in which she lives is full of oak beams and panelling, and during our discussion we sat in a room so furnished, her office-cum-library.

It is possible that Penny Jordan personifies the ideal image of the romantic writer.

I didn't specifically want a career. Girls in my day didn't normally have careers, they normally worked until they got married, then left and had a family.

When Steve and I got married, we decided, for financial reasons, that both of us would need to continue working. Until then, I hadn't thought I would have to, and I had no intentions of having a working career.

My schooldays were nothing exceptional. I went to a small grammar school and managed to get three O-levels; I don't know how I achieved that miracle. Then my parents sent me to a secretarial college in Wortham, which is near Manchester, because I don't think they knew what to do with me. From there I went to work, for short spells, at the London and Lancashire Insurance Company, two small firms of solicitors, and then at the Midland Bank.

I enjoyed working at the bank very much, mainly because I was working for a manager, and dealing with people. I was there quite a long time so I got to know most of the customers quite well. It was all very personal then, but we still kept records. We would see their whole lives developing, with all their ups and downs. It was all very interesting, but nowadays it's become quite mechanized, or so I've heard from friends. Without that personal touch you had with the customer, it isn't as interesting as it was. People tell you that banking is boring. It isn't boring at all, nothing dealing with people is ever boring.

I actually started writing when I was thirty, so for a long time I wrote and worked. And I did both for quite a while, but I finally left on Christmas Eve, sixteen years ago.

Here, then, is another who began her writing career while working full-time in another occupation. It seems such an obvious way to begin, but not all authors agree that it is; Jeffrey Archer, for example, believes that you cannot do both successfully. His view may be an exception though. Certainly, few bestselling authors have started without first having had another career.

Penny started writing in 1976, but it was some time before she had anything published.

> I always wanted to write and I thought when I was thirty, if you are going to do anything with your life, now is the time.
>
> There wasn't a specific reason. Steve was working hard, and we'd moved house and did not go out very much, so I had lots of time on my hands which I wanted to fill.
>
> I was a great starter, but not a finisher, and my thanks go to Steve and one particular brother-in-law, both keen readers like me, who thought it would be of value if I could actually manage to finish something.
>
> You spend a lot of time thinking, well, I'll do that one day, I'll do that another day, and suddenly when you're thirty you think . . .

She paused for a moment.

> You know, I didn't specifically think I could do it, but it was the achievement of actually sitting down and writing something, and finishing it. That was the achievement. That was the goal, and it seemed very, very, grown-up to sit down and actually finish something.
>
> And that gave me a degree of confidence, but I didn't feel really confident until I had a book out.

She paused again, and our conversation returned to her school days. Penny disclosed that one of her problems at school had been that, though she naturally wrote left-handed, she was often forced to do so right-handed. Perhaps this pressure affected her results – clearly, she was no scholar, though she did excel at English. Even then, however, she did not enjoy the set writing.

> You always had to write to order. You'd be given a subject, and they were never subjects that I wanted to write about.
>
> It wasn't until I actually sat down and started using my imagination, instead of daydreaming, that it really all started to flow. And I did daydream a lot, especially through French lessons, about the stories I had read in books, and continuations of them.

I used to read a lot at school. All sorts of books, but as far as comics were concerned we were only allowed to read *Girl* and the *Eagle*. There weren't many around, either, but I had a lucky find when I was about eleven. We had a neighbour whose son left home, and I was handed all his comic annuals, and his *Just William* books. I simply read those straight though. But at school we went to the library twice or three times a week, then I used to read father's library books, my sister's and my own. Everything from *Orlando The Marmalade Cat* to Alastair Maclean.

Penny graduated into writing through her own efforts. She joined a local writers' group, where the varied subjects tackled stimulated her interest, though not many of those attending the course were writing fiction. But, like Clive Cussler (see Part 3), she did seek advice from a writing school.

I paid for the course, but it really was a waste of both time and money. I knew that my dialogue wasn't right, it didn't flow easily and the whole thing was stilted. I actually thought, maybe a writing school would help me polish up on that, but in reality it didn't. It was so basic. It was less helpful than what I knew by instinct, which wasn't an awful lot. So, you know, I agree with the majority. I don't believe those courses can teach you to write. I think it's simply commonsense.

Why had she chosen romance for her fiction? She was happily married and with a good job, but with time on her hands and a lingering desire to write a novel; she could in fact have chosen any subject.

Ah well, I love romance. Especially historical romance. I don't like everything, there has to be a happy ending, though.

I like Barbara Taylor Bradford's books and I liked Georgette Heyer, so when I started, I had a try at that sort of thing. Not specifically trying to copy her work, but you tend to write what you admire.

Eventually it came over me that it would be really nice to have something published, and of course, by this time I had read enough, and knew enough, to know that it's very difficult for an unknown writer, especially for someone like myself. And I'd read somewhere, a women's magazine I think, that Mills and Boon were always looking for new writers. I had read a lot of their books and I thought, why don't I try?

Then followed a long period of time when I wrote three words, three lines, or three chapters. You know, for months, perhaps, I wouldn't touch the typewriter, then I would stay up all hours of the night writing. Sometimes, the idea would dry up and it would be thrown away, or put into the drawer. Eventually I got something finished and I sent it off to them.

They had it for about three months, and I thought to myself, that's a waste of paper again. It was between Christmas and the New Year and I must have had a sudden surge of decision-making, so I telephoned them, and a voice said, 'Oh yes, we've just written to you about it, and we'd like to publish it, but it needs a few alterations.'

I nearly fell out of my chair. I couldn't believe it.

I would have liked to have written historical fiction, but it was the fact that I knew that Mills and Boon were looking for new writers. If I'd read that someone was looking for historical romance, I would have gone down that alley, but I didn't.

Penny's break into writing is far from unique; Mills and Boon has an excellent record of attracting new writers. *Falcon's Prey* was published in October 1981. It was the first of her one hundred and seven titles, all of them published by Mills and Boon or by an associated imprint. There is, however, at least one major difference between Penny Jordan's career as a top-selling novelist and those of others: she has never employed a literary agent.

I asked her how, after writing numerous romantic novels, she viewed her good fortune?

I consider that luck was one of the most important factors in my success. I was in the right place and at the right time. There could be a thousand people who could have written that first novel equally as well, or as badly, as I did, but I had the good fortune to send it in at that specific time.

And my luck included a great editor, Jackie Bianchi. She edited my first and subsequent books, but sadly she was killed in a car accident.

It is a curious fact that the titles of Mills and Boon romances do not tend to have the same importance as titles of other genres. (Among Penny's novels are *Bought With His Name, Desire's Captive, Passionate Protection, Stronger Than Yearning* and *Valentines Night*.) Book titles are normally considered very important, as

Hailey, Cussler, Michener and others stress, but with romantic fiction it is the publisher's reputation and the author's style that matter most.

Sadly, there was no launch party for her first novel, but since the publishers produce so many new titles each year, a party for each new novel would be impossible. When *Falcon's Prey* was published, it was just another title among the many on the Mills and Boon shelves. Penny, like all authors, went down to her local bookshop to see it on display. That was very satisfying, but without a party, and without any major coverage in the local papers (and such novels are very rarely reviewed in the national press), her career as an author got off to a very unpretentious start.

> Even now, but especially then, it's more the brand-name that counts. People have specific writers that they like or don't like, but it's Mills and Boon that counts, not the writer.
>
> I think it's quite common with Mills and Boon, when they take on a new writer, to have to publish several titles before the writer builds up a following of readers. I really don't know anything of this side of the business, but I think they bring out so many of each one [writer] and they won't know, until they get the returns, how well it's sold or not.

Readers may not be familiar with the term 'returns'. Bookshops generally order books from publishers on a 'sale-or-return' basis, and if after a period some are left unsold, they can be returned to the publisher for credit at the price at which they were bought in. A publisher can thus see a stock of, say, 10,000 copies leave his warehouse, only later to have, if he's unlucky, several thousand copies back. It is as galling for the publisher as for the author, not least because it affects the author's royalty payments.

It takes Penny about a month to complete a novel, though she wilts if it does not fall right first time. She seldom goes back and rewrites, or 'patches', as she calls it. More often she turns her mind to something else, in apparent contradiction of the determination writers need if they are to finish a book.

> I don't go over and over it, or rework it. That's just not me, which is why I'm struggling with this long book which I've just done. I'm having to patch and alter it, and it's absolute murder because of the intensity of the concentration.
>
> I do set myself targets. I said it would take me six weeks to complete the corrections and I hope to finish next week. That would be four, and if I don't finish it, all hell breaks loose. If I don't make my own target, I'm unliveable-with.

. . .I do gabble and rush things, and it's the same when I write. People who know me say they can see a lot of me in the novels, but it's not deliberate.

Often the views that I propound for the heroine may not be specifically mine, but I accept that the characters, such as they are, have a bias towards my own characteristics because it's easier that way. I write more of what I want to write, rather than what I think the public would like to read, but there are things that I would like to write that I haven't written.

Of all my novels, I've enjoyed writing *Loving* the most, and another recently, about an older heroine and an adult child, but they all must have a happy ending. I wouldn't write anything different, because I like that.

I write what I think is a good story simply because I enjoy writing it, but I have little idea as to why they are so successful.

Someone I know who regularly reads Penny's novels tells me that the men described in her novels are always vulnerable in some way or other; as a result, readers cannot help but feel sorry for them. It may be that other readers identify in some way with her characters and the situations they find themselves in.

Penny writes many more novels than are actually published, for, surprisingly, Mills and Boon sometimes turn her work down. She is the only author I have interviewed to have been regularly published by one firm over a period of years, and yet to have had some of her work rejected (one report quotes her success rate as 80 percent.) As you will read elsewhere, most authors usually leave their publisher if one of their typescripts is turned down.

Naturally, whenever Mills and Boon reject a novel, they give reasons: 'not enough sparkle', say, or 'the storyline's too heavy for a light romance', all of which can be very helpful to a writer, if somewhat disappointing. Penny told me that she simply 'flings them into a cupboard', since they are of little use to any other publisher, having being written specifically for Mills and Boon. This surprising piece of information started me wondering whether other Mills and Boon authors received the same treatment. If so, there must be hundreds of near publishable typescripts stored away – and suitable, perhaps, for another publisher? It may be that, in an attempt to emulate the world-famous Mills and Boon formula, someone will well publish them one day.

Penny's output is high. She can, as has been said, write a novel a month, providing she is not working on a saga. Each is about 55,000 words, considerably smaller than a conventional novel of around 85,000 words, but slightly longer than Cartland's average of 50,000. Clearly, it is difficult to ensure that each new romance has a fresh storyline, and that the plots or characters in any two books do not repeat themselves – what a cynic might call 'the Barbara Cartland syndrome'.

Penny readily confessed that she does not go back and re-read her earlier titles.

There's little point. I can remember the basic plots, but with romance there are only so many – or, if you like, there's only one plot.

I'm probably repeating myself all the time, but it's repeating it with a different story, and with a different set of characters and a different emotional basis. I always emphasize the emotional basis. That's the important thing.

Then I give the heroine a career, as it were. When I worked, they [the novels] often had office settings. Now I'm at home . . . they tend to have a more country setting. I've one heroine who earns a living doing baskets of dried flowers, and one who repairs tapestries. They have the same story, boy meets girl, and the happy ending, but they are all different.

I don't create the characters as such. They just grow up around the emotion.

I'm influenced by what's going on around me and I'm happy with what I do. For example, I'm not after any literary award. Recognition for me is people going out and buying. I'm not trying to write something of literary merit, I'm trying to write stories. There's a big difference.

Writing perfect English and writing a bestseller are two completely different things. It's like a painting. One can be a beautiful object itself, because of its colour and the way it is constructed. Another can be a painting of a scene that draws you into it. The first stands in its own right for its colour, shape and form [but] – as a literary work – the latter will draw you into it because it will tell a story.

The actual use of the language isn't the primary function; telling a good story is the primary function. If the story holds the reader's attention, it doesn't matter about the language.

To anyone wanting to be a writer, I would say, 'Sit down and do it. Give it a try.' And read a lot.

If you just want to write, you can write what you like. The pleasure is in the writing. But if they want to get it published, if they want to earn a living at it, that's a totally different concept.

I wouldn't recommend anyone to sit down cold-bloodedly and say, 'I want to earn my living writing.' It doesn't work that way.

Penny's view that writing perfect English does not automatically confer bestsellerdom is supported by most of the other authors I interviewed. However, before anyone deduces that any standard will do, they would do well to remember that a typescript has to be easy to read, and that the more editorial work a publisher has to do, the more expensive the book is to produce, and thus the higher its price in the shops. Penny was clearly very fortunate to have her first work published so easily, but luck – although she had already admitted that the timing was important – was not the only factor in her success.

I think, if you said to me, 'why have you succeeded out of the hundreds of others who could have done the same thing and not succeeded?' for me, it was the simple thing that I was in the right place and at the right time. Or I'd submitted the book at the right time.

Then and since, I've had marvellous editors, which is a terrific boon. They do help, but I realize that people might misconstrue this help. People imagine that with Mills and Boon, you are told what to write. That isn't true; you're not. And you are not given a formula and told, 'Here, this is what you can do.'

Penny may not have been given a definitive formula, but Mills and Boon go out of their way to help aspiring writers, perhaps more than any other publisher. The company provides written notes about the so called formula in an effort to help the author meet current demands of the romance market, and these demands have changed in recent times. One result is that they receive over 4,000 unsolicited typescripts a year, many times more than they publish. They have some 350 authors whom they do publish, whose ages range from the twenties (I believe the youngest ever signed up was eighteen) to the seventies. Interestingly, Mills and Boon report that this is also the age-range of their readership, something that should encourage any reader with even the vaguest of romantic story-telling inclinations.

Once writers are accepted by them, and once their novels have acquired a sound following, they can look forward to seeing at least 100,000 copies printed of each title, for Mills and Boon claim to have more than half the UK market readership.

Whether they do or not seems irrelevant to Penny, for with over one hundred titles to her name, worldwide sales of 50 million copies and novels ranked in the top group borrowed from public libraries, she has achieved the dreams that so many others harbour. Would-be romantic novelists should take heart from this, and 'have a go'. Mills and Boon are still looking for new authors.

Molly Parkin

Love All, Up Tight, Full Up, Write Up, Fast and Loose, Switchback, Up and Coming, A Bite of the Apple, Love Bites, Breast Stroke, Molly Parkin's Purple Passages, and others.

Molly Parkin's name featured often in the media during the seventies. Although she now describes her novels as 'comic-erotic', they caused many an eyebrow to be raised then. Sales never reached those achieved by other authors of bestsellers; nevertheless, they were very popular, but she ceased writing them in the early eighties due to a total alcoholic breakdown, and consequently has not appeared in any recent bestseller lists. Why, then, include her in this group?

She has recently taken up her pen again, but her ideas have changed radically with the passing of time. Wishful authors, dreaming of writing a bestseller, often consider emulating successful authors and their themes. Molly is, however, a writer who has been to the top, and to the bottom. Can the hopeful author gain by her experience? She believes so.

She was very much a precursor of authors like Jackie Collins and Judith Krantz. She had ten novels published between 1974 and 1983, and though she was not involved in the glitzy movie world like Jackie Collins, she managed nevertheless to shock people with her books, in interviews, and on radio shows. The popularity of her novels eventually declined, suggesting, perhaps, that familiarity breeds contempt among readers, at least where salacious material is concerned. During the heady years of her success she became notorious for her outrageous behaviour, to a point where she once appeared the worse for drink on the BBC's television show *Pebble Mill at One*. This only served to increase her notoriety. The *Sunday Mirror* later carried a critical comment by the programme's editor, Peter Hercombe: 'It upset a lot of viewers, Molly should have told us she'd been drinking.' To which the writer adds her own postscript: 'it should have been bloody obvious when I arrived!'

As a writer, Molly resolutely maintained her style, and her popularity has waxed and waned as a result. Her novels outraged many readers at the time, but her second book, *Up Tight*, also proved to be too offensive for some booksellers. It was banned from display by W. H. Smith, who ruled that it should only be available from 'under the counter' if specifically requested. Hatchards and Harrods also refused to have anything to do with it, but these decisions were more to do with the jacket illustration rather than the contents. She is, therefore, someone whose experiences any aspiring writer should take into account; having reached the top, what steps can they take to avoid their books becoming unpopular?

Much was written about Molly Parkin in the seventies in interviews, articles and reviews, and in comments about her marriages and behaviour. She described her career as being of three ages, although nowadays it would perhaps be more appropriate to say four ages, for she has been a player of many parts in addition to that of author. In her first 'age' she was at various times an art teacher, painter and a boutique-clothes designer; her second 'age' saw her as a fashion editor, columnist and restaurateuse; her third, as a novelist; and her fourth, as a raconteuse, broadcaster and stage artiste.

When we finally met at her West London flat (finally, because it was almost a year before my original letter was delivered to her, and I had almost given up trying to make contact), evidence of her past occupations was everywhere. The small room was filled with memorabilia, unfinished paintings and artist's paraphernalia. However, writing clearly beckoned again, for in the corner was a new word-processor . . .

Most of Molly's formative years were spent in the suburbs of north-west London, Dollis Hill and Willesden, where her father, a frustrated painter, took any jobs that were going. She had the misfortune to contract acute mastoiditis at the age of seven, and spent months in hospital recovering. Following a spell of convalescence in Yarmouth, she was taken to live with her grandparents in Wales. Pontycymmer, where she was born, lies in a small, typically Welsh, valley, overshadowed by coal mines, a few miles from Bridgend.

Her grandparents were ardent members of a Nonconformist chapel. This Welsh chapel background, as Molly refers to it, did not come as a huge culture shock, however, for even when she was with her parents in London she had had to attend chapel regularly; three times on Sunday. It was the same at Pontycymmer, too.

> I liked the serenity of being with those old people. I liked their con-
> versation and the way they talked about philosophical matters
> around the fire-grate. And we used to have the preacher come round
> and stay in our house. My grandfather was senior deacon there, and
> I sometimes think that my enforced leisure, sitting in chapel for
> hours at a time, really fanned the flame of my imagination.

These enforced periods of inactivity allowed her active and fertile mind to imagine all sorts of characters, situations and story lines. It was an art that she was later to put to good use.

I remember very well in my first school, and that was in London, the progressive teacher described imagination. I must only have been about five, I think, and she asked us all to shut our eyes, and to try and imagine what she was about to describe. 'Those of you,' she said, 'who see what I'm talking about have imagination, and you are to put your hands up, whilst your eyes are still shut.'

I put my hand up, and when I opened my eyes, to my horror I saw I was the only one in the class. All the others turned and glared. She brought me out to the front of the class and said, 'Now this is a child with imagination. She'll probably be a writer one day.' I remember her saying it very, very, clearly, and I hated it because after that, I became known as the teacher's pet, which caused antagonism in the playground, so then I, in order to court popularity, started to become very naughty. That pattern continued, I'm afraid, thereafter. I needed to play the court jester.

Molly's family always expected that she would either go on to university and study English, at which she excelled anyway, or to a newspaper and become a journalist. Her own schoolday ambitions were to become either a painter or a writer, but an unusual set of events set her on a course for art.

Writing was the school work that Molly enjoyed most of all, and at the schools she attended in London and Wales she was always top in English. However, at her last school the English teacher consistently marked her work down, which came as a shock. Molly was not this teacher's pet, but her attitude became cast into one of permanent contempt after one particularly unusual essay:

I remember, I did an incredible piece of writing, which was meant to be, you know, the 'most important' or the 'most exciting' day in my life. I did my entry into the world as a foetus. I did not know much about it, of course, but the teacher, who came from Roedean, called it disgusting, giving me nought out of ten. I even brought my art into it as well, the 'bloody passages' as it were, but that did not seem to make any difference. I thought it was a brilliant piece of writing, but I can obviously see it's strange – and shocking – for a schoolgirl to think like this. She continued to mark me consistently low and, because I was still coming top in art, I was then geared to art school. When my matriculation results came though, I got distinctions in both Englishes [i.e. literature and language]!

Molly went on to study art first at Goldsmiths' College in London, and then at Brighton School of Art. Her studies finished in 1953, and her first real experience of work, aged twenty-one, was as a qualified art teacher at Silverthorn Secondary Modern School at the Elephant and Castle in London. It was a very rough working class school but the paintings she got from the girls were strong and gutsy. The other side to reaching her majority was that she visited every smart night club she could find.

Among the men she met was Michael Parkin and eventually, in 1957, they were married. She started to paint again, giving up the teaching job she so enjoyed. She was always a serious painter. Then she found that she could sell her portraits and landscapes to Liberty's, which could not get enough of them. Her husband encouraged her to paint more and more and there was a great demand for her work. The critical acclaim came when the Contemporary Arts Society purchased a large abstract which hung in the bowels of the Tate Gallery in 1962. But she enjoyed her settled home life, and had two daughters, Sarah and Sophie. Sadly, her marriage survived only eight years . . . and life on her own again soon brought her back to reality for, as she said, she 'became very poor overnight'. What was worse, her painting Muse had left her. She was to suffer an 'artistic block' which would last for the next twenty-five years.

In search of work, especially creative work, she turned her hand to designing hats and bags for Biba, the then trendy, and very popular store. Again, she met with a degree of success, which led her to start her own boutique. Her ability to anticipate trends in design caught the eye of the fashion experts, but her introduction to *Nova* came by a circuitous route. At that time, to become a top fashion editor required both experience and reputation – of which Molly had little – and vacancies were few and far between. At a dinner party held by Len Deighton she met Clive Irving, who worked for I.P.C., the publishers of *Nova*. Whether it was a party conversation piece or not, Molly had the opportunity to describe her experiences in art and how she was now using her knowledge of colour in clothes and fashion.

Molly must have made a big impression, for a day or so later, she was offered the job of Fashion Editor on *Nova*. (Very much phenomena of their time, the late sixties and the seventies, both Biba and *Nova* are now defunct.)

> You know, I didn't write at all until the final year in art school, and then I started writing because it was to do with the diploma and my training to be a teacher. They were flabbergasted then, and asked why I had never thought of going in for writing, as many of my efforts were read out to fellow students. But I really didn't do any serious writing until I joined *Nova*.
>
> There, I worked purely as a visual person to do features on fashion, and I persuaded my friend Mary Holland, who was a journalist, to

write the text for me. They were just little pieces to accompany the visual sixteen pages of colour, but the editor, Dennis Hackett, eventually discovered this and said, 'I'm not paying you to be fashion editor *and* paying Mary to do your pieces. That's crackers. I listen to you talk and you have a magnificent command of English. So do your own.'

It took me two weeks to write the next piece and I was petrified, but when he read it, he said, 'That's brilliant, you must write your own.'

After a time I left to join *Harper's & Queens*, another fashion magazine, and I didn't write again as we used simple captions to the pictures. So my first piece of real writing, strangely enough, was for *The Sunday Times*.

I said at the interview with Harry Evans, [editor] of *The Sunday Times*, 'I really can't write, I'm not a writer.' And he said, 'I like that honesty, and modesty – no one on this newspaper can write any-way...' 'But you really don't understand,' I said. He explained that what he really wanted was my expertise as a fashion editor, and my reputation had preceded me.

He never believed me though. My first week on the paper was sheer horror. When I had done the visuals, Hunter Davies, my boss, said to me, 'Now type up your piece, Molly.'

'But I don't type.'

'Well, write it longhand then.'

'But I don't write,' I replied. 'I did tell Harry, you know, but he didn't believe me!'

'What do you mean, Molly? This *is* a newspaper. How the bloody hell did you get this job then?' He went on like this, and my acute humiliation, lack of confidence, and embarrassment reduced me to tears – it was a time I don't easily forget.

'You are not sitting around in my time. Next week, I want you to interview two working-class girls, one up north, and one in the south. Find out what they spend their money on and what they wear. That'll teach you to write.'

This was yet another hurdle. Although gregarious by nature, with the ability to mix easily, she had not actually interviewed anyone for a press article before.

When I finally got to see the first girl, I said to her, 'I'm terribly sorry, I don't know how to do this.' Her reply didn't help me at all. 'Well, I can't tell you either, I've never done an interview myself.'

'Well then, shall we start at the bottom and work outwards? For instance, how many pairs of knickers do you have?'

'Thirty-six.'

'Never! I have one pair on, and one pair in the wash. How do you reckon to have thirty-six?' I started writing notes furiously.

'Well, I have a pair of white cotton next to the body, you know, for health reasons. Then I wear a pair of tights, and because of the miniskirt, I have a problem walking upstairs with blokes looking up, so I wear a pair of frilly or flowered ones on top of my tights.'

We went on from there, and when I got back with this riveting material I showed it to Hunter Davies, who promptly accused me of making it up! 'No, I haven't, that's what she said.'

'It's fabulous, but I don't know if *The Sunday Times* will wear [*sic*] this.

But it got published, and this was how I became known for doing interviews.

Fashion features, interviews, and a background as a painter hardly indicated that she was destined to become a novelist. Surely she could not have found the confidence to write novels just from having been good at English at school, and writing odd articles for a Sunday newspaper?

I had become very frustrated working on *The Sunday Times*, though I have to say that, as fashion editor, I found doing the interviews most enjoyable, and the most successful items I did were the interviews with people about their clothes.

I felt stymied by the constriction of having to write those interviews as the interviewees expressed themselves. I used to ask very recherché questions in order to get different and more original answers. When they weren't forthcoming I thought it would be better if I made them up.

Meaning to say, that I was starting to drift towards wanting to write fiction! At that point I was confident of my skills as a writer.

It was a wonderful training, writing for *The Sunday Times* then. My editor, Harry Evans, and others, helped. It just knocked you into shape.

She was voted Fashion Journalist of the Year in 1972. At this point in her career Molly had thought about writing a novel, and the more she thought about it, the more it preyed on her mind. She talked about it incessantly at work, but it was not until she decided to take a break that she did anything about her dreams, and then it was her editor, and not an agent, who provided that all-important introduction to a publisher. Again, working in journalism seems to have been an important factor, as it was for Sarah Harrison and Barbara Taylor Bradford.

It might have been a very different story. Molly did have a literary agent, Hilary Rubinstein at A. P. Watt. He looked after numerous novelists, but used to take the time to see her every six months. Their talk turned naturally to 'that novel', and he would encourage her to get on with it. Molly needed more than encouragement, however – she needed a financial incentive. Her answer to Rubinstein's encouragement was usually, 'Why don't you just give me a fiver to do it? As a carrot in front of my eyes.' But she always got the same answer: 'That's not how it's done, Molly, you've got to write a synopsis and a couple of chapters . . .'

> Saying it that way, I never did it, but I was still keen to start.
>
> They were getting a little tired of me and my aspirations at *The Sunday Times*. So in the end I started to write one [novel] when I took a summer holiday, but it came out in verse. I don't know why.
>
> I think I wasn't confident to tackle fiction – for example, how to set the plot – but I did know how to rhyme, and it ended up as humorous piece of work.
>
> My editor, Hunter Davies, on the 'Look' pages, had lunch one day with Desmond Briggs [of the publishers Blond and Briggs], and when he came back from lunch he was laughing. He said, 'Desmond has just told me that he is looking for a new novelist and somebody to write non-fiction. I have told him to get in touch with you as you are driving us mad trying to write. You really can expect a call from him!'

This was the most exciting news she had heard for weeks, but there was snag, though it did not dawn on her then. In fact, it did not dawn on her until Briggs actually telephoned.

> When he asked me, 'Can we have a look at what you have written?', that put me on the spot. I hadn't written anything, except all this verse: hardly an impressive piece of fiction!
>
> I took the rest of the week off and wrote 750 or 1,000 words in longhand. That was actually the beginning of my first novel *Love All*, and I sent it off to him.
>
> I learned later that apparently he didn't like it, not at bit; and neither did his colleague, Anthony Blond. He hated it. However,

they gave it to their secretary for an opinion and she loved it, asking where the rest of it was. That made all the difference. Had she not been so enthusiastic, it might have all ended there.

What I heard first from them when they came back to me was that they would like to commission it, but needed to know how the heroine earned her money and what's her financial background? Other questions were asked, but would I write another 2,000 words?

Of course I did. I actually gave them 3,000 words. There was no plot, I just started at the beginning . . . They told me that 65,000 words was the minimum for a novel and I said 'OK'. That was it – and I made a big decision. I went straight to Harry Evans and said I would like to leave *The Sunday Times* now to write this novel!

His reply was, I recall, 'You are absolutely mad, Molly. Nobody makes their living from writing novels. But your mind has not been on fashion lately.'

I said, 'Why don't you give me the sack and a lump of money?' He was sweet enough to do just that, and I left with some £6,000 or £7,000.

It simply did not occur to me that I could not earn my living this way. It just seemed a wonderful opportunity to do just as I wanted to do.

The publishers gave me an advance of £1,000 based on the submission of those 2,000 words or so. I don't know what I thought about that, as I'd had that large sum from *The Sunday Times* to live on through that summer. Then, when the book came out, I thought that it would be gobbled up with film rights [being sold], and I'd be made. It never occurred to me that it would be different.

I was warned though. William Hardcastle interviewed me on the radio, and he said what lunacy it was to just jump off and become a novelist.

It seemed to me then, as it always has, that either you're doing it, or you're not doing it. I'd never really managed to do two things at the same time, although after the first novel was finished and I was working on the second, I was forced to do a lot of journalism to support the novel. I thought to myself that whilst on *The Sunday Times* I was a fashion editor, then I stopped being a fashion editor and then, in my mind, I became a novelist.

This is another great debating point. Jeffrey Archer is one author who believes that if you are setting out to write, then writing must become a full-time occupation. Molly obviously shares that view, but their opinion is definitely a minority one, judging from the views of other authors I've met. Besides, the fact that she had to write articles and features for newspapers and magazines while completing her second novel is further proof that anyone who wants to become a full-time writer is best advised to start by writing as a secondary occupation.

Molly had by this time married again. However, having the higher income in the household put stresses on her which were quite unpredictable, and which have not been mentioned by other authors. Spouses take a natural interest, but few have taken quite such a strong role as Molly's husbands. As with her first career, when she was earning huge sums for her paintings, her husband became too commercial, so her second husband, Patrick, became more than just a reader.

> At the end of the day, my husband would say, 'Right. Give it to me.' And he would actually count up the words to make sure there were a thousand. He'd say things like, 'that raised a laugh,' or that 'raised not much of an erection there,' or 'and I don't know about that, Moll. That's not very sexy.' And I would have to try harder the next day.
>
> I had decided, because I always thought that everybody had a sex life and that it's funny, and I've got a sense of humour, that sex was very easy to write about, but the humour of it is very difficult to write.
>
> So I had to do as much research as possible. I studied the human-ists, the sensualists such as De Sade and the surrealists.

Since all writers bring some of their own knowledge into their writing, it crossed my mind that she must surely have first-hand experience of the sexual romps she describes.

> I think all my books are, to a degree, autobiographical. Well, ob-viously, there's a starting-off point, and then, you know, I have these flights of fantasy on top of that. You see, I did have five years between marriages and I did gain a lot of experiences then. We call it a sort of literary research of a romantic nature!

Her first novel, *Love All*, was launched upon an unsuspecting reading public in 1974. Perhaps fortunately for some, the bookshops were not flooded with copies at first, but Blond and Briggs had naturally sent out review copies, inviting comment and coverage. Comment they got, although perhaps not quite what they had hoped for. If Molly had made any enemies on *The Sunday*

Times, they were now presented with a golden opportunity; a caustic review appeared, one which most authors would be offended by. It also left little to the reader's imagination and made it clear that the reviewer did not like the novel at all.

Other reviewers did not agree. The *Telegraph*, *New Statesman* and *Evening Standard* gave it rave reviews with the result that many thousands of people bought the book. Molly's publishers seemed nervous about it, though, for they decided to forgo the circus of a launch party. Perhaps, too, they thought that, being a top fashion editor, she already had a large following of readers, and that since she had a high public profile, a launch party was not necessary. To a certain extent she shared a similar start to her writing career with Dick Francis, Barbara Taylor Bradford and Jeffrey Archer. Like them, she was well-known in her field before becoming a novelist. People bought her first novel to see just what the fuss was all about, especially as it soon became known that it was sexually forthright and outrageously shocking.

Not to be cheated out of the traditional celebrations, Molly's friends at Biba threw a party to launch the book and the event naturally attracted publicity. She gave numerous interviews, knowing how to present herself from her own encounters, and achieved many column inches in the national press as a result. In addition to this extensive coverage, the high-circulation magazine *Cosmopolitan* carried a lengthy, if censored, extract from the novel. Molly also appeared on *The Russell Harty Show* with the result that the first edition sold out almost immediately, proving a point familiar to all publicity people: that television appearances virtually guarantee huge sales. Molly told me that she thought the publishers had under-ordered from the printers, which may or may not have been true; from the publisher's viewpoint, however, the book was a huge success from the start.

The publicity arrangements included signing sessions at various bookshops, a hazardous experience for many writers because things can go horribly wrong: it is not unusual for a new author to be humbled by the public's absence. In Molly's case, however, it was rather different.

> I did do some rather unsuccessful signing sessions, because I naturally wanted to see the novel in as many bookshops as possible, but people used to gather, like a herd of cows, at the other end of the bookshop and not come forward! The shop owners used to say that my hats scared them off – but they would buy the book after I had gone.

Despite this awful experience, she does believe that signing sessions help sales. Word-of-mouth recommendation also helps, but the public had recognized that she was just being her natural self in what she wrote; besides there is nothing quite like a reputation for raunchiness to help push up a book's sales. Flushed with the success of press interviews and the kudos she had earned, Molly threw herself into her second novel.

If my first novel was immensely difficult, then my second was impossible to write. Most novelists will say that, because everybody has one book in them. Anybody. The milkman, the traffic warden, because they have got their experiences of life.

The second novel sorts the men from the boys, and the girls from the women, because then you are becoming a professional novelist. Especially if you can finish the second, the third and so on. Someone once said 'up to ten', but I wilted at that.

I thought that there just had to be an easier way of doing the second, because I had done the first one in longhand and it had taken so long. Then I did a little piece of journalism, one of many because I was known for doing interviews for *The Sunday Times*. This one, though, was for the *Radio Times*, who were carrying pieces about romantic novelists, so I went to interview Barbara Cartland. She told me: 'Don't ever write, or learn to type or do any of those sordid things. Darling, you should be like me, lie on a white couch with a white fur over you, look across the meadows and trees, and just dictate it all. You'll like that, Molly.'

So I went home and tried to do what she had told me, though I did not have the white couch or the white fur. My second husband, Patrick, thought it was a good idea, because if you are paying someone to come in for four hours each day, you have just got to sit down and dictate, however unwilling you are to write that day.

I sent the result off to Blond and Briggs and they sent me a horrible letter back. It was *very* critical, like that of a school teacher marking you bottom; the first novel, they said, was lovely, but this was awful. I took against them immediately. I never forgave them for being so insensitive, so I just went to another publisher.

Did she blame Cartland for misleading her? Not at all, she said, for she went on to 'dictate' five more novels. As I wrote in the chapter on Barbara Cartland, so much has been written about her that it is hardly surprising that she has influenced so many others. However, what works for one writer will not necessarily work for another – something ambitious authors should bear in mind.

It seems that most of the authors I've met have had some help from literary agents. Molly's first encounter (with Hilary Rubinstein) did little to inspire her, but in writing her second novel she had the help of another agent, Irene Josephy, who ensured that it was published just a year later.

The book was *Up Tight*, and it proved to be remarkable for reasons other than purely literary ones. There cannot be many authors who have had their novels banned from display by W. H. Smith.

> We had real trouble with *Up Tight*. I had asked my old photographer friend, Harri Peccinotti, who worked with me on *Nova*, to photograph a girl for the front cover. What I wanted was a frontal close up of a girl in her knickers, fifties knickers with broderie anglaise and a bit of lace at the bottom. What we ended up with was a girl in knickers all right, but in the see-through seventies style, and with nothing left to the imagination.

No wonder W. H. Smith felt it too risqué to put on the shelves, and no wonder that publishers would not let her choose material for any more jackets. She was not pleased and, as she said, 'immediately took against W. H. Smith.'

When Michael Joseph published her third novel, *Full Up*, the jacket carried an illustration which she describes as sexist:

> They were silly girls posing in suspenders and everything, so old-fashioned, and my later publisher, W. H. Allen, did the same. I hated those covers, it's the wrong image. What I wanted was Beryl Cook's paintings, or something along the lines of those comic seaside postcards. They [the novels] were supposed to be romps, sexy romps.

Success as an artist and novelist was bound to result in strongly held views, and having played so many more and different roles than other authors, what advice had Molly to offer ambitious writers?

> What I would suggest any wishful novelist to do, is to mix amongst your own kind, because it is such a daunting and horribly lonely job. You're stuck on your own and you've no feedback from anybody. I'm glad that I did.
>
> One novelist did tell me, I think it was Beryl Bainbridge, or Fay Weldon, or Bernice Rubens, all of whom I was friendly with, that when you hit 30,000 words, it's a watershed. Especially with your first novel, but it can happen with any novel.
>
> 30,000 words *is* a watershed, and you ask yourself, what the hell am I doing this for? I can't go on.

That happened to me, and thank goodness they helped. I went down to St Ives, just for the summer, for the kids to be with Patrick, my husband then. When they had gone off for the day, I made myself write 1,000 words, regardless of whether I was suffering from a hangover, illness or domestic disasters.

It worked, for that is how I finally got 65,000 words written for *Love All*.

Twenty-five years have elapsed since she started writing, and with fifteen titles to her credit, she can certainly call herself a practised author. Over the intervening years she has matured, however, and gained a greater experience of life. I mentioned at the start of this chapter that she had taken up writing again, but is she, I wondered, intending to continue from where she left off?

I'm not going to write the same books as before. There's a much more serious writer in me now. I now want to write a blockbuster and my new agent, has been most helpful. I'm very pleased to say that I have a publisher for it.

POSTSCRIPT

Molly published her autobiography in 1993. *Moll – The Making of Molly Parkin* is a full account of her life and loves. Her novels are mentioned but, like many other authors' biographies, there is scant background to how that author became a writer.

With the benefit of hindsight, Molly recommends any writer to secure the help of a literary agent as soon as possible, for in her experience they can be worth their weight in gold.

Dora Saint ('Miss Read')

Best known, under her pen-name 'Miss Read', for Village School, Battles at Thrush Green, No Holly for Miss Quinn, Village Affairs, Gossip from Thrush Green, At Home in Thrush Green, and forty-five more.

Dora Saint is a truly English author, unassuming and unpretentious, avoiding, like Penny Jordan, the limelight of hype and publishers' publicity. She prefers instead to live in the heart of England's countryside where she can lead a rural life in harmony with nature. Nevertheless, her books are widely read and loved; proof, perhaps, that word-of-mouth recommendation does work. She has a huge number of devoted aficionados waiting patiently for the next instalment of life in Thrush Green or Fairacre. Her popularity is reflected by her regular ranking as one of the authors whose books are most borrowed from British libraries. In recent years, she has earned the maximum possible under the Public Lending Right agreement.

For her, as for several other authors, writing is a second career, but unlike, say, those of Dick Francis or Jeffrey Archer, her first career was not one that attracted either headlines or public attention. She was, as she told me, simply 'an uncomplicated teacher'. Her success is thus the more significant, and must surely encourage other writers.

Dora Saint lives with her husband, Doug, a retired history teacher, in a country house near the village of Great Shefford in the Berkshire Downs. Its setting, in well manicured and colourful gardens, is a haven for the local bird population for nuts and titbits are always available. Her love for the countryside and her passion for rural traditions is obvious to any visitor.

Dora's empathy with the countryside originates from her early childhood. Brought up in South London, her first experience of school was at a typical London County Council establishment; fifty to a class, a concrete playground and surrounded by noise. This was not to last, for in 1921 and when she was seven years old, the family moved to Chelsfield. The village lies close to the Kent border in what was a fruit growing area. It was a time when children could walk to school in relative safety, and for Dora this meant a mile or so along country lanes. What made the greatest impact were the sights and sounds of nature, of animals and birds and the smells of crops and wild flowers. She loved it all.

This fascination explains why, many years later, she enjoys writing about country life; it is a subject she knows well. Her books are renowned for portraying rural and, in particular, village life in England as we should all like to remember it, particularly in the south, where it is rapidly disappearing beneath the mass of urban developments.

Dora Saint has a unique ability to let her readers see and share her world. She could also very easily be the 'Miss Read' of her novels. Matronly in appearance, she inspires confidence and oozes good sense. Above all else, she is a practical and level-headed person, qualities you would expect of a headmistress.

So why did she start to write? Was it something that she, like so many others, had always dreamt of doing, or was it a side-effect of teaching?

When I was at school, I had great difficulty in anything connected with mathematics and so on, but on the expression side, I found it fairly simple. I always thought, like thousands of other people, one day I'll do a bit of writing. Certainly, I wanted to be a reporter on a paper when I was in my teens. That would have been bliss.

And I said so to my father. He was horrified, and he said (and I'll always remember his expression), he said, 'that's much too rackety a life for a girl.' So I went into teaching instead.

I had quite a few years as a teacher, but later when I had time, after I was married, I used to think about the idiotic remarks you made when you were teaching. I recall, when teaching infants and getting up a little play, that I said, 'I'm looking for two trustworthy frogs.' I thought, I must be mad; I mean, what would they think? It was that sort of thing that sounded amusing, so by that time I had definitely decided to try my hand at a light essay.

One of the most prestigious magazines at the time was *Punch*. It also had an element of humour, so I thought I would try *Punch* first. It was hard work, but I used to send them something about once a fortnight and, as regularly, they came back, sometimes with a comment or two which helped.

I wasn't upset that my efforts were not accepted to begin with. I went on the principle that you must expect to be rejected. I thought that this was a sensible way to face it. And it's the advice I give to any beginners, so that if you are accepted, the joy is doubled.

And after trying for about eighteen months, they took a little article called 'Last Week's Film'. This was followed by several other small articles, but I remember 'Plasticine for Forty' was the beginning of a series of articles about the humorous aspects of teaching.

They were virtually all monologues. Me talking to a class of forty children about their Plasticine, saying idiotic things like, 'Hold up worms'; 'Hold up baskets'. And comments like 'It's time you put that down, you've done sixteen crumpets already'; 'Well turn it over and make the holes on the other side.' The sort of thing that the late Joyce Grenfell would say.

H. F. Ellis, who was the literary and deputy editor of *Punch* from 1949 to 1953, recalled in *The Sunday Telegraph* in 1978:

> She was one of my favourite contributors because she had no arrogance at all and didn't feel her work was sacrosanct - in fact, I think she was very aware that at about 800 words her pieces were extremely useful editorially, and never minded revising them. In a way, she was, and is, like Jane Austen, in that she writes about what she knows and never goes beyond it.

I next asked Dora when it was that her career as a writer had really taken off. Was it in the fifties?

> No, it was the late forties. About 1947. I tried to widen my scope a bit. When the articles came back from *Punch*, I used to try sending them elsewhere, naturally. Sometimes I was lucky, but often not because writing for *Punch* was very particular. I did occasionally get things into *The Lady* and *Country Life*, then *The Times Educational Supplement* wrote asking if I would do some reviewing for them, which I did.
>
> After a while, I said to the editor [of the *TES*], 'It's about time you had a light essay in your paper. I'm doing articles about town and country schools for *Punch* at the moment.' 'Send me some, then, and let me have a look at them'; which I did, and he told me that he would have had this, and that . . . I started regularly for the *Times Ed.* and I must say they never sent anything back. They were wonderful.

As a reviewer, she was supplying nothing more than a small, if essential, proportion of the paper's information. But though it did not fulfil her teenage dream of becoming a reporter, to many would-be writers, however, such a job would be very welcome. It was a small point, but her work was seldom credited to her by name, and only occasionally by her initials, D.J.S.; an aspect that would disappoint most writers at the start of their career.

But she was certainly blazing a trail, for it was then unheard-of for the 'Times Ed.' to carry essays. Persuading the paper to start publishing these was, in retrospect, the turning-point in her writing career, not least because it led to her next big break. Felicity Kinross of the BBC Schools Department asked her to write a script or two for their radio programmes. As it turned out, this was not a one-off request, and she wrote for the BBC on a regular basis for several years. *The Observer* published 'Thirty-One and a Donkey' in 1953, and it in turn caught the eye of Bob [the late Sir Robert] Lusty, then working at Michael Joseph. Whether it was the headline of the piece that caught his eye is not known, but the title does typify Dora's ability to recall the magic of youth.

> When I was a child, we used to play a game that you had to see and count thirty-one horses, but if you saw a donkey in the middle of counting them – over a period – you had to start again. In the village where I used to go to school I was about eight – there was always a donkey cart outside the pub on a Thursday, so if you were collecting horses, as you came in sight of the pub you said to your friends or neighbours, 'I'm going to keep my eyes closed, lead me into school.'

Whatever his reasons, in November 1953 Lusty asked her to call on him at his office. It proved to be yet another turning-point, as she recalled in the book published to celebrate Michael Joseph's fiftieth anniversary, *At The Sign Of The Mermaid* (1986):

> . . . and Robert Lusty asked which papers I had appeared in.
> '*Punch, The Countryman, The Times Educational Supplement, The Lady.*'
> 'Quite reputable papers,' he said meditatively. 'Really quite reputable.'
> 'Short essays, of course. Not much more than 850 words. How long should a book be?'
> 'Oh! About 70,000,' he said casually.
> I fell back, stunned, upon the mini-sofa. When I had struggled up again, I said I could not possibly write so much.
> 'Why ever not?' he asked, astonished. 'You won't find the length difficult once you begin.'
> He continued to try and reassure me until we parted.
> In numbed despair I sought normality in Dryad's craft shop next door, among the wooden beads and raffia.
> And a week later I started on *Village School* . . .

Dora recalls that, when they met, Lusty said to her, 'We're not commissioning you to do this job, but if you would like to write a book, we shall look at it with interest.' After he had accepted the book, he pointed out that she was not yet a 'known author', so perhaps she ought to use a pen-name. He suggested 'Miss Read' as it was written in the first person, which, for a book about school life, sounded most apt. 'Make it more of an autobiography,' he had added, though he could not have guessed just how her enchanting and evocative stories of rural life would capture the imagination of millions. Cynics might say that this was a piece of publisher's luck, others that it was a stroke of publisher's genius. Either way, it is a prime example of a publisher recognizing that intangible quality which sets one author apart from others.

Lusty was never to commission Dora Saint, neither then, nor for any of the titles that followed. Granted that commissioning fiction was not the convention then, and especially fiction by an unknown author, it is still very surprising that once she was successful, her publishers did not feel it necessary to bind her to them with contracts. 'Miss Read' has never been commissioned to write another book. However, like the majority of publishers' contracts then, there was a clause in hers that gave Michael Joseph the first option on her next title. So once a contract had been issued for a book she had delivered, she did have a publisher to turn to, which pleased her. Michael Joseph have published every title since the first.

I asked Dora if she thought of sending her first book to any other publisher.

No, I didn't. But when I sent the first five or six chapters to Bob, he was rather lacklustre about it. He said it hadn't got the sparkle of the essays. Naturally it hadn't, which I quite appreciated.

For one thing, I was feeling my way and desperately worried about the length of the book. Was I using up too much material in those five chapters? Was I not putting enough in? I simply did not know. I was used to a journalistic approach, very astringent. I was really at sea with the length.

That's why I divided the book into three terms, the school year, and each term into eight chapters. That way, I got some idea of how much I was putting into each chapter. That was my bannister all through that first book.

This approach to 'pacing' a novel is sound advice for anyone planning to write a book. Her novels are, on average, about 65-70,000 words long, and make about 220 pages in paperback form. Her methodical structuring of her books has not only been a major help to Dora in maintaining pace, but it also makes for much easier story-telling.

To achieve this, Dora turned to something familiar – the school exercise book. Writing her novels longhand, she planned to end a chapter by the time she reached the staples in the middle and finish the next chapter by the last page. Thus twelve books would make a full length novel.

Most of her 'original manuscripts' have since been bound into volumes and they are a testimony to her precise style of writing for there are hardly any corrections or amendments to be found!

Village School was finished in October 1954 and published the following year; it was the first of more than fifty titles published over the next forty-two years. Since then, none of them has been out of print for long. 'Miss Read's' success is all the more remarkable because, unlike other authors setting out on their second career, she did not have an agent to help her, nor did she have the benefit of a 'literary' spouse.

Among the titles published, Dora has penned two short autobiographies in which she describes her early years: *A Fortunate Grandchild* and *Time Remembered*. [Recently re-published in a single volume as *Early Days*.] But curiously, neither covers her teenage years, the events that lead up to her career in teaching and, in turn, writing.

As she had taught English in her teaching days, I therefore presumed that, like Craig Thomas (see Part 3), she did not have any problems in expressing herself. Had this really been an advantage when she started to write?

Not really. As a teacher, you can express yourself and you are conscious that you have got to get something across. In that way it enriches your writing, perhaps. You are using your brain quite differently with writing, but I don't think that being a teacher was a great help.

Writing those light essays was, in fact, much harder to do. You had to be so concise. And my experience with Schools Radio programmes proved to be most helpful.

I started off writing [for radio] for the five-to-ten year-olds, about nature because I was a country writer. Then I wrote fiction. We did a long series for children, the eleven-to-thirteen year-olds, who were what, in my day, we called backward. Nowadays all sorts of funny terms are used.

They wanted a story which would also teach them a thing or two, but the subject matter had to be of interest to that group. The vocabulary had to be simple, so they would understand.

Village School was favourably reviewed in several papers. Her old employer at the *The Times Educational Supplement* telephoned her, congratulating her and pulling her leg at the same time. She had achieved a hat-trick, he told her: her first book had appeared in concurrent issues of *The Times*, *The Times Literary Supplement* and *The Times Higher Educational Supplement*. It was an intoxicating moment, though 'Miss Read' was then, and remains, 'anaesthetized and remote from reviews.'

> About reviews generally, and this may sound conceited but it is not, and I think you'll find a lot of writers are like this. By the time you have done the book, you are not at all interested in it. So, if they praise the book, you're very pleased, you're grateful; and if they slam it, you don't really care much because you are not really interested in it any more. It's the book that you are currently working on that matters.

Many authors I've met are convinced that to become successful, writers must discipline themselves to work at a regular time each day; indeed, this is necessary just to complete a novel, they believe. 'Do you set yourself a routine for writing?' I asked.

> No. But determination is the main thing. To my mind you've simply got to plug on, and keep on, and on and on. If you are going to write, and you want to be accepted and marketed, you've not got to take any notice of rejections.
>
> As a housewife, and as a mum in the earlier days, I found I couldn't possibly keep to office hours. In any case, part of the time I was teaching. Only here and there. But if they wanted a supply teacher in any nearby rural school, I would push off for a week while someone was away ill. So, for a time, it was a very fragmented life I was leading.
>
> On a good day, I write for about three hours in the mornings, but the hours are very varied.
>
> I used to tell Bob Lusty, or Michael Joseph, that I would finish the book by March, or April, and give myself a certain leeway. That would allow me to take holidays, and not to worry too much if my daughter was ill and I had to take time off to look after her. I could never work a nine-to-five routine.

These comments are very significant, coming from the author of more than fifty books. They are, too, at variance with the views of the majority of successful writers.

Fans of 'Miss Read' will know all about the two villages she created, Thrush Green and Fairacre. Most of her novels recount the daily happenings of family life in these villages in the days before such places succumbed to modern 'amenities'. Each book takes the story of their lives a step further. These are fictional villages and characters, but where did she get all her ideas and material?

About ninety-five percent of the material comes from my memories. If I come across something technical that I don't understand, I seek help. For instance, in one book, I wanted a public enquiry. That was all Greek to me, so I started to telephone people I thought might help. The Town Clerk provided the answers. I must say that people are marvellous about telling you the proceedings. And the same thing happened when I wanted to find out recently how, at a police station, an identity parade would be held.

I have never had any difficulty in getting help, but generally I write about what I know.

I do wonder, however, whether this sort of help is always so freely available to the aspiring author, although clearly that must depend on the subject chosen.

Something which has fascinated me throughout all these interviews, and which I am sure has crossed the minds of many readers, is why some authors who have written regularly over a period of many years remain popular, while others do not. 'Miss Read' is one of those few authors who, while following the same theme throughout her books, has engendered, and kept, a loyal readership. I wondered why?

First of all, there is this great basic longing for the country in everybody. Certainly the people who read my books have it.

My novels have a collection of characters that's not too big, and anybody with any 'savvy' knows that you don't want a great big cast when you are writing something to hold your reader's interest. All my characters have ongoing lives and it's the serial aspect in my books, just as it is with *The Archers* on the radio, that holds the reader's attention. They want to know what happens next.

I've got the human element, and the countryside background, and from my point of view you're then halfway there.

But I'm not good at plots. I start with place first of all, then I consider the characters. There are a collection of characters in both villages, and I find that I can make perhaps one person the theme of that book. In one of my recent books, it was the two schoolteachers at Thrush Green and their adventures that became the main story; how they were going to retire and how they couldn't find a house.

Then I brought in other people to keep them in the reader's eye, as well as covering the main story.

I don't know whether the next book will be about Fairacre or Thrush Green because I haven't thought about it. But when I do, I will take one of the characters again and follow that particular one.

Above all, I consider the reader. I'm conscious of keeping the reader's attention very clearly.

'Miss Read' clearly writes on the subject she knows and loves best, but it is abundantly clear that not only does she write about what she wants, she also happens to like her subject as well. The dilemma facing many aspiring writers is whether to tackle a subject they know nothing about, because they imagine that it might make a good story; or to write about their own experiences, which they feel may interest people, but which seldom do.

I once read in *The Writer's Handbook* that Ruth Rendell had posed the question: '. . . I wonder where I would be now if I had aimed to please a public rather than suited my own taste?' But further on, Samm Sinclair Baker advised in an article 'How To Sell': 'Write what interests most others, not just what pleases you.' This conflict of views will doubtless remain unresolved.

'Miss Read's' novels will surely go on selling for many years to come, but which title, I wondered, had given her the most satisfaction?

Oh, without doubt, *Village School*. It has also been the most successful, possibly because it was the first one and people, if they want to start reading me, go naturally to *Village School*.

I'm told, some years ago, my books have passed the two million mark, and a number have been translated into German, Japanese and Russian. Surprisingly, they sell well in America. I get a lot of letters from there. I don't know why, possibly because they like to find their roots, and that sort of thing.

I receive several hundred letters a year, about a dozen a week or so, and I answer all of them by hand. I very rarely get a critical one, but once I received a letter to tell me that one of my characters had committed bigamy on page 247! I checked, and he certainly had, so I replied that I would be putting this right before the next printing. That character now dies in an air crash.

Writing a book is very hard work; it takes me at least eight to ten months to finish one and it nearly kills me! I feel very guilty if I haven't written . . .

Dora Saint's novels evoke nostalgic emotions in all those readers who have spent some or all of their lives in the countryside, and in readers who long for the country and an escape from the hectic pace of modern life. All her books contain a number of fine line drawings, the majority by the late John Strickland Goodall. Goodall contributed to her novels from the beginning of the series and, as she says, his work encapsulates and enhances the magic rural world she describes so vividly. Some of his illustrations appear in colour, but most are pen-and-ink drawings.

He had been working for the *Radio Times* when he was introduced to Michael Joseph by his agent, the late R. P. Gossop. John had told me in a letter that his Victorian training had a major influence on his style, and this in turn suited the never-ageing characters and scenery of Thrush Green and Fairacre. It was work that he clearly enjoyed doing.

Would the novels have been quite so successful without Goodall's illustrations? Almost certainly. The appeal of Dora Saint's work lies in her sharply observed evocations of a vanished time, appealing to the yearning for the countryside that lies within so many readers. Here, then, is a lesson that aspiring writers might take note of – that to win a mass readership, books must appeal to the masses.

However, unlike other authors whose books achieve worldwide sales, Dora Saint's novels appeal mainly to readers in the United Kingdom though as she has said, some have been translated into other languages. The cumulative sales from all her editions have now reached five million copies: a total that is all the more impressive. So what advice would she offer someone aiming to become an author?

> Well, I should be completely practical about it, and tell them to write a synopsis about what they've got in mind. Send it with a covering letter to the first publisher they think would like to have their book. If they express an interest, then go ahead and do it.
>
> I would say, keep the thing as simple as possible, not only in language but in format. Keep the reader in mind.
>
> Be practical too. Don't send a horror story to a publisher of agricultural books. Send it to the right publisher.

Dora Saint's current novel, *A Peaceful Retirement*, suggests that this is to be her last. All good things come to an end, but her legions of ardent readers will certainly miss the goings-on in Thrush Green and Fairacre, the next crisis, the colourful descriptions of the seasons, and the ways of country people. It is an era, either consciously or unconsciously, we all seek to hang on to as the pace of life quickens still further. To these pressures 'Miss Read' is the perfect antidote.

PART THREE

ADVENTURE WRITERS

Jeffrey Archer

Not A Penny More, Not A Penny Less, Shall We Tell The President?, Kane and Abel, A Quiver Full of Arrows, The Prodigal Daughter, First Among Equals, A Matter of Honour, A Twist In The Tale, Honour Among Thieves, Twelve Red Herrings and *The Fourth Estate.*

Jeffrey Archer,[*] one of the more ebullient and extrovert of authors, has come a very long way since his first book was published in 1975. His phoenix-like rise to fortune and glory in the literary world must appear, to some ambitious authors at least, to be the stuff of dreams. Twenty-two years and eleven bestsellers later, an obvious candidate for this book, I sought him out.

Just how far he has come was evident when he invited me to meet him at his London apartment overlooking the Thames, almost opposite the Houses of Parliament. The views through the large panoramic windows of the L-shaped living room were magnificent, and the room itself was no less imposing, with its modern furnishings and original works of art on almost every wall. As we started to talk about his status as an author of bestsellers, I mentioned my links with publishing and, in particular, author's relationships with publishers. Perhaps I should have known better for he brazenly announced about his then forthcoming book, *A Twist In The Tale*:

> I think I must be one of the few authors who have called a publisher's board meeting. It was held here, in this room, for my new book . . . I said, 'I would like you to publish [in hardback] at £9.95; and you to produce one million paperback copies at £2.95. These are the dates that you will publish on; and this is what I require from you.'
>
> And I'm very fussy about how many words appear on the printed page. I went through the sample pages with Jamie Wilson, [then] Hodder and Stoughton's production director, as I don't like crunched-up pages or the wrong print.
>
> I've never asked them to do anything I knew they could not achieve, because I've studied them closely for the last ten years.

---

[*] Now Lord Archer; he was created Baron Archer of Weston-Super-Mare in 1992.

The thought that other authors might adopt this attitude must surely send a shiver down the spine of every publisher. Few writers have had the temerity to 'advise' publishers in such a forceful way, but the fact remains, however galling it might be to his publisher at the time, that Jeffrey Archer has been proved right more often than not.

Hardly a week passes without there being an article about him or interview with him in the press, partly because he is extremely effective in achieving publicity, and partly because he is very newsworthy. He is, as newspaper editors will admit, 'good copy', though one cannot necessarily believe everything written about him – events are often grossly exaggerated.

Jeffrey is, therefore, a very public man. His achievements, as well as his failures, are all well documented. He is a man of conviction and ambition, so that when he decides to do something, he gets on and does it; at the same time he has the knack of doing it better than many others. He would say 'better than all others', but what cannot be taken away from him is the credit for his drive and determination to succeed.

It may, however, come as a complete surprise to readers, as it did to me, to learn that Jeffrey Archer, raconteur, sportsman and one-time art gallery owner, never set out to become a writer. His sole connection with the literary world, and it is a very tenuous one, was that his mother was once a journalist for the *Weston Mercury*. Apart from this, there was little to suggest that his talents might lie in writing entertaining novels.

As a schoolboy, Jeffrey was not academically gifted, nor did he acquire many qualifications. He passed his 11-plus, but records do not show any A levels. He did, however, developed a natural aptitude for athletics and was a very able sprinter. After leaving school he trained as a physical education teacher, and went to Brasenose College, Oxford, whose Principal, Sir Noel Hall, was destined to play an important part in Jeffrey's writing career.

Perhaps the only early sign of a literary bent came when, in the last few months of his time at Brasenose, he wrote a sports column in the university newspaper, *Cherwell*, under the heading 'With The Blues', though he did not mention this to me as being significant.

He won a Blue for the 100-yard and 220-yard track events, and even set a university record for the fastest 100 yards. His athletic successes only served to make him more ambitious. He was, and is, an extremely energetic man; he tackles any task with overpowering enthusiasm, which inevitably rubs off onto anyone who comes into contact with him. A typical example was when, in 1963, he answered an advertisement in *Cherwell* for an appeal by Oxfam. The charity had decided to try to raise £1 million, a fantastic sum of money in those days. He volunteered to help by organizing undergraduates to do some of the collecting and, fired by his enthusiasm, they managed to raise £136,000.

In 1966, while still at Oxford, he met and married Mary Weeden, a very accomplished academic. Whereas Jeffrey had few notable scholastic achievements, Mary had many: her command of English, for example, may have proved very useful to him. As other writers have discovered, it is a great advantage to have a spouse with such talents on whom to try out ideas, and who can read and comment on the end results.

I mention Jeffrey's charity work because it seems that, flushed with his success in raising money, he elected to stay in that field, which led to his eventual employment with the United Nations Association. He then formed his own company, Arrow Enterprises, with the sole purpose of raising more money for charities and other well-respected organizations. He succeeded where others had failed. Amongst his major triumphs was an event in aid of the British Council for the European Movement; for them he raised £750,000, and in so doing, met and made friends with such notable people as Ted (now Sir Edward) Heath, Geoffrey (now Lord) Rippon, and the late Lord Mountbatten. There were many similar events, but although his personal wealth was accruing, he cannot be said to have been learning to write.

As must be clear, confidence is not something that Jeffrey lacks. With a growing ambition for both money and influence, he leapt at the chance of entering politics. Starting in local government, he became, in 1967, the youngest member of the Greater London Council. This led him to put forward his name as the Tory candidate for the safe Lincolnshire seat of Louth to which, in 1969, he was elected by a majority of 10,727. This was 727 more votes than he had predicted – the point here being that, although many people dislike his over-confident (his critics say 'bumptious') manner, he is nevertheless nearly always right in his calculations. Nor can one fail to admire his achievements.

At another of the many charity events he organized, Jeffrey met an enthusiastic industrialist, Anthony Bamford, whose father had started the earth-moving machinery firm JCB. Over the months they became close friends, but it was a friendship that was later to cause Jeffrey much personal anguish, because of a decision to invest money in a Canadian firm, Aquablast. It is a sad story, for events were to prove that the 'investment opportunity' was a mirage, but its consequences were what motivated him to start writing.

In 1972 he had received a confidential financial tip. Aquablast had acquired the rights to manufacture a newly invented device which reduced pollution from car exhausts. The invention did not work as effectively as first thought, but the rumours surrounding it were very bullish. To hopeful investors, it was expected to earn millions worldwide, establishing the company as one of the all-time greats. It would also earn shareholders a fortune.

So, carried away by the idea that he would at last achieve another of his ambitions, that of becoming a millionaire, Jeffrey borrowed capital to invest in Aquablast. His enthusiasm was infectious, and Anthony Bamford lent him further capital to invest. They bought shares when the price was at a high point.

Naturally, this type of invention had to be tested, and initial reports were encouraging. However, not all the reports agreed and there were difficulties in establishing a patent in America. The share bubble burst, and Jeffrey lost everything – with the money he owed Bamford, the total exceeded £350,000, a debt of nightmarish proportions. Bamford, of course, eventually demanded his money back, finally seeking a remedy through the courts. Jeffrey, unable immediately to repay the loan, was confronted with the prospect of bankruptcy.

This was a major setback to his career in politics for, faced with litigation, he was forced to withdraw from standing for Louth in the forthcoming election (the second in a short period of time). It was very galling because Louth was still a safe Tory constituency, and he would undoubtedly have retained his seat. He felt that it was hardly his fault that the money had been lost. His friends noticed the rapid change in his behaviour – no longer ebullient, he became, unsurprisingly, a very subdued man. Quite apart from having to depart the political scene, any dream he might have had of becoming a minister, or even prime minister, vanished like a puff of smoke. And on top of everything he had no money, either. Here was a truly daunting prospect.

Owing such a huge sum of money, with no easy way of raising it, became a huge millstone around his neck. A less determined man might have wilted, but not Jeffrey. He quickly calculated that the odds against his earning sufficient sums to remove the millstone by conventional employment were enormous; it would take for ever, even if he could command a salary of £20,000 to £30,000 a year. He needed to restore his pride and repay his creditors much more quickly than that.

Anyone who has heard Jeffrey Archer address a public meeting will know that he can hold people's attention, and usually without any reference to notes. His confidence, and his delivery of both a message and relevant anecdotes, is undoubtedly first class. Whatever one's political views, when he speaks in public, he commands the undivided attention of his audience. But however great his skill in telling anecdotes, he certainly had no experience as a writer of novels. Perhaps his training as a PE instructor, and politician, helped give him the confidence to try.

While he was in these dire financial straits, several people prompted him to write a book. One of those was David Niven, the son of the late, and much-loved, film actor. Jeffrey records his appreciation for the younger Niven's help at the beginning of *Not A Penny More, Not A Penny Less*. He added:

> I wanted to make a film originally and I didn't think I could write.
> So I wrote fifty pages for him [Niven]. It may have been twenty-five, but it was a very small number. I sent it to him, he read it and
> said 'It will make a fantastic book, Jeffrey, but you must not sell it to
> a film company, because if you do, they will pay you £500, or a
> £1,000, for the idea. They will do it themselves and no one will ever
> believe you had anything to do with it at all.' I said, 'I'm not capable
> of writing a book.' 'Nevertheless,' he replied, 'go and do it.'

While this may not have said much for the film industry's probity, Jeffrey
thought it sound advice, despite the fact that he had few qualifications and
little apparent ability. He made a simple decision to write a novel, one that
just had to be a bestseller. He believed that producing a bestseller was nothing
to do with writing, it was all to do with telling stories – something he was able
to do.

What sets Jeffrey Archer apart from all the other authors I interviewed is
that he sat down to write a novel that would make him a fortune. He was not
interested in just being published, in seeing his name on the spine of a book.

I had read that writing had not been among his early ambitions, but I
wondered whether, like many aspiring writers, when he was writing his first
book he had daydreamed just for a moment of becoming a famous author?

> No. I wrote the first one never thinking I would write another. Very
> much a one-off. I never intended it to be a profession or a serious
> pastime, and I don't consider it [to be so] now.
>
> Many years later, Susan Watt, a very distinguished editor from
> Collins, told me, 'You are a story-teller, Jeffrey. It does not matter
> whether you wrote, "Once upon a time there were two men sitting
> in a flat and one man took his pen out . . .", they are going to read it.'
> I did not realize this. I've been telling stories all my life. I have been
> a raconteur. It never crossed my mind that people were prepared to
> pay, let alone pay millions.

He had never read any 'how-to-write' books, nor had he any intention of
attending any courses before he started his first novel. He did not have time to
devote to training; what he had to do, he had to do quickly. He has, in any
case, strong views about writing schools.

> It's a farce. You do your own thing. People write to me from all over

the world and I say to them: sit down, and write a story about what you know about. If you live in a small village, write a story about your village. If you are good at it, we'll all read it. It doesn't matter where you are or what you're doing, a good story-teller just tells a story. *Kane and Abel* couldn't be more simple.

He did, however, seek advice from a few talented people. In the first place his wife, Mary, was on hand to read and comment on his work. Another adviser was Sir Victor Pritchett, who told him: 'Don't worry about the fact that you have to do ten drafts of your book, I do about twelve.' At this point in the interview he showed me the fifth draft typescript which was then his latest book. I can vouch for a fact that parts of it were heavily rewritten.

I always say to people who write to me, you must get away from your husband, or wife. Go away, or get rid of them [*sic*]. You can't write just after breakfast and just before lunch. Maybe at the weekend. You have got to write your first draft flat out for six weeks, or four weeks, or whatever it takes you, and any interference is only going to stop the flow and get it wrong.

Otherwise, you will produce a piece of work even you will admit is not good enough. The one thing you must do, is to write the best you can do, and if you fail, well at least you can say you gave it your best shot. If you say you could have made it much better, that's no good to anyone.

I also think it should be a second career, not the first. Thirty-three or thirty-four would be an ideal age to start.

When he started writing, he begged the use of Sir Noel and Lady Hall's house in Oxford, and they generously offered him a room where he could work amidst the peace and quiet he sought. Not for him the typewriter; he wrote everything in longhand. At that time though, he did not have a publisher in mind, nor had he any idea as to how the publishing world worked.

Despite the shattering of his political life and his personal life, luck had not quite deserted him. He was introduced to Deborah Owen, a talented and highly regarded literary agent, who also happened to be the wife of Doctor David (now Lord) Owen. At the time, Owen was the Labour MP for Plymouth Devonport. Through her contacts and her efforts, Jeffrey's months of hard work were to bear rich fruit.

She liked *Not a Penny More, Not a Penny Less*, even in its unedited form and not just because it was a fast-moving story; it was also told with charm and warmth. Above all, the novel did not depend for effect upon sex or violence, a feature (or rather, a lack of one) that Deborah actively sought in potential bestsellers. The plot concerns four men who, having been defrauded in a classic stock-market deception, team up to reclaim, by fair means or foul, all their money, not a penny more, and not a penny less. The first half of the book reflected its author's own recent and bitter experience, but the second half was pure imaginative story-telling. It was Jeffrey's real-life, and much publicized, experiences that gave the book its air of authenticity. Deborah liked it enough to offer the typescript to several British and American publishers, but it was Doubleday in the States who accepted it first. That was in 1975, and in the same year the Swedish and Japanese rights were also sold – a very good start.

Some sixteen British publishers had turned the book down, however, before Tom Maschler of Jonathan Cape accepted it, paying a small advance. But when the UK edition came out in 1976 it did not become an instant bestseller, though its publication attracted attention. Something else had to happen to make the sales really soar. That 'something' could be called luck, but it really had more to do with the effective publicity machine that Jeffrey had built up during his political career.

As the first few months of 1976 passed, he worked hard at promoting the novel. In America *Not a Penny More, Not a Penny Less* had sold well, if unspectacularly, though at least the film rights had been bought in January by Warner Brothers. In Britain, however, Cape had sold the paperback rights to Coronet for a respectable £10,000 (Coronet, a Hodder and Stoughton imprint would feature more prominently in Jeffrey's life in years to come). The results of his hard work now began to show. Money started rolling in, and within months he was able to convince those who needed to know that he would be able to repay his debts, and soon. He did. According to one report in the *Irish Times*, he had expunged his debts within nineteen months.

Though he had never intended writing another book, he now set about enhancing his good fortune. Two years later, *Shall We Tell The President?* was published. It was a much harder job than he had at first anticipated, but Cape published it in Britain, and then his agent sold the American hardback rights to Viking for a reported £250,000.

As in his first novel, the storyline is straightforward. Set some six years in the future, the novel tells of five men who learn that the President of the United States is to be assassinated. Four of them are killed, and the fifth only has six days in which to prevent the assassination. The name that Jeffrey chose for the President in the original edition (it was later changed) was Edward M. Kennedy. When *Shall We Tell The President?* was launched, in October 1977, it received poor reviews in America, and it might never have become a bestseller but for one stroke of luck.

In retrospect, in seems coincidental, but it is the sort of lucky coincidence that Jeffrey enjoys. In securing Viking as his American publishers, he was handed a first-class publicity story, one which even he could not possibly have engineered. For Jacqueline, the widow of President John F. Kennedy, was one of Viking's consulting editors. Viking, whether intentionally or not, let her know of the book, and that they intended to publish it, but when the *New York Times* carried a crushing review that ended with the comment that anyone involved with the novel's publication should be ashamed of 'herself', it seemed that the criticism was as much aimed at Jackie Onassis* as at the publishers. She did in fact then resign, though whether as a consequence of the fuss or not has never been determined, but her action implied that she objected to the book in some way or other. Further, her resignation suggested (though it may in fact not have been the case) that she found it too embarrassing to be employed by a company which had published a book whose subject was so close to her own tragedy. Whatever the case, her action provided impetus and fuel for the talents of the publicists involved, and mass-media coverage followed, with Jeffrey's book as the focal point. Sales soared. He was now well on his way to becoming the author of a bestseller.

The book went on selling and selling. Five years later, though, he wrote yet another bestselling title, *The Prodigal Daughter*, in which the central character, Florentyna Kane, becomes the first woman President of the United States. Current editions of *Shall We Tell The President?* carry a note stating that he has now changed the name of the original fictional President, Edward M. Kennedy, to Florentyna Kane to provide a natural connection with earlier titles. To Shakespeare's question 'What's in a name?', Jeffrey Archer might perhaps answer 'a bestseller'.

Jeffrey's attitude to being commissioned provides yet another insight into this intriguing man.

> I take a pound advance and I do what I want to do. And I deliver when I want to deliver. I've never been commissioned in my life, and never will be. I wouldn't allow it.

Jeffrey also has strong ideas on how books should be sold. Whenever his political work takes him to a new town, it is quite likely that he will visit the nearest bookshop to see how many of his books are on display. If they are well represented, fine; if not, his publisher is likely to hear about it within the hour.

Just how well do his books actually sell? I asked him, as I had other authors, for details of the numbers sold, and which of the novels had sold the most. He produced the following figures from a book in which are listed details of sales of his various titles (the figures which follow will now be out-of-date but it was

---

* Jackie Kennedy remarried in October 1968, to Aristotle Onassis.

the way he told me that seemed important):

> *Not a Penny More, Not a Penny Less* – One million, nine hundred and forty-two thousand. Coming up for two million.

'One point nine million', I said aloud as I wrote it down. For the purpose of recording volume sales, rounding the figures made sense to me. But not to Jeffrey. He hectored:

> My Prime Minister [then Margaret, later Baroness, Thatcher] would have you for that. If you want to be accurate, one million, nine hundred and forty-two thousand.

I felt suitably chastened. He continued.

> *Shall We Tell The President?* – One million, eight hundred and thirty thousand.
> *Kane and Abel* – Two million, eight hundred and ninety-two thousand. I hope that book will be the first to sell three million.
> *Quiver Full of Arrows* – One million, one hundred and fourteen thousand.
> *The Prodigal Daughter* – Two million, three hundred and forty-four thousand.
> *First Among Equals* – Just past the two million mark.
> *A Matter of Honour* – Only been out seven months and we've sold one million, five hundred and twenty-eight thousand.
> That's just the UK sales, the world sales I just don't know. Five million have gone to Japan – they love good stories – and thirty million into America. About a hundred million worldwide.
> The books get into about 120 countries now, and many have been translated, too. Into twenty-three languages to date, including Thai, Icelandic and Indonesian.

Significantly, none of the other authors interviewed was so specific about sales.

I mentioned that his overall sales were approaching those of Arthur Hailey. 'Ah,' he replied, 'but he's written more books than I have, and been going much longer. Are you going to see him, too? If you do get out to the Bahamas, and get to see the room where he works . . . Well, I'll say no more. It's what every author dreams of.' (I did, and he is right.)

Given his energetic approach to the marketing of his books, I wondered how he dealt with correspondence from fans.

I believe that if anyone has taken the trouble to write, I will respond likewise. I answer every letter. [I then asked how many he received.]

Oh, about hundred a week. Perhaps, when a new book comes out, the number reaches three or four hundred. When my play was performed the numbers rose to a thousand, but it can go up and down very quickly.

For a man who is extremely well-known, and for a man who always likes to be the first or the best, I thought he was playing this aspect down − I could not believe that he received so few letters. As you will have read elsewhere, other high-profile authors receive many, many more. Knowing this prompted me to mention one writer who, I knew, got more, and whom I had seen not too long before. 'That compares with Roald Dahl who, I understand, receives well over ten thousand a year,' I said. Later, I checked this point with Roald Dahl, who then told me that he normally received about 30,000 a year, which was far more than he had told me when I met him. Of course, the vast majority of letters Dahl receives are from children all over the world who love his work.

Jeffrey Archer is a man of many talents. He will tell you that anyway, but it is true. For example, where other authors may just have thought about writing children's books, he sat down and wrote two.

I was prompted to write them because the boys at their school had been saying, 'Your father's a famous author, but where are his books?' So, I wrote two, only for fun, when my children were seven and five − *Willie Visits the Square World* and *Willie and the Killer Kipper*. But I only had a thousand printed of each and gave them as presents. [I asked him if he ever thought of taking it further.]

I've never desired to. I don't want my readers to be fooled by this.

I reminisced for a moment about *The Life of Our Lord*, which Charles Dickens wrote for his grandchildren. In 1934 my father, Michael Joseph, then a literary agent and long before he set up his own publishing company, sold the little book to the *Daily Mail*. It fetched an incredible £40,000 then − about £1.5 million pounds today. And all for only 14,000 words . . . Jeffrey remarked:

That is astounding − it makes me look feeble. I've been offered £200,000 for three of my short stories. Pretty well a record, but that makes me look very feeble.

What he added cannot really be set down here, except to say that he seemed to be was extremely miffed at being upstaged by history.

Though he has not, as yet, written any mass-market children's books, he has turned his pen to plays. His first, *Beyond Reasonable Doubt*, opened in 1987 at the Theatre Royal in Bath, and had its West End debut at the Queen's Theatre.

Then, encouraged by this success, in April 1988 he bought a controlling share in the London Playhouse Theatre. It would have been natural if his next play, *Exclusive*, which opened in September 1989, had been staged there, but in fact it was not, opening instead at The Strand.

Jeffrey Archer, as must be clear to readers by now, accomplishes almost everything he attempts. Had he ever failed at anything?

> I can't write a sex scene. In my first book there was one four-letter word, and my mother saw it and told me off about it. She asked me to cut it out. I did, to please her, and it was the only four-letter word in the whole book.
>
> I wrote one sex scene and when Doubleday saw it they just laughed at me. They said, 'You don't need it. You are a story-teller.'

POSTSCRIPT

Lord Archer has gone from strength to strength. Sales of his novels continue to grow. By 1996, for example, sales of just one title, *Kane and Abel*, had exceeded 20 million copies. It is not surprising that other publishers sought to publish his novels. He has written three more bestsellers since, *Honour Among Thieves, Twelve Red Herrings* and *The Fourth Estate*.

In January 1993, he left Hodder and Stoughton to join HarperCollins, a move that was sealed with a two book contract, said at the time to be worth a fortune. In September 1995, Jeffrey was reported to have received £15 million for his next three books with possible extra earnings from film rights.

For aspiring authors everywhere, Jeffrey Archer's account will be doubly encouraging and it goes to prove that if you have the ability and will to succeed – and the contacts – almost anything is achievable.

Tom Clancy

The Hunt For Red October, Red Storm Rising, Patriot Games, The Cardinal of the Kremlin, Clear and Present Danger, The Sum of All Fears, Without Remorse, Debt of Honour, Executive Orders, Marine and eight others.

Thirteen years ago, Tom Clancy was a full-time insurance salesman. He had his own business, which specialised in selling policies on cars and boats; at that time, the idea of writing a book remained a schoolboy dream. Nowadays all that is behind him, for he is a full-time writer with nine bestsellers to his credit, and a tenth well on the way.

He has earned himself a unique reputation for writing tales all too authentic and chilling – which display a detailed knowledge not only of current military intelligence, but also of little-known contemporary strategy. 'All too authentic', experts felt, because his detailed descriptions of submarines, especially Russia's then state-of-the-art nuclear Typhoon Class, and of America's stealth aircraft were far too accurate for their peace of mind.

When *The Hunt for Red October* was published in 1984, John Lechman, then US Navy Secretary, is believed to have thundered to colleagues, having read the book, 'Who the hell cleared this?' Other officials commented, too. US Secretary of Defense Caspar W. Weinberger, whose job it was to know about such matters, occasionally reviewed books. Of Tom's novel he wrote, in the *International Herald Tribune*:

> There are lots of spy novels, and novels involving military technology, but I don't call to mind many, if any, that compare to Clancy's *Hunt For Red October*; based on accuracy, ability to communicate, narrative skills and plot. It's hard to stop reading this book.

And when *Red Storm Rising* came out in 1986 the technical details were so realistic that the Pentagon suspected that the author had seen classified material.

Tom Clancy stresses, however, that all the so-called secrets he exposed are available through sources officially accessible to the public. As Michener's books are didactic in content, so Clancy's are an exposé of future warfare using today's hardware. His readers could be forgiven for believing that Tom has years of military service behind him. That is not the case, however, for he was excused service, having been born with severe myopia.

Neither in high school, nor at Loyola College in Baltimore, did he give any indication of the huge successes to come.

> I didn't set any records at college. It's true I did get a degree in English, but that's due to the encouragement of the teachers. I don't think there's an English teacher in the world that doesn't encourage you to write. All mine did. And there were a lot of good teachers, some Jesuits and some civilians . . .
>
> I wasn't into sports, because I wasn't terribly well co-ordinated. I was also a puny little kid. I didn't really finish growing up until college. And I was just a scrawny guy in high school.
>
> Despite the encouragement, I didn't get involved in *Blue and Gold*, the school literary magazine, but I did have some stories published in it.

Authors whose early literary efforts appear in school magazines sometimes turn to writing letters to local newspapers. Did he, I wondered, do the same?

> No I didn't, and I didn't want to become a reporter. My Dad did not like reporters very much. Sports reporters especially. It greatly annoyed him that he had to pay for his football tickets, and they got in for free. And he knew the game better than they did.
>
> So I never held the journalistic profession in high esteem until I actually got to meet some of the people in the business. They turned out to be some pretty good folks. My first exposure to reporters was after all this success, and for the most part, the people I have met have been pretty damn good . . .
>
> When I went to England for the first time, I was disappointed by the newspapers over there because they are so small. I mean, they are puny little things compared to what we have here, but I was impressed by the prose. You guys evidently have better English teachers. The depth of coverage was kind of disappointing, although your James Adams, on *The Sunday Times*, is probably the best defence reporter in the whole world.

If journalism was out, what had made him take up a career in insurance?

> I graduated from college in 1969, and my wife and I were engaged to be married on second August of sixty-nine. I needed a job in a

hurry, and it was simply the first decent job offer I received. But in 1980 I took over the business and by the time I had it paid off the loans, and by 1985, I didn't need it any more.

But I wasn't the best insurance agent in the world; I mean, I made a living and met my payroll. Fundamentally, it took me thirty-five years to find my niche is writing. Writing is the first really disciplined activity that I've been able to do.

No doubt the success of *The Hunt For Red October* helped confirm this view. Once again, however, here is evidence that it is very important for an aspiring author to have a full-time job until he or she has become established as a writer.

Tom Clancy was in his early thirties in 1985, and he had what most of us would call a comfortable life ahead of him. He had a steady job, a loving wife and two children, two cars, a mortgage, of course, and all the other commitments and constraints that go with family life. His job had its ups and downs, but by and large it treated him well. So what was it that made him seek the challenge of writing a novel?

Quite simply, he told me, it came about because, during one of his rare moments of idleness, he began to ponder on what he had achieved in his life. This is something that everyone does from time to time, but in his case he realized that he was caught in a middle-class trap of his own making, and that there was no easy way out of it. He would have to remain where he was in order to earn enough to maintain the payments and meet all his other commitments.

In 1986, Father Sellinger of Loyola College, noting Tom's success, invited him to address that year's graduates. This was the moment at which Tom focused his mind in an effort to account for his sudden change in life. He told them:

> There is a defence against the trap into which you are all about to embark, and the defence is within yourselves... Nothing is as real as a dream. The world can change around you, but your dream will not. Your life may change, but your dream doesn't have to. Responsibilities need not erase it. Duties need not obscure it. Your spouse and children need not get in its way, because the dream is within you. None can take your dream away.

This may explain his motive for extricating himself from the self-generated rut, but it was his life-long love of military hardware that provided the impetus for his new career as a story-teller. He had the necessary attributes of a thriller-writer: a vivid imagination, a proven ability in English, and a new slant on a storyline. Some years earlier – on 8 November 1975, as he recalled – he had read a most unusual news item. Members of the crew of the Soviet frigate *Storozhevoy* had decided to defect to Sweden, though most of them were killed in the mutiny. Because the story was so out of the ordinary, it stuck in Tom's memory. In time, his imagination converted the frigate into a submarine, and the plot for *The Hunt for Red October* began to take shape.

As Tom's interest in the United States Navy grew, he bought more and more books on that and allied subjects. His growing appetite for anything about naval history, defence trends, and maritime affairs led him to join the United States Naval Institute, whose headquarters, conveniently, are based in nearby Annapolis. The Institute publishes a wide range of authoritative titles under the Naval Institute Press imprint, and since members of the Institute are allowed to buy those books at discounted prices, he saw a distinct advantage in becoming a member.

In April 1980 he went to the Institute's annual meeting. What he heard and saw there was to have a profound effect on him.

> I saw essentially a kind of great big exercise in informational incest, where people in the Navy were telling each other how important the Navy is. Hell, they already know that. The idea is that they should tell the taxpayers how important the Navy is, then they'll support the people in uniform.

So incensed was he by the occasion that he wrote an 800-word article for the Institute's journal, *Proceedings*, in which he castigated the admirals and the speakers alike, and called much of the meeting 'a singular waste of time'. Considering that he also reproached the Institute for not promoting the Navy's importance, it is perhaps surprising and greatly to their credit that they supported him so strongly in an accompanying column. Naturally, one effect of the article, and of the fuss it caused, was to put Tom Clancy's name firmly on the map.

This was one of two articles that he had published in *Proceedings*. The other, a three-page piece on the MX missile, appeared in July 1982. Apart from these, he had had nothing published since college, and was anything but the archetypal author.

> I didn't have sufficient intelligence to know that it was a matter of confidence. There's an old Japanese proverb, 'A blind man fears no snakes.' I just went ahead, not knowing what the problems were.
>
> I thought that was as far as that letter and article would get, but the following year, I met a naval officer, Ralph Chatham, who

offered some criticism. So I invited him down to my office. This was on the Monday, after Argentina had just gobbled up the Falkland Islands. [Friday 2 April 1982.]

Ralph's a sub driver by profession, and we got talking. He told me some sea stories, about life at sea, and what it was like to drive a submarine for a living.

Well, the idea for *Red October* had been rattling around in my head for some years, and on the basis of the stories he told me, I figured I could write the book. I knew I could look up the technical stuff easily enough; the hard part was getting into the heads of the guys who drive a submarine for a living.

Tom Clancy's knowledge of submarines, fighter aircraft, and other weaponry is authoritative. He understands missiles, for example, in the same way, that dedicated motor-racing fans know their cars, or that computer buffs know their chips. Like so many such aficionados, his interest started in his youth.

I've been a technology freak all my life, back to when I was in first grade. Gadgets fascinate me.

Historically, military technology tends to give a leading edge. If you look at the history of aviation, all the important events in aviation have come from the military side and spread over into the civilian side.

Medicine's the same way. One of the hot items in the United States is trauma treatment; treating people who are shot, or crunched up in automobile accidents. If you are going to get mashed up in an automobile accident, this is the best place in the world, here in Maryland, because they will fly you to the shock trauma centre in Baltimore. A lot of the technicians there came out of the Vietnam War.

Committed to writing a novel, Tom began his research, reading a variety of unclassified books which, though they were not to be found on booksellers' shelves, were nevertheless available to the public. He also bought a war game, *Harpoon*. This had been devised by Larry Bond, a naval analyst, and the accompanying rule-book explained a strategy for war between American and Soviet fleets of nuclear-powered submarines and other vessels. This strategy, which was used by the Navy's cadets in training, was most helpful to Tom as an important source of reference data, but he had little idea at that time as to what it was like to live and work in nuclear submarines, or, for that matter, how nuclear power worked. Not far from where he lives, however, there is a nuclear power-station. Through some of his insurance company's policy-holders, several of whom were ex-submariners working there, he was able to acquire the vital background details that make his novels so convincingly accurate.

Two years after that fateful annual meeting at the United States Naval Institute, he began to write *The Hunt For Red October*. Two drafts later, he sent it off to the only publisher with whom he had had any contact, the Naval Institute Press. Their forte, however, was (and is) largely academic non-fiction with an emphasis on all matters naval, and fiction was not a feature of their lists. True, he had been encouraged to finish his novel by one of their technical experts, but that was no guarantee of publication.

What he was not aware of, though, was that they had made a major decision to start publishing 'wet' fiction, an unusual move for a publishing house so steeped in traditional non-fiction books. The board had set standards, of course, and it had been agreed that any novel taken on must not only be well written, but should make a contribution to naval literature and advance the understanding of sea power. Tom's novel met these criteria. Delighted to have his work accepted for publication, he readily took the Naval Institute Press's editorial advice, making a number of changes at their suggestion.

> At the time, I didn't think I had sent it to the wrong publisher, because I never anticipated the degree of sales that we were going to have. They did, but I didn't. The only thing that made me think about going to another publisher was when they told me that the Board of Control [equivalent to a board of directors] might vote not to accept the book. And after going through six months of submission and rewrite . . . they finally accepted the book, and offered me an advance of $3,000. I talked them up to $5,000, but I make a little bit more than that now!

Tom Clancy was really very lucky indeed for, by convention at least, he was doing it all wrong. Not being a well-known − or even a proven − author, he was, on the evidence available, submitting it to the wrong type of publisher. Nor did he have a literary agent, something which, while not essential, does tend to be an asset. He just had a conviction − like so many writers − that he would one day succeed in getting his work published.

The initial printing was 16,000 hardback copies, which is very high compared with the UK's average of about 2,000 for a first novel. Demand rose swiftly, and two reprints each of 5,000 copies were put in hand shortly after the initial printing. Tom thinks that by the end of 1984 his publishers had printed about 30,000 copies.

But can this runaway success be entirely put down to luck? All publishers send out review copies, and NIP were no exception. But they were comparative strangers to publishing fiction, and because *The Hunt For Red October* was the first novel on their list, they gave the book more publicity and promotion than their traditional non-fiction titles usually received. Copies were sent to senior naval and diplomatic personnel, as well as recognized reviewers. Amongst these was Reid Beddow, an editor for the *Washington Post*'s Book World, who wrote a very favourable review. Promotional copies of new author's works tend to get passed around faster than more mundane books, if only to show that the donor has 'found' a good new read, and in this case, because the book exposed much of current naval intelligence and strategy, it was passed around the nation's military leaders with alacrity. Tom recalled:

> Jeremiah O'Leary, an editor with the *Washington Times*, received a copy, read it, and liked what he read. He went out and bought a copy for his friend Frank Cortez, the American Ambassador to Argentina. He in turn gave the book to another friend, Nancy Clark Reynolds, who was flying out there, to drop off at the embassy. This was in November 1984 and on the flight she read it, and liked it too.
>
> When she returned to the States, it was the Christmas season, so she bought a whole case of books to give out as Christmas presents. One went to the President, because she was an old friend of the Reagan family.
>
> The President took two or three days to read the book. It was quiet that Christmas. When he told *Time* magazine that he liked it, boom! It just went. It jumped on the bestseller list in March of eighty-five and stayed there for twenty-nine weeks as a hard-cover. Then the hard-cover was knocked off by the paperback. That *was* pure luck.

A few good reviews undoubtedly help, but a personal recommendation from the nation's leader is the ultimate accolade. Reagan's admiring comments worked wonders, not so much because he was the President, but because he was a man who enjoyed the full-time attention of the media, so that many of the millions of supporters who had elected him took notice.

Word-of-mouth recommendation, especially amongst political and military opinion-formers, helped Clancy win the battle for supremacy in sales.

> I'm convinced that word of mouth is the only factor that sells anything. I guess TV advertising sells soap and Kleenex and that sort of thing, but in the book field, you don't advertise on TV.

The only advertising for books is someone buying a book and reading it, saying 'Hey, this is pretty good', and telling the guy on the next desk. The plain truth is that I don't think that anybody anywhere knows how to sell a thing . . .

The only book review that counts is the one you get from the public, and the obligation you have as an author is that when someone spends $20, or whatever, on buying your book, then he's getting his money's worth. I'm in the entertainment business.

What is writing, but entertainment?

Tom has been described as a 'wargamer', a devotee of hypothetical or historical warfare played out on computers or on boards, usually as a hobby, although the military use wargames in training. It was his friendship with Larry Bond, who devised the wargame *Harpoon*, that helped him towards starting his next book, *Red Storm Rising*. Not only did Larry Bond became a good friend, he become the godfather of Clancy's son, Tommy; their common interest, apart from Tommy, lay with war games.

Larry's a good guy and takes his role as godfather very seriously. He was over for Tommy's first birthday party in eighty-three, and in a quiet moment he started talking about a little project he had going called *Convoy 84* which was going to be an extended wargame. Testing to see what it was like to get convoys across the North Atlantic in the face of modern weapons, air-to-surface missiles, nuclear submarines, and all that.

We started kicking ideas back and forth, and I said, 'Hell, I've just finished one book. This sounds like fun. Why don't you and me write a book, on this subject, doing a damned wargame?' He agreed, and we shook hands on the deal and that was it.

Essentially, it's used as a database, and the game is played at military colleges all over the world. It comes complete with a rule book and technical digest . . .

That handshake was to prove to be another money-spinner, but although they agreed to share the earnings, only Tom's name appears on copies of *Red Storm Rising*.

Brimming with enthusiasm, Tom is someone who believes in doing rather than talking about doing. With one book just published, he did not wait to be commissioned before starting his second. Meanwhile, elsewhere in the close-knit community of publishing, literary agents were as usual on the prowl for rising stars.

I remember that I met Rob Gottlieb, who eventually became my agent, on Memorial Day [30] May 1984. I was at the American Booksellers' Convention at the time. He had got hold of some galley proofs [of *The Hunt For Red October*], and liked them so much that he went out of his way to find me. In fact he chased me, just like a gigolo chases an heiress, for the next six months or so. I finally signed up with him in January 1985.

The deal I had with Rob was that he could represent us (I was working with Larry Bond) to everybody except the [Naval] Institute [Press]. We would represent ourselves to them. Further, if the Institute came within twenty percent of the offer we got from the trade, then we could give the book [*Red Storm Rising*] to the Institute.

So we sent off the same package of material, both to the Institute and to Rob, who then sent it off to G. P. Putnam's Sons. And Putnam came back with an original offer of $325,000.

Any aspiring author should note that these events took place about three months after *The Hunt For Red October* had hit the bookshops. It is worth remembering, too, that his first novel, which had attracted an advance of just $5,000, had not, at the time Putnam made their offer, yet appeared on the bestseller lists! Either Rob Gottlieb was a very effective agent, or Putnam's management were more than alert to the potential of *Red Storm Rising*. Nevertheless, Tom went back to his publisher at the Naval Institute Press:

'Look,' I said, standing in the doorway, 'this is the offer we have received.' 'They offered you $325,000 for that?' was my publisher's response. I was a little offended by that, by his reaction, in fact. I then said, 'Do you want to make an offer?' He just said 'No.' 'You're sure?' I asked. 'Why don't you come within twenty percent, and you can have the book?'

They declined, and so another publisher won the day and the golden prize. On the face of it, his original publishers seem to have thrown away a first class opportunity to make money, but there is another side to the tale. The Naval Institute Press is governed by its non-profit tax status, and is precluded from making any monetary offer, regardless of size, in competition with a commercial, and therefore tax-paying, publisher. In offering to let his second book go to the Naval Institute Press at twenty percent less than the best offer, Tom seemed generous though he would, of course, not be paying fees to his agent.

And, curiously, the contract for his first novel did not have a 'first option' clause, which obliges a writer to offer his next book to his publishers before offering it elsewhere.

Tom's experience with his second novel is a powerful argument for employing an agent. Some authors seem to endorse their involvement, whilst others shun them like the plague. On balance, much depends on whether a writer has the confidence, the knowledge, and the business acumen to deal with publishers, and even then it is most unlikely that a first-time author would have the sort of reputation in publishing that the best agents command.

* * *

I met Tom Clancy at his home in Maryland. He writes, not in some small corner but in a what most readers would describe as a library. His must have held several thousand titles. Three walls are covered with bookshelves from floor to ceiling, so that he has to use a ladder to reach the upper shelves. He clearly likes books – books on all subjects – though there is, of course, a predominance of military books. His fascination with military history began when he was very young, but his interest in weapons and military memorabilia is also clear: he proudly showed me several handguns he had lying around the room, as well as military caps and other mementoes. Photographs of himself aboard fighting ships adorned the wall, as did several of President Reagan, each bearing a personal inscription.

As you would expect of a gadget-minded expert, he writes on a personal computer. Authors seem either to love or hate computers, but those who use them, like Hailey and Cussler, seem to take to the technology with ease. In Tom's case, he edits on screen rather than relying on marking printed-out pages. Most writers, however, tend to carry out obvious editorial changes and correct mistakes on screen, then print everything out in order to 'see' where it all falls. Either way, it is a matter of personal preference.

Computers do have several advantages, one of which is a dictionary in the program against which text can be verified. Clancy is quick to admit that one of his failings is poor spelling, and he makes frequent use of the spell-check program.

> My spelling *is* really abysmal. All the way through *Red October*, I had misspelt 'numerary.' At least once a page all the way through the manuscript. I've never been a good speller and the current program I use has a spelling checker which gets rid of most of the bad ones.
>
>   Syntax. My mechanical knowledge of English is pretty good. I don't necessarily write the way I talk. I had a lot of good English

190

teachers, so I know the mechanics fairly well. I have a thesaurus, but it is not built onto the program. I very rarely need it. I mean, I do have a fairly firm knowledge of the language.

And for that matter, I've never read any books on how to write. It's like reading books on how to play golf. There's only one way to play golf. You swing the club and clop the ball. The only way to learn to write is to write, and keep doing it until you get it damn right.

One of Clancy's laws of writing is that you always have to kill somebody in the first chapter. The first chapter, or the first sentence, has to grab the reader.

Red Storm starts off, 'They moved swiftly, silently, with purpose, under a crystalline, star-filled night in western Siberia.' And *Patriot Games* starts, 'Ryan was nearly killed twice in half an hour.' What you want to do is to get the reader to think, 'hey, what's going on here?'

When I met Tom, he was waiting for his new home to be completed. Sited on Peregrine Cliffs with a marvellous view over Chesapeake Bay, he drove me there to see it, and later showed me the architect's drawings. The house was to have two offices, one a 'command room' in which he would write, and one for his secretary. Clearly he plans more technological thrillers.

And, of course, there will be a full-size shooting-range. Those who have shooting as a serious hobby know that it is a very disciplined sport. Writing, he says, requires the same approach:

You can always come up with a reason not to work today. I mean, no matter what you do, whether you drive a truck, or you're an accountant, or a cop, you can always come up with a perfectly good reason why you should stay at home and do something else. It's the same thing for a writer. I suppose the principal requirement for a writer is determination.

I start when the kids get kicked out of the house by eight o'clock on their way to school. I start off by editing what I did the previous day. This sort of gets your brain synchronized with what you are supposed to be doing. I work through to lunch. I sometimes work a little after lunch, but generally, I don't. I do most of my work from eight to noon.

Has all the success gone to his head? Well, no, not entirely. He recalls going to his local printer to collect a batch of new stationery, and being brought down to earth with a bang. 'What are you doing now that you have given up your insurance business?' the printer asked. 'Writing,' replied Clancy. 'Gee, where can I get your book?' The fact that *The Hunt For Red October* had been in the bestseller list for months seemed to have passed the printer by.

Sales have been dramatic, beyond the dreams of even the most ambitious writers:

> In a hardback edition, *Red October* sold 380,000 copies up to May 1988, and 130,000 of those were after the paperback came out. 4.3 million paperbacks have been printed in the US.
>
> *Red Storm* has sold over a million hard-covers – roughly. *Patriot Games* – somewhere in the million range in hard-cover.
>
> These are all US sales; worldwide, I just honestly don't know.

His total sales are, of course, now much greater, especially since *The Hunt For Red October* was made into a film. The huge success of the film brought new impetus to sales, but the global totals are, in a sense, irrelevant, for his success has made him a very wealthy man. Money has not affected his writing, but his perception of wealth has definitely changed.

> My object in writing *Red October* was not to make a lot of money. It was to see my name in writing on the cover. I wanted to write and if you care about what you are doing, you're going to write the best book you possibly can.
>
> When the Acquisition and Rights editor of the [Naval] Institute [Press] called me after I had sent in the second draft she asked me, 'How much money do you expect from this?' My brain just stopped, and went on hold for a few seconds, then I said, 'I don't know. I've never thought about it.'
>
> I lost two nights' sleep wondering if I was ever going to make any money out of it. It's crazy, isn't it?
>
> Now I think a million-dollar contract is peanuts, but you know, money has got to be the most destructive thing in many ways, because if ever you start thinking you are entitled to it, then you turn into an idiot. Money can destroy your perspective . . .

Clive Cussler

Mayday! (*Mediterranean Caper* in the US), *Iceberg*, *Raise The Titanic*, *Vixen 03*, *Night Probe*, *Pacific Vortex*, *Deep Six*, *Cyclops*, *Treasure*, *Inca Gold*, *Dragon*, *Sahara*, *Shock Wave* and *Sea Hunters*. Sales in excess of 70 million copies worldwide.

As you will read elsewhere in this section, Joseph Wambaugh writes about police work; Dick Francis about racing; and Tom Clancy about military technology. Clive Cussler's story-telling speciality is sub-aqua adventure, stories of unremitting pace, tension and technical know-how. Reading his novels, it is easy to believe that he is an experienced diver. He is just that but, perversely, he lives far from the sea in Arizona.

In researching the biographical notes I had collected, I was immediately struck by one curious fact. Clive Cussler's first published title (*Mediterranean Caper*; *Mayday!* in the UK), which came out in the United States in 1973, was not the first novel he had written, but the second. *Pacific Vortex*, his first, was not published until four more titles had appeared. With this exception, his career closely parallels those of other bestselling writers. Firstly, because he broke into writing from a full-time job (in advertising, in his case), then because he had written small pieces for a local newspaper, though he certainly wouldn't have called himself a full-time journalist.

An almost myopic determination to complete whatever has been started seems to be one trait that all top authors share. As trite as it may be to say so, writing is a lonely occupation, not least because there is frequently no one else around to offer encouragement, or even to talk to. So where, I asked, did Clive attain his drive, and what did he think led him eventually to become an author?

> During my schooldays I was good at English, but just lousy in science and algebra, and geometry and calculus were wholly beyond me. So I stared out the window and daydreamed.
>
> My main love was archaeology. I could rattle off Egyptian dynasties like most boys can rattle off winners in a World Series. When I got to Pasadena College, I thought, hell, there's no money in archaeology, which is true, there isn't, so I switched to journalism.

I took typing, because in the senior years, we had a choice of subjects. As a friend of mine and I were big on automobiles, there was no need to take autoshop. I could weld and cope with most mechanical problems. I never cared for woodshop, so we got this bright idea to go with the women, and really meet some girls. So we took Home Economics and Typing. The girls there were often mad with us, because our cakes rose higher than theirs. I often look back on that and laugh, because I learned typing because of a love for women.

Journalism appealed to me, until a reporter came out to talk to us one day, and somebody asked him how much we can expect to make, and whatever it was, I was making more than that by working part-time in a grocery store. So then I began to think about business.

But first Cussler enlisted in the Air Force, where he worked as a flight engineer and mechanic. His service took him to Korea, and by the time he completed his duty, he had been promoted to sergeant. His tour of duty also took him to the Pacific, where he was based for a time in Hawaii. It seems that most ex-servicemen, when reminiscing about their overseas postings, give the impression that they had ample time to relax and enjoy their surroundings. In Clive's case, it was the sea that he turned to.

With a friend of mine, I bought what we think was the first aqua-lung in Honolulu in 1952. We just took it back to the base, pumped in about 600 pounds of air, strapped the thing on and ran into the water. No instructions at all. All this was well before formal training and related associations were formed, but I spent many hours exploring and making discoveries under water. It was all great fun.

Many ex-servicemen will also testify, however, that life can be very boring after the programmed activities of military life have come to an end. Clive not only experienced this boredom, he also lacked the necessary motivation and drive to establish a career for himself. As he explained, he simply drifted into advertising. Before that, though, he and his service comrade and diving buddy had run a gas station on the San Bernadino Freeway, just outside Los Angeles.

We had that for about three and a half years. I could write a book on that. If you talked about being robbed, held up, and had cars crashing into the station . . . there were accidents all the time!

During weekends, we had that urge to discover things and we used to tramp around the deserts of Southern California, looking for lost gold-mines, ghost towns, anything we could drum up, and yes, we did have our moments.

Once we found an old airplane that had vanished in the war, with the bones of some fellow still there. It had come down in a gulley and never been found. Then we found the bones of an old miner, which the Sheriff's Department identified as a lost prospector from about 1926. And we found some artefacts from a colonists' expedition from Mexico of 1776. It was really all very fascinating, so I guess that's where I got the bug to look for anything that was missing.

After a while, though, I began to tire of the business. Then I saw this advertisement for a supermarket advertising manager. I went to see them and claimed I had lots of freelance experience, which wasn't true, I didn't know the first goddamned thing about it. When I got there, I was asked to lay out an advertisement, so I went down – I had a VW then – bought a newspaper and copied the general layout of some other supermarket ad.

I showed it to my interviewer, and he said, 'That's not very good.' 'Well, it's the best I can do on my lap in the VW.' 'In that case,' he said, 'it's pretty good,' and he hired me.

My first day was a bit of a problem. I had to lay out a new advertisement, and the supermarket, Richards Lido Markets, at the entrance to Lido Island on Newport Beach, was more like a nightclub, very gourmet, and put out some very unusual advertising for the grocery trade. I told the fellow, who had moved up from the job I took, you have a certain 'style', why don't you just lay out this advertisement, to give me the idea of how you do it? Fortunately, he agreed, and I watched him and that was enough. From that point on, I could do it myself. Then after a few months I started doing the work my own way and winning awards in the supermarket category. I seemed to take naturally to advertising and that led me eventually to my own agency.

Clive is a very modest man, but he is also typical of the successful authors I met because, after my prompting, he went on to tell me that he had actually won several awards, including the Ford Foundation Consumer Award for 1965/6 and the Los Angeles Advertising Club Awards in 1965 and again in 1967; the former for the best promotional presentation and the latter for the best one minute live television commercial. A brief examination of his biographical information reveals that he has won many more such awards.

His initiation into journalism came when he did some freelance writing for the *Globe Pilot* in Costa Mesa, California. He supplied some recipes for a cookery column, but he also had fun writing a column about restaurants, calling himself the 'phantom diner'. Naturally, his research work had to be covert, and all the bookings were made in his wife Barbara's maiden name. His identity may have been a secret, but he was quite well paid for the pieces, about $100 a time, and, naturally, with a free meal included. It was a job that he took seriously for, as he readily admitted, he was in a position actually to ruin a restaurant.

He found supplying recipes to the paper almost as much fun, although events conspired on one occasion to cause him acute embarrassment. His pieces were published under the pen-name of 'Sally Salamagundi', and it was never very clear to him, or his boss, just how many regular readers he had. Then one day he omitted a vital ingredient – and found out, with a vengeance!

> I was still the advertising manager, so I did this piece for the home-maker page, tying in with the specials and the advertisements for the groceries. But all the women who read my column had absolutely no idea that it was actually written by a man who couldn't cook.
>
> The fellow from the newspaper would come on the deadline day, and I'd just clip the recipe together, and give it to him. One day, he called as usual, and I'd completely forgotten to do any preparation. I panicked, and just cut out the nearest recipe and handed it over.
>
> It was the same day, coincidentally, that my boss called me in, and accused me of spending too much time and querying whether it was all worth it. I said, it's hard to tell, I think people are reading the column, but you never know.
>
> Immediately after the column was published, I got over seventy phone calls from irate women. Each time I had to apologise and explain that 'Sally was away on holiday.' Writing under a pen-name, I could hardly say anything else. The problem was that, when I handed over the recipe – it was for Oatmeal Cookies – what I had missed was that halfway through it read, 'continued on page 20.'

From advertising groceries, he set up an advertising partnership with Leo Bestgen to form Bestgen and Cussler. It was, by American standards, a small agency, employing just two other people, and they specialised in newspaper, magazine and radio work, being too small for television contracts. No sooner had they become established than Clive announced that he wanted to move on to one of Hollywood's big-time agencies. He and Bestgen parted on very amicable terms, leaving him free to join D'Arcy Advertising in 1965 as copy director. There he put together copy for advertisements for Budweiser, Ajax detergents, and General Tires. The work did not satisfy him, though; married and with two children, he found that he became bored with time on his hands after the children had been put to bed. It was then that the idea of writing a book really germinated.

His career in advertising continued, however and he became, first, advertising director for the Aquatic Marine Corporation, and then vice-president and creative director of Mefford, Wolff and Weir Advertising. Creating winning storylines and catchy headlines, he was clearly talented, and seemed set on achieving fame and a degree of riches. But like James Herbert (see Part 1), he found that life in advertising did not totally satisfy him.

So where and when did the confidence to start writing a novel come from? After all, there is a huge difference between doing small pieces for the local paper and writing full-length books.

I don't know that I even thought about whether I had the confidence, it never really entered into my mind. Nobody ever encouraged me, but coming from advertising, I looked at the problem from that angle first. What kind of book should I write? I didn't have that great American novel burning within me, or a story of great-uncle Harry who came across the prairie in a covered wagon.

I finally struck on the idea of a series, after I had studied all those series characters – James Bond, he was in his prime; Dean Martin as Matt Helm was a hit. Having never written a book before, I studied other authors, and their style and rationale. Once I'd created the concept, I just plugged on through until it was finished.

My first idea, which went into *Pacific Vortex*, was based on Fu Manchu, and my villain turned out to be a yellow-eyed big character who lived under the sea off Hawaii. Dirk Pitt was just a secondary protagonist at the time, and as the story unfolded, I killed off just about everybody but Pitt.

The next book, which was *Mayday!* in the UK, and *Mediterranean Caper* over here; Pitt just came in and took the whole book away. I never did go back to the evil villain.

But, you know, I was unlike many writers. If you talk to most new authors, they think their first story, or book, should be chiselled in marble, and they never can figure out why it never gets published. I didn't really have any misconceptions, I thought that I would, well, just give it a try. I'm fortunate in being one of those people who, whatever they start, are driven to finish it. Crossword puzzles, or writing a book, if I start, I finish.

I was between advertising jobs, and contemplating writing again, when my wife said, 'If you want to write stories about the sea, then why don't you take this job?' The pay was poor. In fact, I remember, it cut my salary by two-thirds, but it meant working in three or four different scuba-diving shops. I did the promotions and all kinds of fun stuff, but when business was slow, I would sit at a card-table in the back of the shop and that's where I wrote *Mediterranean Caper*. OK, we had *Pacific Vortex*, that wasn't getting anywhere, but I thought *Caper* was good enough to get published.

It was really a better book and I did have some help. I went out to bone up on English versus [as opposed to] creative writing. You know, people always asked me, when I was young, did I have a teacher who inspired me? I never did, but I did have an excellent teacher on one of those creative writing courses at Orange Crest College. She did inspire me: her name is Pat Kubick.

I remember the first time I took chapter one along, it was a big breakthrough day, 'cause I had never really talked to other writers, or anybody else. If you've ever been to one of these creative writing courses, you will know that you get up and read your poem, article, or whatever, and your classmates just go animalistic, and tear everybody's efforts to pieces.

I've seen women go into sobbing fits because somebody has criticized their work, and there would almost be fights. We had this – oh she really was an awful old lady – who would rip the hell out of anybody who read out their work. So I sat in fear when the first chapter of *Caper* was read out, where the old plane appears and strafes the modern American jet base. At the end I thought, here it comes, but not one hand was raised. As the teacher looked around, I thought, I'm really in deep trouble now, she turned to the old bat and said, 'Don't even you have anything to say?' She looked up and said, 'No, it's good.' And I knew I had arrived.

So I finished *Caper*, and at this point I figured I needed an agent. I contacted some friends in Hollywood; I knew a lot of people in the public relations business, and they gave me names of literary agents in New York. I got devious at this point, so rather than just sitting down and writing the usual letter of query and the sample chapter, I went out and printed 500 hundred sheets of stationery and envelopes as the 'Charles Winthrop Agency'. I used to live on Winthrop Drive when I was a kid, and I always thought that it was a classy name.

I used my father's address in Laguna Hills and wrote to the first name on the list. He happened to be Peter Lampack, then a junior literary agent at the William Morris Agency. I wrote, 'Dear Peter, As you know I primarily handle motion-picture and television screenplays, but I've come across a couple of book-length manuscripts which I think have a great deal of potential. As you're aware, I'm retiring, would you like to take a look at them?' About ten days later, Dad says, 'There's a letter here from a man called Peter Lampack. Shall I read it to you?'

It read, 'Dear Charlie, Sure, if you say so. I'll take a look at the manuscripts.' So I mailed them off. A few days later another letter came. 'Dear Charlie, the first manuscript's pretty mediocre, the second one's pretty good. Where can I sign this guy Cussler?'

I almost fell off my chair! I fired off this letter, telling him where to find Clive Cussler, and he wrote introducing himself. He sent me his contracts, which I signed. That was 1969.

It wasn't easy to get a publisher. Peter never gave up, he struggled through 1970 and 1971, and in 1972, apparently, his boss said, 'Get rid of Cussler, he's not going anywhere.' Peter said 'No, I think he's got something,' and he finally got *Caper* placed with a small house. They published 50,000 copies and sold about 32,000.

A year or two later, *Iceberg* came out and they paid me 5,500 bucks. Published 5,000 copies and sold about 3,500. Then came *Raise The Titanic*.

Lampack is a tough negotiator, so tough that I never had the courage to tell him the story of Charlie Winthrop, but when he sold the film rights to Lew Grade we celebrated in style. This was a real coup. We were in New York at the time and with Barbara, Peter, and his wife, we went to dinner. Later on, I said to Barbara, 'Now is the time to tell him. I don't think he'll drop me now, I'm one of his biggest clients.'

When I finished, he laughed himself under the table and said, 'Oh my God! I always thought Charlie Winthrop was some guy I met when I was drunk at a cocktail party.'

That's how I got an agent . . .

Cussler is a very determined man and, whether at work or at play, he applies the same dedication to the job in hand, as his hobby of hunting shipwrecks demonstrates. It is a pastime that combines his interest in archaeology with his passion for underwater adventure. When we met, he claimed to have found only nineteen wrecks, but press releases credit him with thirty-four historical findings, amongst which are two Civil War ships – the Union's *Cumberland*, and the Confederacy's *Florida*. Whenever he does locate a new wreck – and he has been seen searching the North Sea and around the coasts of Scotland, Denmark, Holland and France – he never claims salvage rights. His satisfaction lies in finding and identifying those wrecks. It is a costly business, upwards of £30,000 ($55,000) a trip, but thanks to his *alter ego*, Dirk Pitt, who has earned him millions of dollars, he can afford it. His other, and no less expensive, hobby is collecting vintage and classic cars.

* * *

All authors will, if they are truthful, admit that they are exhilarated when their first book comes out. They dismiss the hundreds of hours it has taken them, the lack of sleep, the missed social events. It is the culmination of all their dreams, their ambitions. Few will ever confess to their egos getting the better of them after publication (and this certainly happens to some writers), but fewer still would share experiences like Clive's:

> My big fantasy, since I started writing a book, was that some day I'd be walking down the street, or on a bus, or any place where I'd see someone reading one of my books. Once I saw someone with my book in their hands, I knew I had arrived. This was a dream I had for years, long before I was ever published.
>
> Well, *Caper* came out, but only 32,000 were sold across the country, so I didn't see anyone reading a copy. Then, before I had finished *Titanic*, I went to have lunch with a friend, who had to visit his attorney. It was still lunchtime, and whilst he was in signing some papers, I wandered up and down the hall. Nearly everybody was out, but I walked around a corner and I just happened to look into one office where there was a very attractive girl secretary. She was what we call 'brown bagging', eating sandwiches and an apple at the desk, and she was reading a copy of *Iceberg*.
>
> I mean the sun burst out, harp music played, drums rolled, trumpets, the whole works. My God! I just staggered in and I kind of mumbled, 'How do you like the book?' 'It's pretty good,' she replied.
>
> Then, like a complete turkey – and oh, how I hate myself now - I said, 'Would you like me to inscribe it for you?'
>
> 'Inscribe it?'
>
> 'Yes, I wrote the book.'
>
> Now, you can imagine you're sitting in an office in Denver, Colorado and you're reading a book, and some guy comes in and says, 'I wrote it!' Would you believe him?

She got up from behind the desk, slithering around me, clutching the wall like I had the plague, and got to the doorway. She gave me a withering gaze and said, 'What are you? Some kind of asshole?!'

Like those *Tom and Jerry* cartoons, where the mouse hits the cat with a sledgehammer, and he cracks and crumples up, that was me. So, if you see someone reading your book, never, never go and talk to them.

He has another strong tip to pass on, too, one which stems from being too frank with a publisher. The events he told me about took place some years later, when he was not only better known, but far more able to command high advances. It is, perhaps, worth retelling this cautionary tale, for it may benefit some aspiring writer, if ever he or she achieves bestseller status.

> I went to lunch with Lou Wolfe, who was then President of Bantam [the American publishers], and while we were sitting there I told him that I always appreciated being with Bantam because I'd always hoped my paperback line would be with one publisher. And I said that I had to tell him that I would probably have taken a little less money just to stay with Bantam.
>
> The guy went into shock. Well, I thought, it's just a statement. No big deal.
>
> 'I'll have you know,' Lou said, 'I was always willing to pay you more!'
>
> 'So what,' I replied, 'I always earned out. I have *always* earned out, so what the hell difference does it make?' [meaning that he always earned more in royalties than the advances paid to him by the publisher.] That stuck in Lou's head, because when we came to him with the manuscript for *Deep Six*, they offered me $200,000 less than they offered me for *Night Probe* – and *Night Probe* did quite well.
>
> My agent tried to increase the offer, but they stuck, and Lampack and I gave it some thought, recalling the problems we had had with our previous publisher, and we agreed to throw it to the open market.
>
> Another publisher was quick to offer a million dollars, and once Lou heard about this he said, 'I'd have paid you that.' And I replied, 'Then why didn't you?'

When the typescript for Cussler's third novel, which he had simply entitled *Titanic*, was finished, Peter Lampack sent it to the publisher of *Mediterranean*

Caper in the usual way. Sadly for the publishers, they turned it down on the grounds that 'it was a little too heavy, and paper costs have gone up.' Peter then sent it off to Putnam, who wanted a massive rewrite, which Clive refused to do. Then it was given to Viking, who took it on as it stood, paying him an advance of $7,500.

He still has that rejection slip. In the light of the book's huge success, it is more than an amusing memento; it is another bad dream for publishers who turn down typescripts which later turn out to be bestsellers.

The sinking of the RMS *Titanic* in 1912, with the loss of some 1,490 lives, is arguably the worst single peacetime shipping disaster in history. The disaster made a huge emotional impact on seagoing travellers, both at the time and afterwards. Several films, fictional and documentary, have been made, and many books published since the liner collided with an iceberg and sank, all fuelling the public's interest. By 1976 the disaster had become a legend; by then literally hundreds of thousands of people had heard something about this ship.

Then, in 1976, a new book was published, apparently reviving the story. *Raise The Titanic* was just the story to entrance readers (many of them already familiar with or fascinated by the historical facts), because it was almost believable. (In some ways it presaged the work of Dr Robert Ballard who, in September 1985, actually located and filmed the wreck of the *Titanic*, later publishing a vivid and evocative pictorial account, *The Discovery of the Titanic*.) Once Cussler's book had caught the public eye, sales soared, and its success increased the sales of his earlier novels.

One factor, perhaps, helped single him out for fame and fortune. Like Frederick Forsyth with his *The Day of the Jackal*, Cussler also used a true story as a basis for his fictional theme, a story of which there was already a firm awareness in the public's mind. A marketing person might say, albeit cynically, that the author wrote the story in order to take advantage of this wide readership base.

Publishers, writers, and booksellers might also say that had the novel been published simply as *Titanic*, the fortunes of Clive Cussler might have been very different. Between leaving its author and appearing in the bookshops, the title was changed. Several authors have confessed to being unable to think of catchy titles for their work – even ex-advertising people . . .

> Yes, I think my titles stink! I don't know what it is, I just can't title a book. It was the sales department [at Viking], when they were ready to do the jacket, who came back and suggested that they could get more mileage out of *Raise The Titanic*. They were right.
>
> *Vixen 03* was a stupid title; I wish now, I'd named it *Quick Death* which was the nerve gas they used. *Mediterranean Caper* was a ghastly

title; that was my first [published novel] so the editor picked it and I didn't argue. *Iceberg* was OK, *Cyclops* probably isn't too bad. *Treasure* is good.

When I think back to my days in advertising, when we really sweated on a headline, and the more money there was on the account the more we sweated, I feel guilty about titling. I know I could do better.

Although *Raise the Titanic* is probably Clive's best-known title, it is not the most successful. By the spring of 1988, *Raise The Titanic* had sold about 145,000 in hard-cover, and had gone to number two in the bestseller lists, where it was listed for twenty-six weeks. *Cyclops*, published in 1985, sold 235,000 copies but was only on the bestseller lists for thirteen weeks. *Treasure* was running away. When we met, Clive thought the sales had already reached 300,000 to 400,000, but today, this total exceeds six million copies, and of all his titles, *Inca Gold* is his personal bestseller.

His books have been translated into over forty languages, from French to Hebrew, creating a loyal following of readers all over the world. Whenever novels are translated, they earn both the author and the original publisher useful sums in royalties. Cussler complained to me, however, about a practice, also mentioned by Hailey and others, that his novels are produced, without permission and in breach of international copyright agreements, by unscrupulous publishers – or 'bootlegged' as he described it ('pirated', a UK publisher would say), in India, China and Burma, to name just three countries. These publishers pay no royalties at all, while the prevention of pirated editions is notoriously difficult.

Overall, he believes that, with foreign rights sales (which are often difficult to quantify precisely), his global sales have exceeded 70 million copies in all editions. Not a bad record for someone from the advertising world, who found a literary agent by the exercise of his creative flair!

The action in all of Clive Cussler's books takes place in or around water, whether lake, river or ocean. His chief character and *alter ego*, Dirk Pitt, is very much a part of the magic formula that has made Clive's books so popular, and he has a definite opinion about the merits of continuing the same character in a series of titles.

Major publishers used to tell me that I was nuts to keep the same hero in each book. Pitt's a fun character, but he is a phenomenon I've never figured out, because unlike Ian Fleming's books, where people thought of James Bond instead of Fleming, readers think of Cussler instead of Pitt.

Everybody said 'You'll never make it with a series in hardback.' We have, but I can't explain that. Fleming never did very well with Bond in hard-cover.

Aficionados of Cussler's stories will know that Dirk Pitt works with the National Underwater Marine Agency, or NUMA. Readers may, however, be very surprised to learn that this organisation really does exist; indeed, it is the financial base which permits him to sail on those expensive sea searches. As Clive explained:

> It's a non-profitmaking foundation. The original trustees were going to call it The Clive Cussler Foundation because it's supported by my book royalties, and I said, to hell with that, and they called it NUMA instead.

The fact that NUMA and its work genuinely exist undoubtedly lends an air of authenticity to his novels; one element that has made them so popular. But he shares with a great many other authors the dread that one day the reading public's taste may change. It is a fear to which he readily admits:

> I could change. I could take a pen and make up anything that the public wants to read, because I have the old advertiser's ability. I'm not pegged in, if somebody came out with a really good new plotting style, and it was a huge success, I bet I could switch right into it, with a little play of my own and go on with Pitt.

The 'pen' in this context is a word-processor, Clive being an author who has taken to the latest technology. When he is writing, he disciplines himself to work rigid hours, knowing that authors must have that determination if they are ever to succeed. He works the same hours as he used to when he was in advertising: 'nine to five – with an hour off for a Martini.'

His first two books were written in the evenings, and at weekends; he firmly believes that any ambitious author should begin by writing in his or her spare time. It seems only common sense to retain a full-time job, for writing is not an occupation from which anyone can immediately earn a living; indeed, only a small percentage of published writers actually pay the rent from their work. When Clive set out to write *Raise the Titanic* he was still employed full-time at Mefford, Wolff and Weir. After the huge success of that novel, and only then, was he able to give up his job.

Clive sets himself a daily target, normally achieving about 1,000 words, roughly four pages. If he has a really good day and everything flows, he will achieve six pages, and if not, just two. Naturally, what he writes depends upon the thought and research he puts into a book, but these accrue over variable, and often very long, periods of time. When he has finished the typescript, he is ready to hand it over.

> Right from the beginning, I always stand or fall on the finished typescript. I have never sent a chapter out, or a summary. What the publisher gets, is what he gets.

These are sentiments with which many other authors would agree. However, it is all very well for an established and successful writer to make such statements, but a different matter for the novice.

Cussler's message for eager authors is somewhat unusual:

> My advice? Copy someone else! Find a successful author you idolize in the genre you are interested in and copy, not plagiarize the story, but the writing style. They don't seem to teach writing style on any courses that I have found, whether to use a prologue and epilogue, or whether you want to write in the first or third person, [or] the benefits of flashbacks, or how to divide it into sections.
>
> I try to end a chapter with a hook. Like the old Saturday matinée serials. The reader will probably be in bed when he'll hit that point, but he'll always sneak a peek at the start of the next [chapter], then I'll hook him again.

As I have said, he is very conscious that readers' tastes change with the passing of time. He has even considered killing off Pitt, though everyone keeps telling him that the idea is mad. (I cannot imagine that he will ever do so, for his *alter ego* is also modelled on his son.) He has, however, given much thought to what the change he might bring about in his work.

But whatever the future may hold, Clive Cussler has the last word:

> Writing a book is no different from an inventor inventing a product. You sit there and create this thing. . .

Frederick Forsyth CBE

The Biafra Story, The Day of the Jackal, The Odessa File, The Shepherd, The Dogs of War, The Devil's Alternative, The Fourth Protocol, The Negotiator, The Deceiver, The Fist of God, and *Icon*.

It seems a strange fact, but Frederick Forsyth did not see any television until he was in his teens. For passive entertainment, as was traditional, he read books. His parents encouraged him in this, but he had no immediate ancestors who showed any talents for, or even leanings towards, writing. Mother and father were both shopkeepers in Ashford, Kent; his grandfather had served in the Royal Navy; his grandmother was a furrier in Gillingham; and his mother's father was a garage mechanic. It is hardly surprising, then, that writing was not one of his early ambitions.

When we met at his 190-acre farm in Hertfordshire, he reflected on his early aspirations, those he achieved by his own efforts, and those that were won by chance.

As a schoolboy, his first ambition had been to fly but, more importantly, he developed a yearning to travel, to see the world. He explained that both ambitions originated from his home environment, where his imaginative mind had been fired by the places he had read about.

> I was a voracious reader. Television, well, it had been invented, but we did not have one in our household. I think my parents got their first television when I was in my mid-teens, so my earlier years were spent reading books. Apart from the radio – then called the wireless – and the gramophone, one read. My parents were avid readers. So the three of us, in the evenings, would sit just reading.
>
> I found I went through all the usual baby books. I skipped Beatrix Potter, but read a bit of Enid Blyton. Enjoyed the usual comics like *Beano* and *Dandy*, and later graduated to Richmal Crompton's *Just William* books.
>
> But I was also interested in more adventurous stuff, and I recall taking individual authors and consuming everything that they ever wrote. I had my John Buchan period, and I read *The Dancing Floor*, *The Island of Sheep*, *The Three Hostages*, *Greenmantle*. I did not have a Henty period; I wasn't a great imperialist. Jeffery Farnol – now

unknown. I liked the adventure stories about the old pirates and knights and what I suppose we call period-costume stuff. I just read a lot.

I also became fascinated by aeroplanes. I read all about the First World War fighter pilots: Bishop, McCudden, Mannock; and the Germans, Immelman, Göring; and the French, Garros and Guynemer. I just became smitten with the idea that one day I was going to fly.

From the First War, I graduated to the Second World War, and read all the memoirs of Bader, 'Johnnie' Johnson and Pierre Clostermann. I consumed them all, one after the other. And I retained a lot, too: I have a good retentive memory. So, between adventure and flying, I suppose the only clue in that little boy in Ashford is that there was someone trying to get out and get away, and go places.

It is unlikely that the then nine year-old Frederick Forsyth realized that it was his much-travelled father, with his vivid memories of faraway places, who set him upon a course that would ignite his imagination.

If the young Forsyth was bright and imaginative, he was not academic, though he developed a passion for languages and soon became competent in French and German, and, later, Spanish. Surprisingly, he did not at this time receive any encouragement to write. Not one of his teachers spotted his talent, and the fact that he did not contribute to the school magazine rather confirms that any writing or journalistic leanings were latent.

Although he enjoyed languages, he made a conscious decision not to further his education by going on to university. He spent four years at Tonbridge School where he developed very strong views about the public school system.

Discipline. I didn't like, or enjoy, the discipline, the hierarchy, the rigid and stratified chain of command that pertains in a public school. It didn't suit me. I was always a bit of a loner, and what with my head filled with fantasies of bullfighting and flying . . . At least, bullfighting after reading *Death in the Afternoon*, Ernest Hemingway's classic. Flying, for obvious reasons I've described.

There I was at Tonbridge, with a flair for languages and a profound yearning to get out and see the world. There's one other influence on that.

My father, in the after-war years, used to read every day the *Daily Express*, in the days when it was run by Beaverbrook and the editor,

Art Christiansen. And they had in those days – they don't today – a bevy, a stable perhaps, of forty of the best foreign correspondents. Almost every day I would lean – and I'm talking about a nine or ten year-old – lean over my father's shoulder and read the headlines. Very often underneath would be 'Beirut', and then the date. I would ask my father where Beirut was, and he was enormously patient and helpful. Right, he would say, I'll show you. He would get the large school atlas out and tell me where Beirut was. Capital of the Lebanon, but he didn't just say it was there, and then go back to the paper. He told me about the Lebanon. He'd been through Port Said, he'd been to the Orient, had seen India, even planted rubber in Malaya. A much travelled man. Datelines [in the newspaper] included many and varied places, and he would point out to me where Montevideo, Buenos Aires, Rio de la Plata, Mexico City, North America, Asia, the Middle East, and even Europe were on the map. Today I don't remember the new capitals, because all the African capitals have now been changed, but I remember Salisbury, Blantyre and Lagos. I knew where they were. I could probably name ninety percent of the capitals of the world, because that's where the newspaper correspondents filed their reports from, and I just determined that, one day, I was going to get out of Ashford, and I was going to see them all.

So the wanderlust was born there. The desire to fly was born there; and the desire for exotica, for the sand and sun, and for the red colours of the bullring, were all born there, in that little house in Ashford.

Forsyth left school when only 'seventeen and four months' (he was very precise about that), with the immediate aim of doing his National Service in the Royal Air Force, but he was prevented by his youth. Unlike many others he had some flying experience, having learned how to fly a Tiger Moth (a single-engined biplane).

I wasn't allowed to join the Air Force until I was seventeen and a half. Even then I snipped six months off the legal age of eighteen.

I started at Ternhill, in Shropshire, on an aircraft called a Provost, a Hunting-Percival Provost T1 trainer. It was a two-seater, side-by-side, with a fixed undercarriage. That took up nine months of what's called basic flying, and then we went on to an advanced flying training school at Worksop in Nottinghamshire. That was on Vampires. The Vampire was not originally built as a trainer, it was built as a front-line fighter, but by the time I was being trained it had been superseded by the Hawker Hunter. So the Vampires had been relegated to a training role, and they had invented a thing called the T11, which was another side-by-side trainer.

Not only did he see – literally – a good deal more of England through his National Service, but also other parts of Europe. He managed to hitch a seat on RAF flights to Beirut, France, Germany, Gibralter, Malta and Spain. After leaving the RAF he secured a job on a provincial newspaper, which scarcely seems the best way of seeing the world, if that was his real ambition.

Well, in a sense, I had sated my lust for flying through National Service. I had done it, and got my wings; I had proved I could do it. I was told when I went in, in no uncertain terms, there was no way any small boy from Ashford gets to be a fighter pilot. I had done it, and I had been offered the chance of staying on for a permanent commission, but I decided that I wanted to go on, if you like, to the other lust, which was to travel. And I thought that, as I hadn't got enough money to finance my own travelling, I would find a job that enabled me to do it. That seemed to be a foreign correspondent.

That was my next step, so to speak, on this pilgrim's progress. Flying was buttoned up, I had done it. But I still had no aspirations at all of becoming a fiction writer.

No, I wanted to travel. And how best to do it? So I enquired, how best to become a Fleet Street correspondent, and I was told nobody gets into Fleet Street straight from school, or straight from National Service, you had got to do your time first in a provincial newspaper. I asked around, and consulted the editor of the Ashford paper, the *Kentish Express*, and he was a very nice guy. He took the magazine called *World Press News*, which was the trade magazine of journalism, which I borrowed, and in the Situations Vacant column I spotted an advert for a cub reporter on the *Eastern Daily Press*. I asked him about it and, he said, 'It's a very good paper, but it's a daily rather than a weekly, and most people start on a weekly paper. At least you'll soon learn the discipline of working for a daily paper, with six deadlines a week. If I were you, I'd write off for it.' Which I did, and got my interview in Norwich.

I was really very lucky, for the editor-in-chief was a man who had been a correspondent in the Spanish Civil War and was interested that I spoke French, German and Spanish. He took me on as a cub reporter, but the thing was, I had to sign a three year contract, because they didn't want – as they had had before – people whom they trained up to the point where they were just beginning to pay their way, and off they'd go.

His three and a half years on this paper allowed him to gain all the experience necessary to qualify for a job in London's Fleet Street. He could hardly have imagined that at the time, though, when all he did was to cover such mundane events as swimming galas and cage-bird shows. His days as a cub reporter held not the slightest indication of the exciting life ahead.

In May 1961 he moved to London, an experienced reporter in his early twenties. He joined Reuters, the world-famous news agency which has offices all over the world. It took him just eight months to fulfil his dreams.

> The chance of a foreign posting was something most correspondents dreamed about. I was surrounded by people who were much older than I, and I was twenty-three then. People had been there for years.
>
> Luck – I've had so much luck, so many flukes and coincidences that turn out right for me – a guy put his head around the door of the office one day and said, 'Anyone here speak French?' So I said, 'Yeah. Me.' 'Right,' he said, 'come with me.'
>
> He took me off to the head of the French Desk, who was French, and said to this guy, 'See if this cub speaks French.' So the Frenchman turned to me, and rattled off several sentences in French and I rattled off several sentences back in French. He was a busy man, in shirtsleeves, with bands to hold his sleeves up, tapping away upon his typewriter (we didn't have computers in those days), and he just looked up, and said, 'Hee speekes vair good French. Why?' So then the other fellow who had summoned me said, to him, not me, 'The Deputy Editor, Paris, has got a heart murmur, and he's going to have to be flown home. They are screaming for a replacement.' So the Frenchman said, 'We-ell, send 'eem. E's all right.' And that was it. I was on.
>
> 'When can you leave?' 'Instantly!' I said, 'tonight.' I only had a bedsitter and an MG sports car. No real ties, one suitcase held all my belongings. I garaged the car, paid up the rent on the flat to the end of the week, and I was on the evening plane to Paris.
>
> And that was May 1962, during the height of the OAS* crisis, with Algeria due for her independence on 1 July. Assassination

---

* Organisation de l'Armée Secrète, a secret terrorist group opposed to de Gaulle's Algerian policy. Algeria had been colonized by France between 1830 and 1860, and between 1954 and 1962 had been devastated by war between the Arab nationalists and the French or French-descended settlers, who were supported by the French military. When de Gaulle's Fifth Republic agreed to Algerian independence, many of the settlers and the military put their support behind the OAS.

attempts were being hatched against [President] Charles de Gaulle, and the Foreign Legion had gone into mutiny along with the 11th Colonial Paras, the crack French regiment in Algeria.

I met the French bodyguard around de Gaulle, because I was, as the cub reporter, the youngest, the junior, and given what was deemed to be the most boring job, which was following de Gaulle around. Whenever he left the Elysee Palace for a function or to open a motorway, or go to the Chambre des Députés to make an address to the house, there was this enormous press corps, part French, part foreign, following.

Not because what he was doing was of enormous interest, but in case he suddenly went down with a bullet through his head. Here was a kind of Kennedy assassination that was foreseen, that was awaited on an hourly basis. When are they going to get de Gaulle? When will the gunshot ring out? When will the bomb go off that will blow him to smithereens? Charles de Gaulle wasn't up against a Lee Harvey Oswald, he was up against the cream of the French Army, the best of the best that were deemed to be, the officer corps and the NCO corps of the French Foreign Legion and the colonial paratroop regiments. These were the best. If they couldn't do it, nobody could, surely? we all thought. So there was this enormous press corps following him around and the lofty old man knew perfectly well what we were doing there. We were there to see him die.

Well, in the periods between when he moved in his guarded limousine came the waiting, which every journalist will tell you is part of the job. You wait, and you wait, and you wait. The British, American, Swedish, Danish, Finnish and Norwegian press corps kept themselves to themselves in a single group, and the French in the other. I, because I was bilingual, joined the French group, and there I got to know and listened to the reminiscences of the bodyguards and drivers, and later, when I needed it, I could always call on these contacts, calling in markers, because I'd done favours for them, and they would talk to me about what it was really like to try and protect that man. That is why the authenticity of *The Day of the Jackal* is genuine.

I also knew bars where I could find OAS sympathizers, and because I was curious – not because it made a story, but because I was curious – I would frequent them. I would listen to their side, of how the great traitor de Gaulle had given Algeria away to the wogs, and so on. These were the OAS, the ultra-rights. As a journalist, I found I could move between all segments of society, from high society, the diplomats and politicians, to the underworld, the rebels, and the security service, counter-intelligence, and, amongst them, killers. And I met a number of pretty violent individuals in that area.

Forsyth's career as a diplomatic correspondent for the BBC is another reason why he was able to use his investigative experience as a base for the thrillers he was destined to write. It must be said, however, that just being a journalist and mastering the art of gathering information is not an automatic passport to becoming a bestselling writer.

However, when he became a freelance correspondent working in Biafra,* he was greatly moved by the many children he saw dying as a result of the war and, knowing that the British government of the day supported the oppressors (France, by contrast, supported the Biafrans), he felt compelled to put all that he had seen and learned into a book.

One incidental feature of his experiences in Biafra was that he met arms dealers who were selling weapons either to the Biafrans or the Nigerians (sometimes both sides), and mercenaries who were fighting for the Biafrans. All of them had stories to tell which he stored in his memory, and which were to prove so useful in his fiction.

Back in London on leave, he just happened to saunter down to his local pub, the Mason's Arms in Devonshire Street, where he liked to enjoy a drink and the convivial conversation of acquaintances. Among the friends there was one Brian Seaton-Hunt. Had he not been there, Frederick Forsyth might still be a foreign correspondent.

We got talking and he mentioned that he was an agent, albeit in a small way. I said, 'Well, I'm an author in a very small way.' He asked, 'What have you written?', and I told him that I had just finished a manuscript about Biafra.

Now, the serendipity of the whole thing is that barely a week earlier, he had been talking to Rob Hutchinson [the editor for Penguin's Africa list] who had told him, 'We really could use a book about Biafra as a Penguin Special'. And so obviously Brian Seaton-Hunt said to me, 'I think I know how it can be placed', but he didn't tell me about Rob Hutchinson then. But he said, 'Give me the manuscript.' I did. And we took it to Rob, who said to Brian, 'This is exactly what we are looking for. Good controversy about Biafra.'

Brian, alas, is now dead; he died of a heart attack some years ago. He wasn't an established agent as such, he hadn't got an office, but he

---

* Biafra was an area of Nigeria that seceded from that country in 1967, resulting in a bloody and brutal civil war that did not end until Biafran resistance collapsed in 1970.

aspired to be a literary agent. And indeed, he was acting for another author.

I interrupted, to suggest that had he not met Brian, nor written about Biafra, he would not have had the confidence to write *The Day of the Jackal*.

> I might not, though I think it was quite a different undertaking, because I could write *The Biafra Story* from researches; it was basically reportage. I could write from my researches and from what I had seen, and interviews I had had with people who knew Nigeria much better than I did then.
>
> *Jackal* was quite different, in as much as here I was into fiction, inventing characters, inventing plot lines and sub-plots and so on. So it was different in that sense. I didn't consciously think, as I started to write it, I know this is going to work because I have written one [book] already. I just thought this is going to work because I have in my time picked paperback books off airport bookshelves and read such absolute rubbish. I was sure I could do as well, or better. It was very impudent, but that was the way I thought.

Penguin did indeed publish his non-fiction book about Biafra, though he never saw the proofs or cover designs because by the time the book was in production he was back in Nigeria. He was paid an advance of just £50 for *The Biafra Story*, against a royalty of about 3d (1.25p) per copy (this all happened before the British currency was decimalized). Despite this seemingly small sum, he earned some £350 in all, for the publishers sold the entire run of 30,000 copies.

Most authors whose first book had sold that number of copies would be tempted to continue in the genre that had brought them success. Forsyth, however, like Barbara Taylor Bradford, believed he could write other subjects.

> I found myself, in January 1970, back in this country from the Biafra War, without a contract or a commission, freelance, and therefore unemployed. I was like an actor 'resting', with time to kill, no income coming in, and not much in the bank. I had an idea in my head. I had mulled it over for some six years, from the time I had been covering the OAS attempts to assassinate Charles de Gaulle in Paris.
>
> . . . I had picked so many trashy paperback pseudo thriller novels off airline bookstalls, and after a hundred pages in the middle of a flight, closed them and said, 'This is absolute nonsense. The man does not even know what he is talking about. He hasn't even made an attempt to know what he's talking about.' And that irritated me.

I figured that somebody, somewhere, proof read these manuscripts, and they had been published first in hardback and then paperback, and I had bought them, with my impecunious means, only as a paperback. And I had got through a hundred pages and just simply thrown them down in exasperation. I had a conviction that if I couldn't do better, at least I could do as well.

I felt that if one was going to write a thriller, one ought to make it credible. And credibility, it seems to me, is about getting the facts right, especially where you were going into facts rather than fiction.

So I did just that. I wrote what turned out to be *The Day of the Jackal* without a contract, and [without a] publisher, in thirty-five days in January and February [1970]. And without a clue as to how to get a novel published.

(This did not ring wholly true, for any author who has had one book published must know at least something of the ways of publishers. But he was, of course, back in Biafra when his first book was being produced.) With the novel finished, the first person he went to, of course, was his drinking companion, and agent, Brian.

I really didn't know how it was done. A year later, I had this much bigger typescript, and a thriller novel to boot, and no idea what one does about getting a book published. Who do you go to? Who do you see? I soon discovered that it was a 'catch twenty-two'. If you are a big and popular novelist, you have no trouble getting a top agent. A top agent will have no trouble getting you published. But if you are a 'who's he?' nonentity, with an unpublished manuscript, and a first to boot, then the big blue-chip agents don't want to know.

My work was submitted in sequence to four publishers: W. H. Allen, Cassell, Collins, and then Michael Joseph.

I got rejection slips from the first, second, and third. It was with Michael Joseph for about eight weeks, from mid-July to mid-September, and I hadn't had a word back. It was frustrating, but it was the holiday period, and quite coincidentally – well, not quite – I did actually do a bit of beavering myself. I met [the late] Harold Harris, who was then editorial director of Hutchinson - oddly enough, in the same bar at the Mason's Arms.

Brian had been hawking it around to these publishers, but was getting nowhere. It so happened that Hutchinson then were right across the other side of Great Portland Street [i.e. near the pub], and Harold Harris had dropped in for a beer. Brian introduced me to him, but nothing much came of it. The book was not even mentioned, but I had already by then decided that Brian was getting nowhere, and I thought – wrongly or rightly, whatever – the reason he was getting nowhere was that nobody was reading the damn thing. I didn't think it was that bad.

I thought that if anyone is just reading the first chapter, they will come to the view that this is a book about someone trying to kill Charles de Gaulle who, of course, was then alive and well. Therefore they must think it is a duff book.

What I'll do, I thought, is write a synopsis. So I wrote the synopsis, which covered all the twenty-four chapters in the book in one page per chapter. After that was done, I went back to Hutchinson and I inveigled myself into the presence of Harold Harris, and I said, 'I've got this typescript.' His eyes glazed over, you know, in a sort of disbelief; after all, he was a busy man and had rank after rank of secretaries to protect him from unsolicited typescripts. But being a very courteous man he said, 'I see.' Then I cantered on, saying, 'I don't want you to read the typescript, it's too long, it'll take you for ever. But would you read the synopsis?'

After twenty minutes he looked up [from the synopsis], and said, 'It could be interesting, where is it?' I replied, truthfully, 'It is with Michael Joseph.' He stared at the ceiling for some time and he said, 'It is absolutely out of the question for me to examine a typescript that is in the hands of another publisher. Good day.'

But I read the body language, went outside, got a cab, and went down to Michael Joseph, though by this time it was the lunch hour. I asked at reception for it back, and a junior duly gave it to me. He said, 'Are you formally withdrawing it?' I said, 'Yes I am.' And without any more ado, they gave it to me, the whole typescript, with elastic bands in two directions to hold it together. I literally shoved it under my arm and went back to Great Portland Street, where I gave it to Harold Harris, less than thirty minutes after leaving him. 'Oh, good Lord, have you withdrawn it from Michael Joseph?' 'Yes,' I said, 'yes, I have.' 'Oh, in that case, protocol permits me to read it.' 'Thank you very much. I will be in touch, but can I have your phone number?' That was on a Friday at about two-fifteen.

Brian Seaton-Hunt, who wasn't best pleased by having been circumvented, got in touch with me in extreme perturbation and said, more or less, 'What the asterisk do you think you're doing? I have been informed by an extremely irate gentleman from Michael Joseph that you have withdrawn your typescript unilaterally. If this is to proceed, we can no longer be associated.' I said, 'Well I'm sorry, but they *have* had it for eight weeks.'

This was the Friday, and on Monday Harris called me up and said, 'If you'll be here at four pm with your agent, we'll discuss a contract.'

So I called Brian and told him the news and we duly presented ourselves at four pm. To all intents and purposes the contract was a conventional publisher's contract. In other words, we filled in a few figures. The normal percentages for a first and unsolicited typescript, with an advance of £500 on signature, which took place then and there, and £500 on publication.

The most interesting thing about all this was that Harold Harris suggested that I sign what's called a three-novel contract, which very much enthused Brian – which now changed everything completely. This was the best thing since sliced bread, but there were clauses further down the list about foreign royalties and 'acceptance' [of any typescript submitted]. In other words, if I wrote a load of junk, they could turn it down. The question then arose, and it arose before I left the office, 'Do you have any ideas for a successor [book]?'

This was in the early days, this was September 1970. Bold as brass I said, 'Yes, of course I have, scores of ideas, and just as intriguing as this one,' but actually I hadn't an idea in my head. So I went away, literally to think up another theme.

Brian was walking a foot above the pavement after we left. And he repeated, it *was* extremely unusual for a first-time author, with no name, no renown, no repute, and no track record, to be offered a three-novel contract. It did virtually commit Hutchinson to publishing three novels.

From then on, I was devoting a lot of time trying to think up another theme. And I came up with two. One based on the notion of hunting a missing Nazi; some shades, if you like, of the Eichmann hunt, which had taken place ten years earlier in 1960, and with some shades of Nazi trials that had taken place at that time.

The alternative was a novel based on mercenaries in West Africa. So I wrote up the general idea, on one page, and in the broadest possible brush strokes. Then, about a fortnight later, I went back to Harold Harris and said, 'Which one would you prefer?'

Unhesitating, he chose the Nazi one, which came to be known as *The Odessa File*. I began work on that probably in the late winter, the December-January period. My deadline was 31 December 1971, so

I had got virtually twelve months in which to devise, research, write, and present. That was quite a schedule, so work began next year.

To be fair to Hutchinson, with the success of *Jackal*, they permitted me to vary the other contracts [that is, for the two following books]. For one thing, the £500 plus £500 [advance], a thousand, was superseded before the launch. Advance sales alone went over what I would have been due. I think the book was published at £2.50 . . . I would have had [a ten percent royalty of] 25 pence per book, so £1,000 would have required sales of 4,000 books at counter price. I believe the launch print was 5,000, and then they did a pre-launch [printing] of another 3,000, bringing the total to 8,000 copies.

All in hardback. That was just the UK edition alone. By then, however – by June 1971 when the book was published - some quite substantial foreign contracts had been negotiated. Those, I recall, were Viking, worth $10,000, and the big one, Bantam in America, was worth $356,000. There were others too, in Germany, France and Italy.

Probably five or six quite substantial foreign rights had been sold prior to June 1971. Of course, although I attended the launch party, I was deeply involved in researching *The Odessa File*.

One of the more curious habits of the media is that all too often magazines and newspapers quote dramatically high earnings for authors. Sometimes these are accurate, more often they are not, but reading them can lead other writers to expect high advances for a first novel. One UK ladies' journal which carried a feature about Forsyth commented that he had been telling friends that he expected to earn some £5,000 from *The Day of the Jackal*.

They all laughed like drains, and said, you are out of your skull. It's a one-in-a-hundred chance that a first novel will ever get published at all, then what you'll get for it is between £500 and £1,000 as tops. And it'll die, because that is what first novels do . . . I was regarded as impudent beyond belief, to even think I was going to get £5,000 out of a first novel.

Who laughs now, I wonder?

* * *

After nine hugely successful novels – and ignoring his non-fiction, *The Biafra Story* and two others – had he, I wondered, ever tried to analyse why *The Day of the Jackal* was so popular?

Obviously, I have tried to analyse that since, because people have said to me, 'Can't be your first . . .' All I can come up with – and I could well be wrong about it – but it seems that the formula which I have used since then works. I think there are three things that intrigue.

One, and this sounds very big-headed, but it is very basic, you must have a story to tell. You can't take an episode and spin it out for four hundred pages. You can't take one single rather smart idea, and pad it to a blockbuster. The story must be a pretty big story in itself.

I would say you've got to have what you reckon is a cracker of a story. The idea of knocking off the president is, you know, a fairly big issue, assassinating presidents is big enough for people to say, yes, I believe all this effort would probably go into trying to prevent it. Whereas all that effort might not go into trying to prevent an offence against, say, the Litter Act.

The second one – and this people said to me later – it [the novel] is all innovative, it's never been done before.

I don't know why, but I'm rather a stickler for accuracy. It seemed to me, as a reader, that I was interested in how things worked, how things were done, what the procedures were. I would find it unsatisfying, as a reader, if this bank clerk suddenly whips out a loaded gun, because by and large bank clerks do not have loaded guns and your ordinary chap on the Penge eight-forty-nine am to Cannon Street, or wherever, is going to be pretty hard put to go and get a Colt forty-five. There has to be procedure: how on earth did he get the damn thing? And when people produce these marvellous high tensile sets of burglar tools, I'm intrigued to know where they get them from. So, I thought, if you are going to start talking about false passports, let's find out how you get false passports. So I found a professional forger, and he told me. He was rather displeased later when it all appeared in print, because he said, 'I do have a wife and children to support, and now every punter is going to be doing it.'

I said there are three things that intrigue. The third is that the readers like being taken behind the scenes. I liken it to a stage. Most of us sit watching the television or reading the newspapers, as the audience to a production. We see the ministers on their best behaviour, and we see the civil servants at their most urbane. I take them back and show them the actors without their make-up on. I explain what goes on behind the façade that the captains of industry, politics, senior civil service and military defence show us. The readers seem to think there's something behind the headline, and I'm going to tell you what really happened and which wasn't in the papers.

I did not really believe he would disclose many of his 'trade' secrets. Access to his sources clearly stems from his earlier life as a reporter and foreign correspondent. Investigative journalists, he said:

> . . . can actually move between the police and the underworld. The police mix with the underworld, and the underworld mix with the police. They drink in the same pubs, sometimes they've almost got a one-to-one relationship. Armed neutrality occasionally, and sometimes even open warfare, but they do know each other. The journalist can sometimes move from the highest level of society to the lowest and yet be more or less accepted.

So, accepting that he is able to procure accurate and detailed information from his special sources, does he really believe that it is just attention to detail that ensures his novels become bestsellers? Is that aspect more important to the success of his books than, say word of mouth, publicity, or advertising?

> That's a good one. If publishers could answer that, they would know exactly where to spend their budgets, and none of them can. *Jackal* was clearly word of mouth, by the fact of its having a launch print of 8,000 copies. It wasn't necessarily the sort of book that every reviewer will jump at like the next Le Carré, or the next Jeffrey Archer.
>
> I think that word of mouth was undoubtedly to a large degree the main reason. Later, yes, of course, there was a publicity budget and yes, there were reviews and there were interviews, and promotional campaigns, and now they [his publishers] are actually buying television space, and advertising books on television like any other product. Like cornflakes!
>
> Then you've got paid and unpaid promotion; permeation chat shows on radio or television, like *Start the Week*. It suits the journalist, because he's got a personality on his show, it suits the publisher because he's got his author on the show. It probably suits the author because it may raise his royalties. Then you've got all the paid, purely paid, promotional publicity.

Fortunately, at the merest rumour of another Forsyth thriller, orders start to arrive at the publisher's sales office, but he accepts that all that might change one day.

> Oh, the fickleness of the public. I can't predict what they want next year, and I don't think anybody can. If film makers knew what the rave film was going to be next year, there wouldn't be so many repeats and so many films number two, three and four [i.e. sequels to hit films]. Everyone's looking for a winning formula, film makers are, novelists are; all I can do is to devise an idea that interests me. If it doesn't interest me, I won't do it anyway because I can't sustain the interest to do it.
>
> All I do really is to take an issue I haven't dealt with before, and which very few, if any, have ever dealt with before and yet which is contemporary . . . The *Jackal* was written about events in 1963 but published in 1971, *Odessa* was published in 1972, [and is about] events starting with the assassination of Kennedy in 1963. *Dogs of War* was much more recent, published in 1974 about events in 1970-71.
>
> Only then did I start setting the stories futuristically: *Devil's Alternative* published in 1979 but set in 1981-82; *Fourth Protocol* was published in 1984, but set in 1987 with the then forthcoming General Election, which took place and Margaret Thatcher won again. This one, *The Negotiator*, again published 1989 but set in 1991.

Since he started to write, Forsyth has produced eight stunningly exciting thrillers, as well as his book about Biafra, a short story, *The Shepherd*, and a collection of short stories, *No Come Backs*.

> Of all of them, *Jackal* has been the most successful in numeric terms. After that, it's difficult to make comparisons because the new ones tend to have enormous upfront sales, whereas *Jackal* crept, and then broke from a walk into a trot, and a trot into a canter. If you took a decade, I would say probably *Jackal*, has been the most successful and, oddly enough, then *Fourth Protocol*.

Which, considering all this began with a chance meeting in a London pub, is not at all bad.

* * *

Those who wish to emulate Frederick Forsyth will have noted the reasons he gives for the success of his thrillers. They might also note his advice to others who wish to follow in his footsteps:

Stick with the job you've got. Don't jack in a perfectly good job that pays the rent. Until, at least, you have your first one out, and in print, and you can judge whether you are going to be a professional novelist who can bring up his wife and kids on what he earns as a novelist. A lot of people are one-novel writers, one-story men.

Second – assuming that this chap has decided that he wants to write a novel and he is going to do it in his spare time – prepare. Don't have one smart idea that will actually occupy four sheets of paper; sit down and try and write four hundred sheets about that one idea. Work out your story.

It is very personal; it is the way I do it; it is the only way I can do it. There's no way I could sit down at a typewriter when I don't even know quite what's going to happen. Apparently there are people who can do it that way, and they are brilliant, marvellous. Sometimes it shows, but I find the best way is to prepare it, and what helps to prepare it is a synopsis, about twenty pages. What's going to happen, who is going to do what to whom, the twists and turns, betrayals and conspiracies, until you have a structure. About seventy percent of the preparatory work of a book is the structure. It's not actually the characters, the dialogue, the descriptions of the sunset over Bantry Bay. It's not even the sex, or the violence. It's the structure.

Whether his success is due to the structure of his novels, the detailed research and reputation for accuracy, or word-of-mouth recommendation, he certainly receives lots of mail, and not just from the United Kingdom.

The two most numerous categories in the world are the Germans and the Americans. The British, not so much. They [the letters] fall into basically four or five categories. 'Please can I have an autograph, or a photograph?' 'I liked the book or I didn't like the book.' Or, 'By the way, you have made a mistake.' And, 'I have got a great idea for a novel; what I suggest is that you split it 50/50.' Or, 'Will you come and address the school?' To the ones who wrote and said 'read it and liked it', with no questions, there's nothing to reply about, and to them I give a spiritual thank you. Those asking for an autograph or picture get one.

Those who would like me to write my next book based on some story they have devised get a polite 'Thank you, but I do actually prefer to do my own.' And invitations to speak in public are regretfully declined. I just can't do that sort of thing. One, I'm an appalling public speaker, and I loathe it. I have a profound dislike for it. And I could be travelling the country several times each week to answer all the questions and to give public addresses.

Does he see himself still writing in five or ten years time?

I am not going to say that I am never going to write again. Possibly this is the last book. I don't have the three great aphrodisiacs, of lust for power, for money, or for fame. In America, I'm a freak for not being turned on in quite a substantial way by any of the three. Add to that a lack of compulsion – I'm deliriously happy when I'm not writing. Without the three stimuli, and without the compulsion, it is more or less fluke, chance, that I write at all.

I don't know if I'll even stay with writing. There's television, I mean writing for television, with which I'm involved at the moment, in a project which I find very interesting, I and a partner, two partners actually. One is Murray Smith, who is a top screenwriter, and [Sir] David Frost, who is the upfront man. We three have secured ourselves a contract. . .

POSTSCRIPT

Frederick Forsyth's last remark suggested an impending change in his career, but that was not the case. The 'contract' he had mentioned resulted in a series of six thrillers for London Weekend Television under the banner 'Frederick Forsyth Presents'; and a book linked to the series entitled *The Deceiver*, published in 1991.

Then he suffered a major setback when a financial advisor went bankrupt resulting in the loss of part of his hard-earned fortune. Whether it was this loss, or having had a break from writing, the zest to start again was rekindled. For he later wrote two more thrillers which hit the bestseller lists, *The Fist of God* and *Icon*.

He had obviously remembered his first rule – 'stick with the job you've got. Don't jack in a perfectly good job that pays the rent.' To date, his thrillers have been translated into thirty languages which have contributed to massive worldwide sales of 50 million copies. With these achievements, he hardly has the problem of paying the rent!

1997 marked another high point in his life for he received the CBE. A well-deserved honour.

Dick Francis OBE

The Sport of Queens (non-fiction), *Dead Cert, Nerve, For Kicks, Odds Against, Flying Finish, Blood Sport, Forfeit, Enquiry, Rat Race, Bonecrack,* and twenty-four other thrillers. Worldwide sales exceed 60 million.

In any discussion of modern British thrillers, one of the first names to be mentioned will be that of the former jockey Dick Francis. He has written, to date, thirty-five first-class novels, and many rank him among the best thriller writers of our time. Above all, he is the epitome of someone who, having become highly successful in his chosen career, abruptly quits to take up another. In his case, he had reached the ripe age of thirty-seven, a time when most jump jockeys begin to think about a less dangerous occupation, not least because at that age the body is beginning to take longer to recover from the bruising and broken bones brought by the inevitable falls.

The majority of jockeys gravitate naturally towards training but this did not feature in Dick's plans: he decided to take up writing. He is now in his late seventies, and given his experience of two careers, he was a prime candidate to interview. Why was it, I wondered, that he, out of the legions of ambitious authors, should have succeeded so notably? What was the magic of his appeal?

I went to meet Dick when he was in London on an annual visit from America to launch yet another of his thrillers. His visits to the United Kingdom are usually timed – like clockwork they are so regular – to coincide with the launch of his latest novel, or at other times to watch a classic race. He had, as usual, an extremely busy schedule of publicity events, and he said, with a mixture of resigned glee and complaint, that publicity tours were one of the major burdens that he had to endure, adding (though I didn't altogether believe him) that he didn't like such pressure. Our meeting was thus rather shorter than those with other authors: according to the schedule he described, he was set to be rushed from the Hyde Park Hotel by chauffeur-driven limousine to the BBC for a radio interview with Michael Aspel. After that, he had more book-signing sessions to carry out, and more journalists to meet, all wanting to quiz him about the latest thriller.

Much has been written about Dick's magical transformation from successful jockey to bestselling author. Most reports suggest that he retired while at the zenith of his racing career, and then took up writing but, strictly speaking, that's not true. He was writing his autobiography long before he retired; in fact, he was about two-thirds finished, when he learned that the rules forbade professional jockeys from appearing in print! This prompted me to ask him what had given him the confidence to take up writing.

> It was my wife, Mary, who encouraged me. When the idea of writing my [auto-] biography was being considered, my literary agent – who talked me into the project – suggested that if I didn't feel like doing it, then he would get a ghost writer. We both said that definitely wasn't on.
>
> I'd started it . . . in 1956, and I'd written about half by the following January, when I had to give up riding. My retirement from racing was 'big news' in those days and all the media wanted to interview me – newspaper reporters, television, and the radio; they all asked 'What are you going to do, Dick? Are you going to train?' I didn't want to train, particularly because I felt I could get up on a horse anytime and do a job just as well as anyone else.
>
> I said [to the journalists] I'd half-written my autobiography; I'll see what develops. And the sports editor of the *Sunday Express* got to hear of that. He asked me to lunch and said would I write half a dozen articles on the current racing scene. Well, I did. And I continued writing them for the next sixteen years.

This seems to me to be a classic case of someone turning a dream into reality, just as anyone can (in theory, at least). As he told me, he had no formal training at a writing school, nor had he read any 'how-to-write' books, though his wife Mary, as he says quite freely, did and does help by checking drafts for accuracy, misprints, and errors, as well as ensuring that the plot makes sense.

What does seem to have become clear from my interviews is that most authors who become bestsellers have had direct links, of one kind or another, with publishing. In Dick's case, his wife Mary used to be a reader for a literary agency (and, as will become clear, he made another useful publishing contact during his riding career). In his shoes, any writer would, I think, ask Mary's opinion. That may seem a little unfair to Dick's literary ability, but he is always ready to give her credit for her help, particularly, he stresses, with the research.

Like Frederick Forsyth and many others, his attention and interest were initially caught by the displays of colourful paperbacks at airport bookshops. He used to buy one or two, and soon began to think – a point has been mentioned in many reviews of his career – that if others could write thrillers, then why shouldn't he? He told me that in his early days as a journalist with the *Sunday Express*, he had to travel widely and often. 'At airport bookshops, I'd see rows of paperback thrillers and I'd usually buy a couple to read on the flight'.

* * *

Dick's early education was, by his own admission, rather scant. His mind was always elsewhere – on anything related to horses, riding, and the local hunt. His first experience came when he was only five, learning to ride a donkey on his grandfather's farm in Pembrokeshire. He learned the art of balance by riding bareback, because his father, George, reckoned that it was the best way. No sooner had he gained some confidence than his brother, Douglas, challenged him to jump over a small fence riding bareback and seated backwards! He did, though not without falling off several times first, but for all the painful bruising he won himself the princely sum of sixpence.

After that, there was no turning back. He admired his grandfather, a former jockey who rode to hounds every week in the season, and bred hunters, an occupation at which he was singularly successful. Dick's introduction to the care and handling of foals began on that farm in Wales; there, it can be seen with hindsight, his empathy with and passion for animals had their origin. The magic and excitement of horses and riding fired his imagination, so it was hardly surprising that he much preferred to go riding, or follow the local hunt, than attend school.

After the end of the First World War, his father, who had also been a jockey, had worked at W. J. Smith's hunting stables in Berkshire, which was owned by a well-known riding school in Cadogan Place, London. The significance of this is that members of the Royal Family were among the pupils; as events turned out, Dick was later to ride for royalty. He and his brother spent many happy years learning from their father's inexhaustible schooling and advice, and picking up tips from watching the riding school lessons and sometimes from the stern reprimands the riding master handed out to his pupils. Curiously, however, Dick never ever had even a single formal riding lesson.

It was not long before he began to compete. He was only eight when he won his first event at a gymkhana. Not unexpectedly, given the wealth of family experience and 'professional' advice to hand, he soon collected numerous rosettes for winning events. After gymkhanas he competed in horse shows, with equal success, and at Richmond Horse Show in 1932 he collected a trophy which he still treasures today, a hunting crop presented by Princess Elizabeth, now Her Majesty the Queen.

Even from an early age, Dick craved to emulate both his father and grandfather by becoming a jockey, too. At first he thought he would remain small enough to ride in flat races, but he grew out of that mould, so to speak, leaving him only the option of becoming a jump jockey.

Then came the Second World War. Everyone wanted to do their bit, even those below the call-up age for National Service. Dick immediately tried to join the cavalry, naturally enough, but they did not want him, and he was advised to wait. Having failed in that, he tried to become a pilot, but was turned down for flying training, becoming an air frame fitter instead, a job he learned to hate, even though it took him to North Africa. He bombarded his superiors with a constant stream of requests to be trained as a pilot until they were heartily sick of him.

Persistence succeeded. He went out to Rhodesia and began his training on a Tiger Moth, a period of his career he found most enjoyable. From there, he came back to England and went on to fly Spitfires. Then came an enforced change to Wellington bombers, and he was posted to Silverstone in Northamptonshire. Flying the lumbering twin-engined Wellingtons after the fast and agile fighters was not so nearly so enjoyable, rather like changing from a thoroughbred to a cart-horse, However, the new posting at least enabled him to get home during his leaves, and on one of those all-too-short breaks he travelled to Somerset for a cousin's wedding, where he met his own future wife, Mary Brenchley.

Vast wars affect almost everyone's lives in one way or another. (Roald Dahl and Arthur Hailey were also wartime pilots; Clive Cussler and James Michener served in the Pacific; for all of them, their values and outlooks were changed by their experiences.) After the war he returned to normality, but horse shows no longer held the same appeal. He had become acutely aware of the bitchiness and envy of other competitors and their families. He still wanted to become a jockey, though both his parents disapproved, and it was through his brother Douglas that he found work in the Cheshire-based stables of George Owen.

Dick's first win, on a horse called Wrenbury Tiger, was at Bangor-on-Dee in 1947, though he only got to ride because the first two choices of jockeys fell through. His luck changed immediately, for he won another race that same afternoon on a mount that had previously never showed promise! More followed, and as the season came to a close, he had nine wins under his belt. With his marriage to Mary imminent, he was on Cloud Nine. But then came one of many bumps in his life. Literally. During his last race of the season, on a wet and dismal day, he suffered a nasty fall, breaking his collar-bone in the process. Breaking bones became a habit; his collar-bone eleven more times, his nose five times, his wrist once and his ribs too often to be recorded. Racing is a very dangerous sport, and jockeys soon learn to cope with the pain and inconvenience, otherwise they retire early.

Undeterred by this first temporary setback, he continued to race, and records of his successes over the next decade read like a fairy-tale. He evocatively, if modestly, recounts all the trials and tribulations in his autobiography, *The Sport of Queens*, published in 1957. For the first few years he remained an Amateur National Hunt Jockey, before turning professional in 1948. He rode numerous winners, of course, 345 of them, but not all his mounts came home 'in the frame'. One of those less successful occasions – and he took part in 2,305 races – was at Newton Abbott in 1952, where he rode Hornblower for its owner, the publisher Michael Joseph. In fact, he knew Joseph quite well, having met him several times while schooling horses at Ken Cundell's stables. Years later, this friendship was to prove a useful link with publishing, the sort of contact that seems to be so essential if a writer is to succeed in getting a first book published.

One of the sadder events recorded in his autobiography is when he rode Devon Loch, owned by the Queen Mother, in the 1956 Grand National. Quite simply, he became internationally famous for not winning. It has never been explained satisfactorily, but the thoroughbred belly-flopped in mid-stride, yards from the winning-post, and when well clear of the field. The incident became one of the racing world's greatest mysteries, and one of Dick's most poignant moments.

In all this while, there had been nothing to suggest that he would become one of the country's great story-tellers. As far as academic subjects are concerned, he had had, out of necessity, to become competent at mathematics when learning navigation during the war, but that scarcely involves creative writing. Mary was quick to point out to me during our meeting that as time passed, and his writing experience increased, so both his ability and his spelling improved. She also pointed to the latest gadget they had acquired; lying on the coffee-table in front of us was a portable hand-held computer with a built-in dictionary. 'Nowadays, this proves to be very useful. We're both using it.'

* * *

Dick Francis still looks every inch the slim and fit jockey he was years ago, but he also wears the appearance of a confident author who knows his subject. When we met, he lived in a luxury apartment in Fort Lauderdale, Florida, an address that implies wealth and exclusiveness. (He has since moved to the British West Indies.) Certainly he is now a wealthy man, but he originally forsook England in the interest of his wife's health, for she suffers from asthma and the warm Florida weather allows her a better life. There is a price to pay, however, for they miss the company of their many friends and relatives. So most summers they travel back to England to see them, and to renew acquaintances in the racing world.

All his novels have ranked as bestsellers. To underline this point, the initial printing of *Bolt*, published in 1987, was 75,000 in hardback and 500,000 in paperback! And these figures were despite, or arguably because of, the serialization of the book in the *Daily Express*. When your publisher confirms this sort of print quantity, you know you are amongst the top bestsellers. But why are the books so successful?

To borrow a term from racing, Dick had a head start when he turned to writing. It is fair to say that, at the time of his retirement from riding, anything he did would have been newsworthy. The fact that he elected to take up writing and to work for the *Sunday Express* gave him more than an adequate lead in the publicity stakes. With his racing articles being published, he was to a degree already recognized as a professional writer. Then, of course, there was his contact with Michael Joseph, who had once said that if Dick finished a book, he would publish it.

He wrote his first novel, *Dead Cert*, without leaving his job at the *Sunday Express*, and Michael Joseph paid him the princely sum (at least it felt like that to Dick at the time) of £300 in advance for it.*

It was published in 1962 and, as they say the rest is history. Now, of course, it is a very different story when it comes to advances but, even today, the publication of his first novel still gives him his greatest satisfaction.

Dick has travelled a good deal, and so have his books, for they have now been translated into at least thirty languages. Some of the novels are landmarks, like *Reflex*, published in 1980, which earned him £211,000 for the US paperback rights alone, and was in addition selected as one of the Book of the Month Club titles in America.

While I had been talking to Dick, Mary had been glancing through some press cuttings that I had brought with me. She took exception to one that stated that 'a bestseller's relationship with his agent is like a boxer's with his manager, for a literary career is made, it doesn't just happen.' Having thought about it for a moment, she said firmly:

> That was not the case with Dick's books. His agent did not make him at all. It just happened. He was a very famous jockey at the time and because he chose to write about racing, his book was bound to arouse interest. Later, I think that word of mouth got him a firm readership. After that, the publisher's publicity machine really got going. It was that way round, not the publicity making him a well-known author.

---

* A recent survey proved *Dead Cert* to be a much sought after title by collectors of first editions; the asking price in 1996 was £1,400.

He was certainly major news at the time of his retirement from racing, but Dick interjected that he thought the success of his books was due, in part, to their accuracy and authenticity.

> If there is anything to be done, I hate to see it wrong. If I'm reading a book on any subject and I know that the facts are wrong, then I lose interest. So I assume my readers will too. Therefore Mary and I are always checking every detail. She really is a great help. When I wrote *Flying Finish*, I kept going along to Oxford Airport to find out about up-to-date flying regulations, which are quite different to when I was flying, and they said, 'Why don't you start again? It'll soon come back.' I simply didn't have the time, which was short anyway, having to write the regular articles for the *Sunday Express*. 'Why don't you send your wife along for a few lessons, then?'

So Mary took up flying, and became a very competent pilot. Later on she was to write a book herself, *Flying Start*, published in 1980.

It may be that one reason for the popularity of his books is because they are based on a hugely popular sport, particularly in the United Kingdom, where the actual number of people who pay to go to the races can exceed 4 million. Add to that figure the viewers of televised races and you can see just how large the potential market is for any book based on the Turf. Approximately 1 million people watch the average race broadcast weekly, and this rises to 2 million for major races; the Derby has an audience of over 7 million. Then there are those devotees who attend point-to-points, trials, gymkhanas, horse shows and who go hunting, and the very large numbers of people who like to ride. The reading market is simply huge. A large number of those who have only a casual interest in racing have always suspected that there are criminal goings-on in the sport, and here is an ex-jockey whose books virtually confirm this. This aspect surely has to be a part of their appeal. It is unlikely that a survey has ever been made to ascertain whether the readers of his books are regular racegoers, but it seems reasonable to assume that most of them have been to the races at least once or twice.

Dick Francis is now a very wealthy man, but he stresses that money was never his motivation for writing. He only wanted 'enough money to pay the extra bills', because he had two sons at private schools. I suspect that, initially, at least, this was only a small part of his motivation, but having Mary's experience and support doubtless encouraged him to start his first book.

Unlike many other authors, Dick does not feel that he has to include long passages devoted to sex. Whatever his reasons for this, his thrillers succeed nevertheless. His books fuel the argument that sex scenes are not *de rigueur* in order to achieve volume sales. Curiously enough, few thriller writers include any sex scenes at all; if they are telling a tale that makes for exciting reading, there is hardly any need. It may be that this is actually one reason why Dick's novels are so popular. And, equally do his regular readers avoid novels by writers whose books are known to include sex scenes?

For the last thirty-two years Dick has delivered a new typescript every May, as regularly as the seasons come and go. His publishers are indeed fortunate in this: in the first place, because if an author continues to sell, the regular delivery of new works makes for excellent marketing; and in the second, because these annual thrillers are presented in such a way there is very little editorial work to be done.

For many years, until she died of cancer, Dick used to send his typescript in to Anthea Joseph* at Michael Joseph, who have published every one of his titles to date. Indeed, there is a tacit agreement that so long as he delivers a new typescript every year, then his publishers will keep all his titles in print.

> I remember when, shortly after I had delivered *High Stakes*, Anthea telephoned me to say that I had used the word 'weird' too many times. 'Do you mind if we change one of them to grotesque?'
>
> Sure, I said, that's OK. And that was the total editing I was aware of. Nowadays, my work comes back with the commas changed around. That is because someone else is working on the books, and I change them back again before I return the typescript!

One of the sadder problems that may beset bestselling authors is that, sooner or later, after several titles with the same theme, their sales may start to drop off. The public's reading habits begin to change, or perhaps they tire of the subject. Richard Gordon, who wrote *Doctor in the House* and other similar titles, is a classic example of this. Since all Dick's mainstream titles have been about racing, or have had racing or riding as a background, I was more than curious as to why his books keep on selling despite the fact that they follow the same theme. I had read somewhere that he had once asked his publishers whether they would publish a book that did not have racing as a background, and they had said 'no' in no uncertain terms. Had he, then, I asked, ever done anything more than think about writing a thriller not related to the sport?

> Well, let's get the facts right. It all cropped up one day in a light-hearted conversation over lunch with the late Anthea Hastings, then Chairman of Michael Joseph Limited, and my editor.

---

* Michael Joseph died in 1958 and Anthea married MacDonald Hastings in 1963. Anthea Hastings became Chairman of Michael Joseph Limited in 1978.

I said, 'If I write a book which hasn't got horses in it and it isn't based on the racing world, would you publish it?' Anthea thought for a few moments. 'Yes, we'd publish anything that you write, but we'd rather you didn't do it, though. Your readers would be disappointed.'

But many people ask me if I'm going to write a book outside the racing world. I argue that it's worth staying in the scene as almost anybody and everybody can go to the races. Photographers, bankers, toy manufacturers, pilots, computer people, they all go racing. So I set the scene in their field, and then tie in the racing background.

So what advice would he give a budding author?

First of all, know your subject, what you are going to write about. Familiarize yourself with the subject. Do your research and get the facts right.

When you are writing, try to capture the reader immediately. End each chapter with a cliffhanger. Don't allow your reader to put the book down at that point and go to sleep. Make them want to start the next chapter.

As for style, don't worry about it. It isn't so much that authors choose the style, the style chooses the author. You can't do except what you can do. That is why some people can write and others can't.

His success as a writer continues but recent thrillers have not always attracted rave reviews. This is one result of writing a series using the same theme and reviewers have become accustomed to his work. Success is qualified by continued high volume sales but it was rumoured that his latest bestseller, *To The Hilt*, is to be his last. That is not so, for I have it on good authority that Dick Francis is hard at work on another story.

The hardback sales of *To The Hilt* have been the most successful to date and, interestingly, each title manages to outsell its predecessor. Currently, about one million copies are sold each year in the United Kingdom with an equal number sold throughout the United States of America.

Success can be qualified in other ways. Dick has won several prestigious awards for his literary work; the Crime Writers' Association gave him a Gold Dagger award for best novel and later a Diamond Dagger. The Mystery Writers of America presented him with three Edgar Allen Poe awards for the best novel of the year and in 1996 made him a Grand Master for his lifetime's achievement.

As you can read in other interviews, a number of successful authors create and finish a book in a year, some more frequently. But one inescapable fact is salutary: a reader can consume a novel in a very short space of time. Dick added finally, 'Readers often write to say they loved my book so much they read it in just a few hours.'

Ironic, isn't it, that his year's hard work is condensed into a few hours reading time?

Arthur Hailey

Flight Into Danger, The Final Diagnosis, In High Places, Hotel, Airport, Wheels, The Moneychangers, Overload, Strong Medicine, The Evening News, Detective. Over 160 million copies sold.

Arthur Hailey surprised me by saying:

> I live with doubts, and insecurity. Even at this point, I'm insecure about the book I'm working on; and a good thing too. People seem to think because a previous book was a success, the next one will be automatically. If the public doesn't like it, they'll find out very quickly and word will get around. Nothing is easier than to fall flat on your face if you get complacent.

With worldwide sales of over 160 million copies, I hardly expected to hear that sort of self-deprecating observation, although it sounds like very good advice.

Arthur Hailey is one of the world's top selling authors, and now lives in the sort of style usually only found in contemporary society magazines – absolute luxury, surrounded by all creature comforts and, of course, the latest technology. His home lies in one of the most idyllic places in the tropics, Nassau, in the Bahamas. The house is very private, and impossible for the public to reach. It is set in grounds that overlook a creek where normally, his latest luxury motor-yacht, *Sheila III*, would be moored, although when I visited him it was being serviced – in Miami! Jeffrey Archer had told me that Hailey's study was a writer's paradise, and he was absolutely right. Reached by a covered walkway from the house, the octagonal-shaped annexe is air-conditioned and fully carpeted, and even has a post room and a shower-room! Inside, the ceiling rises to a single point, giving an air of roominess, and the walls, naturally, are covered in bookshelves, some containing reference books, others holding sets of his major novels, with one copy of each foreign language in both paperback and hardback editions. Arthur quite naturally employs the latest technology, using a state-of-the-art personal computer.

Having always harboured the dream of becoming a writer, a story-teller, even at a very early age, his main opportunity came when he was running his own business in Canada. He was aboard a commercial flight when a chilling thought entered his imaginative mind.

1956, I think it was, I was thirty-six and had virtually given up hope of becoming a story-teller. I had mentally given up. I was doing quite well, relatively, in those days. My own small advertising and sales promotion business showed signs of expanding. And then, on a business flight from Vancouver, I dreamed up a play which became *Flight Into Danger.*

It was a totally uneventful flight, as I recall, except that the *North Star,* a DC4B, was the noisiest aircraft in the world. It had four engines which I'm pretty certain were Canadian. There was no way you could sleep and it was a long flight. I got tired of reading and just sat and daydreamed as a substitute for sleep. I guess I've always had that kind of mind. I have it now, because sometimes in bed, or in the shower, I think up a story situation.

I daydreamed a story, and the point was, at that time, 1956, I was a rusty old pilot. I had, during the war – flown and was competent to fly, but hadn't flown since 1947 when I came out of the RAF. I had never flown a four-engined airplane, though I had flown fast twin-engined Beaufighters. I guess I asked myself, if anything could go wrong, could I fly this aircraft? In those days, you thought of it as an enormous thing to do.

Then, I suppose, one thought led to another and I asked myself, what would cause me to be required to fly it? It was a Friday night. I do remember that, and in those days, you had the choice of fish or meat as an in-flight meal. Catholics observed fish on Fridays, but I remember having meat. Suppose both pilots ate infected fish? Could I fly this aircraft? Would the stewardess be able to help me fly the aircraft? Would there be a doctor? I put the pieces together mentally because of those bloody noisy engines. If it hadn't been for them, I'd have probably gone to sleep.

When I arrived, I enthusiastically told Sheila [his wife] about my wonderful idea. She encouraged me, and I sat down to write it as a television play. [It took him less than ten days to finish it!]

I didn't know anybody [connected with television] or anything about writing a play. I simply put the result [then titled *Flight 714*] in the mail, addressed to the Script Department, Canadian Broadcasting Company. Within a week or two, I had a telephone call and they offered me some money. I think they started off with their lowest figure – I think it was $750. I was so excited that I took it. It never occurred to me to negotiate at that point. I was called to their offices, they needed another four minutes to make an hour's broadcast, could I do it? And no other rewriting was necessary. It went on the air in April 1956, and it was an instant success. It was just like a fairy story.

I went on from there and did television plays [twelve in all], and after a while, Ernest Hecht, who was just starting out in business as Souvenir Press [in London], approached my agent, a dear lady who sadly died in 1974, to ask if I'd write *Flight Into Danger* as a novel. I said no, I didn't think I could write a novel, and after all these years I'd finally found something I could do.

The he tried again, and said if he found a collaborator, would I agree to a fifty-fifty percent? Again, through my agent. I hardly thought about it and said, 'Sure, why not?' I've lacked confidence, I think. In some ways, I have suffered that all my life.

The original title, *Flight 714*, had been changed by CBC's Drama Director, Sidney Newman, to *Flight Into Danger*. The story has had a significant effect, for it was the forerunner of many 'air disaster' novels, movies and television films, *Airport*, *Airport 1975*, and the spoofs *Airplane* and *Airplane 2* among others, coming immediately to mind; a veritable industry in itself. Arthur continued:

So I went across to England and met Ernest for the first time. He was operating out of a real crummy place in Soho. They had to lock the doors so the winos couldn't get in. I read the draft [of the novel], made a few suggestions, only minor, and got my contract. Why, I asked myself, didn't I do this myself? It was just this lack of confidence.

Later I made one mistake when the book was coming out in America. At the time, I was working out in Los Angeles working with CBS . . . when I had a call from the American publishers to say that they did not like the title *Flight Into Danger* and wanted a suggestion for a new title for the American edition.

I didn't think much about it, and off the top of my head I said, 'They land on runways – why not call it *Runway Zero Eight*?' Great, they said, and went ahead. That has caused me so much anguish across the years. I still get letters from Americans buying what they thought was a new book when they were in England, and vice versa. They always write to the author, and we have a form of apology letter.

Soon after that trip to England, I had written another play, *No Deadly Medicine*, a two-part hospital play about pathology. That had got me an Emmy nomination, and a lot of attention.

Ken McCormick, who was then editor-in-chief of Doubleday, saw the show, and called Maeve Southgate, my agent, whom he knew quite well, and asked if I would write this as book.

This time, I thought about it and decided to have a go. There it is [pointing to his shelves], *The Final Diagnosis*. I was nervous about it, as I had to take time out to write and I'm a slow worker. I don't like taking risks, especially as we had two children then, but Sheila was always encouraging me, saying, 'Take chances, drop the business and do what you want to do.'

The Final Diagnosis came out in 1959 and it didn't do anything spectacular, didn't get a lot of attention, and I'm not sure whether it was even on the bestseller list, but it was a steady seller and sold well in hardback. It went through a lot of paperback editions and just kept on going steadily, as it has across the years. It was also a Book Club selection. That helped. Then foreign publishers started picking it up, that's how I began to get foreign rights, and when that happened, I made a conscious decision to switch to books.

* * *

Arthur Hailey was brought up in a small 'two-up, two-down' house in Bedfordshire, England. Typical of many in Luton, it was built with the front door opening directly to the street and a toilet outside in the back yard. As any writer will tell you, authors need somewhere quiet where they can think and write. Arthur Hailey started by using the cupboard space under the staircase. There, he could shut himself off from household interruptions. He was, in short, a closet writer, like Joseph Wambaugh.

Arthur's writing career has its origin in his schooldays. Born in 1920, he acquired his basic knowledge at a traditional elementary school, where 'traditional' meant calling the teacher 'Sir', and though free-ranging discussion was encouraged, everybody knew who ran the classroom. True, he was good at English, but again, like many other authors, he is very self-denigrating about his understanding of the English language.

Two things fascinated me at school. One was science and the other English composition. I was never any good at grammar. To this day I have the barest notion of the rules of grammar. I know what a noun is, a verb and an adjective. Every now and again I ask Sheila what an adverb is . . . and I think I recognize a split infinitive when I see one, but I couldn't tell you what's wrong. As for a participle, I haven't the slightest idea what that is.

I was really no good at that, and yet in composition, in a class of twenty to twenty-five, I was always number one.

Having heard similar comments from many of the writers I've interviewed, I cannot help but feel they are simply being self-effacing. However, if it is true, then it should give many other would-be authors tremendous confidence.
Arthur continued:

History fascinated me. I loved that, and geography, which doesn't get taught nowadays. That, too, I liked, because it made me interested in foreign places. Geometry I liked. That made sense because it was visual and I could see it. Then we were doing logarithms, which I remember I hated. I could never see any purpose in them. But I really wasn't good at maths. I wasn't terribly good at multiplication or subtraction. I guess I could get by, but the best thing that happened was, as far as I was concerned, the appearance of the calculator.

This very discerning maths teacher, Mr Swallow, scraped me through mathematics; he gave me a pass mark, which I didn't deserve, and encouraged me to write stories while the others were doing their maths. We kept in touch and I went back to see him after I had published books. I know he took pleasure in that, and I know that he died a few years ago.

* * *

. . . My aim, at school, was to become a newspaper reporter. That was the peak as far as I was concerned. I couldn't see anything beyond that, it never occurred to me that I would write books. I wanted so much to be a reporter, and I remember that the headmaster knew the chief reporter of the local paper, the *Luton News*. Then one morning, just before I was due to leave, with a long face he told me that his friend had died. I don't know if it would have made any difference, but I tried [for a job on the paper] myself and they didn't even consider me, because you had to have been to a grammar or high school.

I tried for the Junior County Scholarship, but competition was tough. They had one for the whole of Luton, which I think had a population then of around 70,000. I came close to the top, and there were two people at the interview, the other was a girl. The girl won.

So he went to college to learn shorthand and typing, courtesy of his ever-encouraging mother, Elsie. Arthur Hailey was not then, and is not now, someone to give up that easily. At the tender age of thirteen he was writing letters to his local paper, for journalism was still his main ambition in life. A minor breakthrough came when he submitted one expressing his frustration about not being able to go swimming at the local public swimming pool on Sundays. He was a keen swimmer and it was a long letter – too verbose by today's standards, but it was an exciting and rewarding experience for Arthur to see it in print.

His first work experience was as a junior with a local firm of estate agents. He was given some typing to do, but he made many mistakes and was reprimanded several times. His dismissal became inevitable after omitting a zero on a selling price for a factory!

Then came the Second World War. He joined the Royal Air Force Reserve with an ambition to become a pilot, but his luck was out once again, since a minimum of a grammar school education was a prerequisite to qualify for pilot training. A frustrated Arthur was assigned to desk duties but his fertile mind could not relax; he continued to write, though much of his output was thrown away. A few poems only remain, but none were actually published until they appeared in Sheila's book. (*I Married a Best Seller*, published in 1978.)

With the heavy losses of pilots in the first two years of war, the rules were changed and a lower educational limit for pilots was announced. He was accepted for pilot training, but as this was the period of Lend-Lease with America, he was assigned to a training school in Americus, Georgia. There he learned to fly on a Stearman PT-17, an open-cockpit biplane similar to the classic RAF basic trainer, the Tiger Moth. He remembers the time well, for every time he flew, he was violently air-sick. It was a handicap he suffered for months which made it difficult for him to learn all that he was taught, and it was a direct cause of him failing his first flight examination. Fortunately, he eventually overcame the problem well enough to qualify as a sergeant-pilot in 1943.

I recount this because it set me wondering – indeed, and it seemed a logical deduction – whether, if he was frequently air-sick, he might not have overcome the problem entirely. All those years later, his subconscious mind might easily have toyed, at least while daydreaming, with potential food problems on that flight from Vancouver; perhaps the embryo of an idea that later inspired *Flight Into Danger*.

A year later, Arthur was back in the United Kingdom and stationed in Perth, Scotland, where the weather, as often as not, was terrible and they were frequently grounded. During these periods he naturally read a lot, but the extra free time also gave him the opportunity to write, and it was here that he had his first major break. He wrote a short story, which he entitled 'Rip Cord'. When I asked him if he had sent it off to a number of magazines, he said he thought he had, but could not now recall which they were. It was the *Courier* that first published this tale, and it was to prove, as Sheila highlights in her book, a pivotal point; a precursor of his destiny. It was submitted on a pot-luck basis and had it been turned down, it probably wouldn't have bothered him at the time. In retrospect, though, this was his lucky break.

He remained with the RAF after the war working, for a time, in the Air Ministry in London. He had access to vast numbers of official Air Ministry files, and it was whilst browsing through these that he had a brainwave. He rewrote and condensed a number of them into a humorous series of brief notes, mostly illustrating the petty and bumbling behaviour of British officialdom. His efforts seemed just the type of article that *Punch* might publish. It did. (Curiously, at this date, 1946, another aspiring writer was just finding her feet, with articles in *Punch* – Dora Saint.)

Two years earlier, Arthur had married Joan Fishwick. She was, however, never destined to play a significant part in his career as a writer. Their lives in the immediate post-war period continued to be affected by numerous petty restrictions. Indeed, one not so petty limitation, food rationing, was not lifted completely until 1954, nine years after the war's end. The die was cast when, in 1947, he decided to emigrate to Canada.

* * *

On arrival in Toronto they found that Canada was not the land of promise that they had first thought. Arthur tried numerous newspaper and magazine publishing houses for employment, including MacLean-Hunter, all to no avail. Not enough experience, and being an Englishman proved to be major drawbacks.

As I have said, Arthur Hailey is not a man to give up easily. Eventually, his first job turned out to be in the real-estate business, but in his determined way he kept in touch with Maclean-Hunter and bided his time. When a vacancy for an assistant editor on a trade journal, *Bus and Truck Transport*, became vacant, his application was successful.

Marring this success was the unhappy state of his marriage, so he threw himself into his new job, often working very long hours. His long absences from home put tremendous pressures on his wife Joan. She led a lonely life because Arthur had the car during the day, and their home was well away from regular public transport services. She left him shortly before Christmas 1949.

At about this time Sheila Dunlop, also a fresh immigrant, joined the typing pool at Maclean-Hunter. Her first encounter with A. H. Hailey was with his voice on a dictaphone, a voice, and a person, she grew to like. With similar interests, and her understanding of a writer's needs, their friendship grew into something more. Unlike his first wife, Sheila had aspirations as a writer, and became an editorial assistant on Maclean-Hunter's *Canadian Homes and Gardens*. By 1951, when they married, Arthur, as editor of *Bus and Truck Transport*, had become an authority on road transport.

Together they continued their journalistic careers, and Arthur increased his earnings by writing as a freelance. His wide knowledge of road transport matters meant that his articles were readily accepted by business newspapers like the *Financial Post*.

Arthur then left Maclean-Hunter for another magazine, *Trailmobile*, where he was sales promotion manager. It was an opportunity that he had initially turned down, but it offered a very attractive salary of $11,000 as a sweetener, and had he finally accepted. This was a very good income indeed for 1953, but the work failed to stretch his writing talents; composing advertising copy for trailers palled after a while. It was then that he made that flight from Vancouver to Toronto.

* * *

With the sudden success of his television play *Flight Into Danger*, Sheila coerced Arthur into leaving *Trailmobile*. Still not fully confident of striking out on his own, he compromised by allowing himself to be retained as a copywriter for *Trailmobile*, and started his own business, Hailey Publicity Services, which, though small, proved to be a successful enterprise. (There is a certain similarity here between his career and that of James Herbert and Clive Cussler.)

It is interesting to look at his career alongside those of Dick Francis (jockey), James Herriot (vet), James Herbert (advertising agent), Jeffrey Archer (politician) and Tom Clancy (insurance agent), as well as others I have interviewed. Like them, Arthur had been successful in a different career long before becoming a writer. This suggests that success in another occupation is often a prerequisite for success as a writer. There are exceptions to this, of course, as in the cases of writers who, so to speak, have always been writers, like James Michener, Catherine Cookson and Alan Dean Foster.

As has frequently been said here, the majority of top authors, though by no means all, employ literary agents. Arthur's writing career was considerably enhanced by his agent, Maeve Southgate, mentioned earlier. He recalled her contribution with affection:

> She had written from New York and we had simply exchanged letters. Then she phoned, and I told her about this agent's plans. Whatever she said made me laugh and, with what she had written to me, persuaded me to go along with her.

Within two or three weeks, and on the basis of what I had said, she set up her own agency, which she had been itching to do for some time. I was her first, and principal, client. She represented me from 1957 until she died in 1973. There are people whom you meet in life who have a tremendous influence on you, and she was one.

I recall one occasion when she was very helpful. I was out in Los Angeles and my play *Diary of a Nurse* was being put on at the premier drama theatre, Playhouse 90. I hadn't signed the contract but rehearsals were under way, and the producer, whom I had worked with on *No Deadly Medicine*, came up to me and said, 'Look, this is a little embarrassing. We don't usually do this, but your agent is being pretty unreasonable. The offer is good' – I think they were paying about $10,000, which was good in those days – 'She's stalling over details, and won't sign.'

I was quite embarrassed about the whole thing. From Los Angeles, I rang Maeve in New York and said, 'Look, these are nice people, and that's a pretty fair price we've got and I think we should sign.' 'Sweetie,' she said, 'you go back and continue to be nice to them and leave the negotiating to me.' Which I did. What she was holding out for was the amount of money I would be paid if this particular play was subsequently made into a series. She got her way, and indeed it was, and the series ran on . . .

With her help, Hailey's career as a novelist prospered. As sales of his first novel, *Flight Into Danger*, rose steadily, he produced, as has already been said, *The Final Diagnosis*, a novelization of his award-winning play *No Deadly Medicine*. Published in 1959, *The Final Diagnosis* became a notable success (despite his very modest comments about its sales, made earlier in the interview), for it was selected not only as a *Reader's Digest* Condensed Books choice, but also by the Literary Guild of America as well. Translation rights were sold for twenty-three foreign language editions, and film rights were sold to United Artists, who produced it as *The Young Doctors*.

By now a full-time novelist, his next book, *In High Places*, won him, in addition to its earnings from royalties and rights payments, a prize of $10,000 from Doubleday Canada in 1962. This novel also attracted a good many rights sales, with twelve foreign language editions being produced.

The story of the success of his next three titles reads in itself like a bestselling novel. He enjoyed three major worldwide successes with *Hotel*, *Airport* and *Wheels* (1965, 1968 and 1971 respectively), each selected as a *Reader's Digest* Condensed Books choice, and each made into a film. *Airport*, the film, had two sequels, *Airport 1977* and *Airport 1979*; *Airport*, the book, appeared in the *New*

York Times bestseller list for sixty-four consecutive weeks, and for thirty of these at number one.

Given his experience of writing screenplays, I would have expected him to have written those for the films of his own books; or at least to have had a say in their creation. Not so. After his early experience of writing a television play, he feels that producing a screenplay takes far too long and is too stressful.

In addition to securing the best publishing and financial deal for an author's work, agents can be helpful, too, by offering advice on all aspects of writing for publication. That was probably, I suspect, another aspect that he came to miss after Maeve's death, for help is something that Arthur is always glad to receive.

> I seek advice because, first of all, I write about specialist subjects. With every book I do I usually, during the course of the year's research, find someone who appears to be not only knowledgeable about the subject, but interested in the process of writing the book. Sometimes I arrange for that person to stay with me. Sometimes I pay them. If it is someone who doesn't need to be paid . . . for example, in *Strong Medicine*, I had a very well-to-do scientist to whom I would not have presumed to offer money, [so] I made a substantial donation to a research project in which he was in-terested. Usually I have one adviser on each book. I don't name them, but I have someone who is helping me, and yes, I have a financial arrangement with that person to read what I write. And to be very critical. To pull me up on the small things.
>
> I think of myself as a story-teller, and if in the course of telling that story you can inform people about particular backgrounds, with which they may be outwardly familiar – about which they don't know the 'behind-the-scene' details – then they become very interested. If you can project that, particularly to people overseas, who are absolutely hungry to know what happens in the United States, then you will succeed.

Sales of his books are phenomenal. He told me that he 'does very well with sales in North America, but income from overseas sales is two-and-a-half times greater than in North America' – vindicating his point about writing for overseas readers' interest.

Since *Flight Into Danger*, his novels have always been commissioned. This may seem a logical course for author and publishers alike, but many authors do not chose to have their work commissioned, like Craig Thomas, or if they do, only accept nominal sums, like Jeffrey Archer. In Arthur Hailey's case, he receives very substantial advances (in the first instance because of his earlier success as a playwright, then because of the sales of his novels) though he could not recall exact sums when we met. For his last book he received some $2 million as an advance against royalties, payable in four stages. He stresses that every author should always read the small print in a publisher's contract very carefully, and in particular should ensure that if the income from the sale of rights has exceeded the original advance by time the book is published, then the advance should be increased.

Publishers' motives for paying high advances can be whittled down to one: they are confident of achieving extremely high sales. They know, too, that such an author will back the publicity effort and take part in promotional tours and other activities, such as book-signing sessions and radio, television and newspaper interviews.

I take part for two reasons. One is that I feel an obligation to the publisher and to the salesman. I was a salesman once myself, and I like to share in that and make my contribution. The other is that after having spent three years on a book, it's exciting to come out in the open when the book is published and participate. Between books, I disappear from sight; I avoid publicity. There's no point in having publicity between books, which is why I never seek it out.

I think one of the reasons why I get attention when any of my books comes out is that I haven't been heard of since the last time. I don't get some literary agent to put my latest *bon mot* in the gossip columns, as I know some writers do.

I've found it easy to go on television and be relaxed. Not everyone does. When I go on television, radio, or even give a newspaper interview, I feel an obligation to them. I have made a commitment. They have given me some of their time. The author, incidentally, can get an enormous amount of time, free time, that you couldn't begin to pay for, so I think I owe something in return.

When I go on a show now, I usually submit a paper in advance, because there are so many books being published and the interviewer is very unlikely to have read yours. I list a summation of points that I can talk about if you want to bring them up. The one thing you must always do, is to make the interviewer look good. It isn't smart to score off the interviewer, and it helps you if you can help the interviewer.

If you can get into a news column for some reason, that's great. The difficult thing about any book is to make people aware that it exists, and that is the advantage of being on television. With every book, I've been on the NBC's *Today* shows in the mornings. The salesmen at Doubleday [his American publishers] say you can measure the effect of that by the people who buy the books.

It takes Arthur three years to complete a new book; each one has had a totally fresh subject, unrelated to the others. *Hotel* (1965) is about the lives of guests and management at a New Orleans hotel; *Airport* (1968) examines a situation where one major problem with an aircraft nearly causes an all-out disaster; *Wheels* (1971) is based on the motor industry in Detroit; *The Moneychangers* (1975) on banking; *Overload* (1979) on the electricity industry; *Strong Medicine* (1985) on the pharmaceutical business; and *The Evening News* (1990). *Detective*, to be published later this year is yet another new subject for the unique Hailey treatment. He, for one, cannot be accused of being a single-subject author.

Where does he get his ideas from?

I really don't think about the public's taste when I choose a subject. I'm much more concerned with my own taste. I never choose a subject unless it is something that will absorb and interest me. Sometimes the subjects have been my own ideas, and at other times they've been suggested by my publishers. And it can be a combination of the two.

When I signed a contract with Doubleday to do a book after the hiatus of my heart surgery [in the early 1980's], I didn't have any ideas for a subject. Sam Vaughan [of Doubleday] suggested the pharmaceutical industry and my first reaction was, 'Ho hum - I don't think this is for me,' But because I trusted Sam's judgement, I decided to meet a few people in that industry. I got caught up and became fascinated, so it turned out to be the most exciting subject I've ever tackled. *Strong Medicine* was the result.

The latest one, *The News* [this was its working title when I interviewed him], was one hundred percent my own idea. I don't know why I haven't thought about it before with my interest in the news, and I'm not thinking about readers' reaction, one takes chances on that.

Having covered his choice of subjects, I asked him how he chose his very succinct titles – like James Michener's, these are also one of Arthur Hailey's trademarks. How much input came from his publisher?

Again, that's varied. I suppose the classic case was *Airport*. When I was writing that, I had on the manuscript, *Surly Bonds of Earth*. That's from the poem by John Gillespie Magee, a pilot killed in World War Two. The salesmen at Doubleday, knowing what [the novel] was all about, started calling it *Airport*. Everybody hated my title except me – I loved it – but in the end it became *Airport*. *Wheels* was suggested by someone at Doubleday over dinner one night. *Moneychangers* was my idea, taken from the Bible [Christ overturning the tables of the moneychangers in the temple, Matthew 21:12], but my agent Maeve didn't like it – she thought it was anti-Semitic, which it wasn't – but I dropped it and called it *Bank* or *Bankers*. Then another author came out with another book – non-fiction, so it didn't clash at all – called *Bankers*. Sam Vaughan telephoned me to say, 'We can't do this, you've got to change the title.' So I came back to my original title and it worked very well.

Arthur Hailey ranks as a truly international author, with worldwide sales exceeding 160 million copies and translations into thirty-nine languages; all from only ten novels. What, then, is his secret? What is it that has singled him out from the thousands of other novelists, and has caused him to rank him so highly? The reasons lie in his explanations, but timing is perhaps one of the most important, and his latest book is, perhaps by design, unlikely ever to date.

What advice does he have for the aspiring author?

Get on with it. There are people who 'talk book', and there are people who 'write book'; talking writers, and writing writers.

Do what research you need to do. Some people don't need to research very much. Pay attention to every small detail because if a reader knows it is wrong, it will ruin the whole book for him.

It helps to be nosy. Read, read and keep reading. Remember, it's a very lonely life, writing.

He does not receive as many letters from readers as some other authors. Generally he gets about twelve to fifteen a week, though those he does get sometimes make most interesting reading. Sheila Hailey reprinted extracts from some of the early letters in her biography of Arthur; some are quizzical, some demanding, some laudatory, but few are really critical. They are, though, the only feedback from readers an author is likely to get, and they can provide guidance for future writing. The number of letters he receives rises to about fifty a week when a book comes out. Sheila assumes the responsibility for answering them as Arthur finds it difficult to keep breaking his concentration on research or writing to reply in detail. He does, however, hold strong views about readers' letters, and was not afraid to air them to me:

> I have a commitment with a reader to deliver a book – a reader did
> not buy, with that book, a piece of me or my time. These things
> [dealing with readers' letters] always take time, and writing
> requires a certain amount of ruthlessness.

Arthur Hailey's post will increase later this year, when his next novel, *Detective*, is published. It is set in Miami, where a Catholic priest loses his 'faith' and becomes a homicide detective. It is a fast moving story and with a very different background to his previous novels, but he told me that this story reflects his own non-belief in any god.

Anyone seeking to know what it is like to be married to a well-known and highly successful author should read his wife's book, *I Married a Best Seller*. Now out of print, it is still to be found in public libraries. It is packed with snippets that point to how he became so successful, but as he told me, he 'went down on his knees to keep some of the details out.' But which details, I wondered?

Robert Ludlum

The Scarlatti Inheritance, The Ostermann Weekend, The Matlock Paper, The Chancellor Manuscript, The Bourne Identity, The Aquitaine Progression, The Bourne Supremacy, The Apocalypse Watch, Cry of the Halidon and thirteen more.

A study of Robert Ludlum's background would suggest that he was destined for a long and successful career on the stage. Unlike most other adventure and thriller writers, he was not a politician, or an insurance salesman, or a graphic designer, or a journalist, or a jockey, or teacher or policeman, but an actor of note, and, perhaps more importantly, a successful producer, during a first career that spanned some twenty-five years.

Any would-be biographer could be forgiven for thinking that the young Ludlum was stagestruck. He made first appearance on stage when he was just fifteen. At twenty, when he left the US Marine Corps, he headed back to the stage, and by the time he had reached the ripe old age of forty he had produced 300 stage productions for New York and regional theatre. Though he has had much written about him as an actor (some journalists have even bestowed star status on him), he is the first to deny that he is anybody special. In fact, he would rather the media did not hype his acting role, though he is less reticent about his ability as a producer, as I was to discover during our meeting.

Naples, in south-west Florida, is a sleepy city of wide, open streets, with a marked absence of very tall buildings. Very few were over nine floors, in complete contrast to the modernistic and high-rise styles of Miami. From my hotel there I set off on a sweltering day to meet Robert Ludlum at his wintertime apartment, which overlooks the beach to the west of Naples.

His home is a writer's dream. Set high up in its block, it has a window which allows him to look out along the coastline. The apartment is decorated in sumptuous style, and even has a marble floor; there was, however, little evidence of his earlier theatrical career anywhere in the place.

My interview with Robert Ludlum was enhanced by an excellent lunch in a nearby hotel. There are, however, risks in carrying out an interview in such a public restaurant with a very well-known writer. Both your meal and interview are liable to be interrupted by friends, or by fans coming over to say hello, and to say how much they enjoyed his books. Ludlum, to his credit, was always very courteous.

Few of these fans, I guessed, would have known about his earlier career in the theatre, though. I suspect that it was his accomplishments as an actor and producer that provided him with the confidence to start out on a second career as a writer at forty years of age. Logically, given his background, he might have started writing plays, or even film scripts, but why novels, I asked?

My wife has always said I was a writer from the beginning. I got sidetracked with minor success as an actor and producer, but I was always scribbling, always working with playwrights. I worked with Bill Manhoff in *The Owl and the Pussycat*; I worked with Murray Schisgal in *The Typists and the Tiger* and *Luv*, and when I say work, in no way did I have anything to do with the writing of anything, but I would work with them.

I was constantly a closet writer. I'd come home from the theatre and I'd sort of look at it all, and think, after a day like this it's either a quart of Dewar's White Label, or else it's sitting down and writing. I felt that, what with having children and everything, it was healthier doing some writing on the porch than it was quaffing an entire quart of Dewar's White Label.

I did my fair share of that, too, but I loved writing and still do, and I think I'd gotten to the point in the theatre where it wasn't how good a show you put on, it was when you got it on, because if you don't get it on by Tuesday eleven o'clock the unions will kill you. Coming from the last of the 1950 liberals, I'm not an anti-union man by any manner of means.

When I had written about three hundred pages of what became *Scarlatti* [*The Scarlatti Inheritance*], I put it down; put off, if I am honest, because of what I had been reading. I am a voracious reader, more of history than biographies. But after a couple of years, I read what I had written and thought, 'Hey now, this isn't bad.' It needs a lot of work, but anyone who works in the theatre knows that anything needs a lot of work, and I decided I was simply going to try, and so I did. And I think, in the words of my wife, when I said I was going to switch gears and try to write for a living, and her words which I'm sure you've heard somewhere, were, 'Well, you're forty years old, if you don't try it now, you may regret it for the rest of your life. . .'

As most authors and publishers know, a first novel will usually only sell about 3,000 to 5,000 copies in hardback, and often fewer. *The Scarlatti Inheritance*, you will not be surprised to learn, sold over 75,000 in hardback and had, by 1977, six years after it first appeared, sold over 5 million in paperback. (These hardback sales were later dwarfed by *The Aquitaine Progression*, which sold over 600,000 copies in the first three weeks after publication.) It was published by World in 1971, when Ludlum was forty-four, a time when most people start to plan their retirement, not a new career. His achievements, however, were such that he could quite easily have returned to the theatre had he failed to get his first work published, which is possibly why he had the confidence to start writing novels.

Giving up one career for writing is no rarity amongst the authors I interviewed for this book. Other thriller writers who have taken to writing in middle age include Jeffrey Archer, Paul Erdman, Tom Clancy, Dick Francis and Joseph Wambaugh, nor should one forget those other writers like Dora Saint, James Herriot and James Herbert. All of these have, it seems, been singled out for fame and fortune – indeed, a few for colossal fortunes – and all are, clearly, the envy of aspiring authors. Their successes provide an incentive for those others who often dream about becoming writers, but who never do anything about it. Reading about the lives of these bestselling authors, their backgrounds, education and upbringing, it is possible to discern a loose pattern which provides a clue to success: an affinity for English, for reading, for story-telling, for fact-finding, and, above all, for being both imaginative and original.

* * *

Robert Ludlum was born in New York City in May 1927. His father died in the mid 1930s, leaving his wife, Margaret, to care for Robert and his sister. Robert grew up in New Jersey and was fortunate to enjoy private education, ending up at the Cheshire Academy, from where he graduated in 1944, and Wesleyan University in 1951 after military service.

Usually there are some aspects of an author's formative years that provide a clue or two to their success as a writer. It may seem strange, but it is not absolutely necessary that you excel at English in order to become a top writer; being able to express oneself is one matter, being able to tell a good story well is quite another. It is apparent that during their childhoods some authors had not the slightest intention of ever becoming writers. Ludlum added more weight to this:

> I think my first ambition was to be a quarterback in [American] football, but although I was fairly athletic . . . [it] was obviously out of the question. Then my next thought was to be a pilot, so I enlisted in the Naval Air Corps for World War Two when I was actually just

sixteen and a half, and then I found out – I read somewhere – that everybody in what they called the V2 programme was being sent to sea because they had enough pilots. I immediately enlisted in the Marine Corps, and I forgot the fact that I'd already enlisted in the Navy – that was quite a problem.

But it was resolved and I stayed a Marine. Then I – of course – went to college as the First Fine Arts Major at Wesleyan University. Then my goal was to be the finest actor I could be, and one thing led to another and I found out that I didn't have the gypsy soul for that.

As a schoolboy, I don't think I was exceptionally good at English. Both at prep school and at college I wrote a couple of stories in creative writing, one of which was published.

Perhaps he was just being modest, but his last point did suggest that he might have been rather good at English. Did he receive any encouragement to write?

Oh yes, from several teachers, but I didn't take them seriously. I was rather good at history, but really terrible in the sciences. Absolutely terrible, as a matter of fact.

At university, there was a fellow [a lecturer] who said to me, I believe it was a chemistry course, he said, 'Robert, I like your acting' (because I had done some acting in the university's theatre), and he said, 'If you promise not to come back for the second semester I'll pass you with a D.'

By the time he had left university, surely he had written something that had been published? Surely he could not just have switched to a writing career at the age of forty without some inkling that he had a certain ability?

The only one I do remember was when I was in the South Pacific with the Marines. I had written some two hundred pages of my impressions of everything, of war, and all that, but I lost it on my discharge in San Francisco.

It was something that I just wanted to do, because most of the time life in the South Pacific was boring . . . It was just something that I just felt like doing, in other words. As my wife always said, in my background there always was the writer, even at a very young age, and I've always been sidetracked until I was forty, and then I decided, 'now I want to try it.'

I lost the manuscript on the Oakland ferry in San Francisco when I woke up with the largest hangover of my life. As a matter of fact, one of the people who got me into that trouble was a young Brit. It was 1945 and the war was just over. We'd just gotten back from the Pacific, and somehow – and don't ask me how – some British warship had come into San Francisco. I don't know how we latched up, but four or five of my buddies and myself and this guy, a British officer, went drinking . . .

I woke up at five o'clock in the morning on the open ferry, sans money, sans manuscript, and sans identification. That was my 'arrival' back to the States.

All of which makes an interesting contrast with James Michener. He, too, had written down his observations whilst serving in the South Pacific (curiously enough, Clive Cussler also served there). But whereas Ludlum had only penned some 5,000 words, Michener wrote a full-length novel, though the former had intended to complete his work, until prevented from doing so by its disappearance. As already recounted elsewhere, Michener's, novel was published, and became world-famous, as *Tales of The South Pacific*, on which the musical and the film *South Pacific* was based. What might have been for Robert Ludlum, had he not lost that typescript, can only be imagined.

* * *

As a fifteen year-old schoolboy, Ludlum first appeared on stage in a performance of *Outward Bound*, and the experience made a huge impression on him. Thereafter, his all-consuming ambition was to become an actor. In 1943 while still at school, he auditioned for a part in a Broadway production. To his utter surprise, he got it, and his ambitions thus became firmly centred on a career in the theatre. He took over from Robert Willey as Sterling Brown in the long-running comedy *Junior Miss*, and then went on tour with the same play, which took him to Detroit, Michigan. There, still keen to serve in the war in some way or other, and still keen to be a pilot, he travelled to Toronto to volunteer for service in the Royal Canadian Air Force, but was turned down because of his age. As the end of World War Two approached, he enlisted in the US Marine Corps, which resulted in his posting to the South Pacific.

After his two-year stint, he continued his education at the Wesleyan University in Middletown, Connecticut, where he obtained his BA with distinction. Thereafter he worked for six years as a professional actor, the beginning of what, by any standards, was a very successful career.

He played many roles in a variety of stage productions, from that of a soldier in *The Strong Are Lonely*, to Spartacus in *The Gladiator*. And he also appeared in various other productions, including Shakespeare's *Richard III*, and Shaw's *The Admirable Bashville* and *Saint Joan*. Although very modest about his career, Ludlum appeared in eight Broadway productions and, more significantly, more than two hundred television programmes.

The first of these was in 1952, as a district attorney in NBC's series *Treasury Men in Action*. He was usually cast as a lawyer or a killer, but after a while he realized that as an actor in these programmes he could not exercise any control over the finished result. He therefore turned his talents to producing for the stage instead, concentrating on non-traditional locations. He started in his new role at the North Jersey Playhouse in Fort Lee.

His exposure on television provided a spin-off when an advertising man who wanted a 'soft intimate voice' to put on a commercial heard him. He thought Ludlum's voice was just perfect. This led to his providing numerous voice-overs for commercials, notably for Ford Automobiles, Braniff Airlines, Tiparillo cigars and Plunge bathroom cleaner. As he once said, this 'was the easiest money he ever made', and a welcome diversion from his stage career. Robert added his own slant on the subject:

> Actually, it takes a degree of discipline to be a good voice-over. Not only that, people write what appear to be superb scripts, but the text cannot be spoken.
>
> I've run across that many many times, and I've said to the director, 'this is fine on paper but you can't speak it this way.' And I will not name the products, but there were a number of products where I rewrote the script myself, and two of them became terribly successful. I loved it when the advertising people dropped in their own credit line at the end, but I wrote the lines.

Then, with the help of financial grants, he founded a theatre in a shopping mall in Paramus, New Jersey, the Playhouse-on-the-Mall. There he put on such productions as *Who's Afraid of Virginia Woolf?* and *Hamlet*, engaging stars from Hollywood and television. The public appreciated his efforts, and the audiences filled the theatre. Full houses brought in the cash, and the theatre's success was patently evident. As his confidence grew, he began to present more adventurous and esoteric productions, but whereas his popular productions brought in audiences – and thus cash – these did not. Since he derived far more pleasure and satisfaction from staging these more unusual pieces, he became quite despondent, coining a colourful and much-quoted epigram in his frustration: 'When you do something exciting and good, you could shoot a moose in the lobby for all the people who ever came.'

His depression with the theatre was the initial driving force behind his decision to take up some other activity. He was also by then in his early forties, an age at which many men seem to change their careers. It may be, too, that his decision had something to do with the realization that we are all mortal, which promotes a deep wish in all of us to leave something more permanent behind us.

Though his career at this time had its ups and downs, he was instrumental in helping others to their fame and fortune. One of the actors in his company, Alan Alda (and incidentally, Robert's tennis partner for four years), was to become a major star in *M*A*S*H*, and go on to parts in other cinema and TV films. Another, Pernell Roberts, played Adam in the long-running television western series *Bonanza*.

Robert Ludlum himself became quite famous locally, and also to an extent, in Hollywood, because many of the actors who came to his theatre worked there as well. Outside these two areas he was not quite so well known, except perhaps amongst the theatrical cognoscenti. Nevertheless, he was carving himself out a successful career, and clearly could have gone on to the top of his profession.

In all, he spent fifteen years as a producer before, in 1969, turning his hand to writing. What may seem curious is that he turned his hand to writing thrillers, rather than plays. Nevertheless, his books encompass a large degree of 'theatre'.

> What I try to do, and it is something everyone in the theatre knows, is [ensure] that the structure of a book is nothing more than the evolvement of one situation into another until there is a climax, with each segment being indispensable because, as with an audience, if you don't want to know what's happening from scene two, or from act one to act two, you're going to leave the theatre. And the actors are on the unemployment line next week.
>
> So I suppose I equate suspense and good theatre in a very similar way. I think it's all suspense and 'what-happens-next'. From that point of view, yes, I guess, I am theatrical.
>
> It was an article in the *Illustrated London News* that gave me an idea for the first book. Because I saw two astounding pictures which made such an impact on me. They weren't adjacent, at least one page separated them.

He had a habit of looking through old magazines, and what he saw in the *Illustrated London News* clearly made a huge impact on his alert and imaginative mind.

In 1918, after Germany surrendered at the end of the First World War, an international agreement was drawn up, known as the Treaty of Versailles

(1919). Among other, often very harsh, terms, this called for Germany to recompense the Allies by paying over 20 billion gold marks in 'war reparations', and France and Belgium later 'occupied' parts of Germany in order to claim their share. Such actions only served to accelerate the already rising inflation in a nation shattered by four years of war, and by November 1923 a loaf of bread cost 200 billion marks, at a time when the rate of exchange with the US dollar was 4 trillion marks. To put that into perspective, in 1914, before the beginning of the First World War, a loaf would have cost 20 marks, and by 1919, 43 marks. Paper money became almost worthless. German children would play with wads of paper notes, and impoverished householders had to use wheelbarrows to cart around enough money just to buy the basic essentials for survival.

What Robert Ludlum had seen at in the *Illustrated London News* was a 1920s photograph of a German pushing a wheelbarrow full of banknotes on one page, and, nearby, another of members of the Nazi Party (then a nascent political force) in full kit with smart, new uniforms and Sam Browne belts. It prompted his fertile imagination to ponder on just how they had managed to get their uniforms, if a loaf of bread cost so many marks. Who provided the money? The result was an imaginative plot based upon the idea of international financiers providing the backing for Hitler – which became his first novel, *The Scarlatti Inheritance*. He was to use the theme of money and Nazis again in *The Holcroft Covenant*.

His first novel was followed a year later in 1972 by *The Ostermann Weekend*. Made into a film which was later released on video as well, the plot centres on John Tanner, a television news executive who invites three couples to his home (not surprisingly) in New Jersey for a festive weekend, in honour of his long-standing friendship with the Ostermanns. Tanner unexpectedly finds himself in the middle of a struggle with both the CIA and an international spy ring, Omega. The novel's tension and pace are maintained by the reader's awareness that the leader of Omega is one of Tanner's guests. The plot underlines Ludlum's deeply held opinion about authority, and his (self-admittedly) almost near paranoiac belief that power and authority are nowadays in the wrong hands. He would surely agree with the nineteenth-century historian, Sir Dalberg Acton, whose famous dictum is much quoted: 'Power tends to corrupt and absolute power corrupts absolutely. Great men are almost always bad men.'

Ludlum had now caught the writing bug and he was quickly into his third book, *The Matlock Papers*. This was published in 1973, as was *Trevayne*, although, curiously, the latter appeared under the pen-name Jonathan Ryder, and published from another publishing house, Delacorte. There is, of course, nothing unusual about writing under a pen-name; many authors have done so, and doubtless many more will do so in the future. So what were his reasons for disguising his name, I wondered?

A certain editor and publisher said that you can't publish more than one book a year because you are then automatically considered a hack. I pointed out that Charles Dickens wrote every week, and that they were wrong. Totally. But I wanted to write this one book, *Trevayne*, and then the other book was *Cry of the Halidon*.

But I listened to them because I was new in the business, and so, had I had a brain in my head, I would have said, 'Forget it. I'm going to write it and put it under my own name. Period.' But I was too much of a neophyte to listen to my own reasoning, which was, 'why not?' Anyway, *Trevayne* was a great hit in England.

But I think the UK treats authors in a much different way to the USA. You both respect us more, and you don't demand of us the kind of – what do you call it? – the only word I can think of is a kind of showmanship that seems to be required here.

In other words, whenever I've done interviews in the UK, they've been with much less hype than anything I do here. Here, maybe it's because I was once an actor and what have you, I feel I must entertain more, you know? Whereas when I've done UK interviews, I can relax a lot more. People don't expect that kind of nonsense, and it is nonsense . . . I call it the 'show-me factor', and I'm not interested in doing it, but I suppose the actor in me just drives you on.

However, and unlike a number of writers, once he had become known as the author of bestselling thrillers, he allowed *Trevayne* to be re-published under his own name. The novel now bears Ludlum's name in large type on its front cover. Another title published by Delacorte was *Cry of the Halidon* but this did not appear under Ludlum's name until 1996, twenty-two years later, when it was published by HarperCollins. His current publishers are not alone in reinstating an author's real name after first publication under a pseudonym: Craig Thomas's name now appears on his *Emerald Decision*, which was originally issued under the pen-name 'David Grant'.

Earlier in our interview, Robert had mentioned his paranoia about abused power; indeed, I had read of this in a number of press-cuttings. Where, I wondered, had it originated?

Where do you want to start? Nixon? Watergate? Good Lord, I could go through British history, our [American] history, I could go back to the Pharaohs. I really think the abuse of power, both elected and appointed, has been constantly evident throughout history. We entrust power to people who shouldn't have it, and there's no way we can ever correct this, but I feel that I've got to raise my voice if I feel that it's wrong, and so I do.

I've read about Margaret Thatcher and the power she wields. I offer no comment at this time, but you may find a book about a female prime minister one day, not in terms of what she's done, [but] in terms of a country's economy.

As his thrillers maintain a certain similarity of theme, if only in the sense that they are highly dramatic, I asked him whether he feared that one day his popularity might wane?

That wouldn't bother me because I write – although I come from the theatre and I need an audience and I respect an audience – I still nevertheless write for myself. I do not write for, nor do I pander to, an audience; I don't try to dissect my audience, as some very well-known writers do, and say 'this is the kind of book I'm going to write because I want to be terribly successful, and I want to make a lot of money.' I don't have to do that, fortunately, and therefore I write with the wind behind my own sail. I write what I want to write.

I am nothing but contemptuous of a writer that does otherwise, because it comes off so false. And I've seen too much of that, especially recently, when there's this kind of 'let's hop on the particular bandwagon and make a buck.'

Ludlum's career in the theatre had provided him with a wide circle of friends and contacts, and it was through these that he was able to get that most important introduction into publishing. He remembered, with affection, his first editor, Richard Marek, with whom he had spent many hours:

He was most helpful as an editor, of course, and a writer who doesn't ask the advice of an editor is a fool.

For someone who definitely writes what he wants to, this is a significant comment. Ludlum, who also confirmed that he, too, had never set eyes on any 'how-to-write' books, is most emphatic about certain aspects of writing thrillers. For example, he determines the novels' titles with care, unlike some others I have met.

I wouldn't allow anyone else to choose the titles of my books. No way!

I will tell you I'm not happy about seeing authors' names set as large, or larger, than the titles, but I'm flattered by it. I see my books in airports all over the place, and when you see the titles, I guess a part of me says, 'Hey, I'd rather see a title', but then on the other hand I'm not in that position where I can say that.

In the theatre we used to have a phrase, your name must be a hundred percent in size of title, or your name must be in print below the title, but still in star status. I'm used to all these things, but I'd rather have my books known for their titles than I would by the author.

Whether it is his trade-mark three-word titles, his exceptionally strong storylines, word-of-mouth recommendation, or a combination of all three, that make his books successful is of little importance. His sales are huge, although he is not sure of the current worldwide total. Reports vary, but at the least, they exceed 50 million copies and at the most they approach 195 million. Either way, such numbers would bring a wide smile to the average author – if there is such a person!

Robert Ludlum is a very modest man, and though I sensed he tends to play down the glory of his multi-million sales, he is quite proud of the way his books have 'travelled'. How did he view his success?

Yes, you are talking about my books being translated into over thirty languages and sold into forty-three countries. So maybe there's a point to the numbers game. It's just that I can't possibly conceive in my mind 160 million copies.* I just can't.

But as to what made these books so successful, I think word of mouth, always. Remember, I come from the theatre, and a great phrase that – and I can't remember whether it was Antony Quayle or Denholm Elliot, both such great actors – but one said: 'What killed the play? Word of mouth.'

I think word of mouth has helped me most, but then luck, timing and a fine agent [no less a person than Henry Morrison] help too. I think I've had publishers, especially my current publishers, who care, and they know how to market a book. That's important, too.

I think that developing a style and maintaining it by consistency and frequency of product helps, but [so too does] avoiding that fine line between under – and over – exposure, too many books too

* Today that figure has risen to 200 million copies sold.

rapidly, because this generally leads to sloppy or unthoughtout work. This diminishes the consistency of style.

Then I don't describe sex scenes either, and that may help sales. To me, I think that it's much nicer, and much more evocative sensually, to use certain catch-phrases, and to allude to certain things that we all know, to arouse an imagination but not to become prurient.

Avoiding sex scenes, at least in thrillers, is echoed by other top authors, and would-be writers should note this advice. Robert Ludlum clearly enjoys writing thrillers and of all those published to date, he has derived more satisfaction from the *Bourne* series than any other.

Listening to Robert Ludlum talk, I became aware of that velvet voice, which had appealed to the advertising executive all those years ago, so much so, that I wondered whether he had ever thought of recording tapes – talking books – of his thrillers.

No. I'd be taking work from an actor [if he read his own work], and I find the authors that do that – including some very good friends of mine whom I obviously will not name – reprehensible. I know how hard it is for an actor to get work, and I would never take the job from an actor. Sure, I can do it, and I've been offered a great deal of money to do it.

As we were talking of money, I asked whether the security of having money made it easier for him to write. Does he think, too, that having money helps someone setting out to write?

Well, I think if you're real poor, I think you're going to grab the first bus that comes along. If you're terribly rich, you're possibly too indolent to really strive. I was in that perfect situation once, as I had enough money to live, though certainly not rich. I wasn't really poor either, but I made sacrifices as a young actor that I never should have made, because I was so poor, and I took jobs that I shouldn't have taken, extras on television and this and that, which categorizes you.

A great director named Sidney Lumet once said to me, 'I keep you working as an extra because I know you've got a wife and a kid, but I'm gonna tell you right now, don't take any more of these jobs as an extra. You're a much better actor than this – hold out.'

I said, 'Sidney, how can I hold out without any money?' His advice was to get myself a job as a bartender and hold out. Sound advice.

So, finally, can he, on reflection, pin down the one feature which he believes is the one most important to his success?

Every author, of course, has a 'beginning'.

It starts with someone in the world of publishing believing in, or at least liking, your work. In my case, it happened to be an agent, the same agent I've had all my life. It might also be an editor, invariably a hungry junior editor, anxious to make his mark by 'discovering' new talent; also because senior editors rarely have the time to pore over the voluminous new material submitted. Remember, senior editors were once junior editors.

Craig Thomas

Rat Trap, Firefox, Wolfsbane, Snow Falcon, Moscow 5000, Emerald Decision, Sea Leopard, Jade Tiger, Firefox Down, The Bear's Tears, Winter Hawk, All The Grey Cats, The Last Raven, A Hooded Crow, Playing With Cobras, A Wild Justice, A Different War. Worldwide sales: 20 million copies.

Craig Thomas is one of Britain's own master thriller writers. Since his breakthrough with his second book, he has acquired an avid group of readers, keen to devour every word that he writes. In this respect, he shares similar good fortune with other famous authors, among them Tom Clancy, Clive Cussler, Robert Ludlum and Joseph Wambaugh. He also shares with them that one rich and exceptional moment, of having had the first novels they submitted accepted by the first publishers they had approached.

Born in Wales, Craig Thomas began his education at Cardiff High School and went on to the University College, Cardiff, to read English, a subject at which he was to excel. A good starting point for any author though, as you will have read elsewhere, not essential. With an MA degree behind him and a yen to continue in the world of education, he became a teacher, ending up at Shire Oak School in Walsall, in what was then the English county of Staffordshire.

He describes himself as the 'boy from Hicksville' who made good, and admits to being somewhat temperamental, impatient and emotional. Exceptionally hardworking – 'a dedicated workaholic' in his own words – he is mercurial but sensitive by nature. He too, like so many others, once daydreamed of becoming a writer, although not as a novelist, but as a radio or television playwright. Over a period of several years, he bombarded the BBC Script Unit with a variety of ideas, including a science-fiction serial and a radio version of part of J.R.R. Tolkien's *The Lord of the Rings*. Each time his submissions were returned, usually with a curt and impersonal rejection slip, until he thought, like thousands of writers in the same situation, that he was attempting the impossible. He had, too, also entered a number of writing competitions, but always to no avail.

His pride was undoubtedly dented by every returned script, but perhaps his training as a teacher guided him because, faced with these constant rejections, he sought advice. This is something that perhaps anyone might eventually have done, but the important factor in his case was that he asked one of the

BBC script editors what he was doing wrong – could the editor advise him? Amazingly, this simple piece of lateral thinking helped put him on the road to fame. There seems little doubt that Craig could have gone on writing little pieces, gone on fruitlessly submitting scripts to the BBC, for many years, but for that singularly important advice.

The script editor's advice was gloriously simple: what Craig was writing was unsuitable for broadcasting. He ought to apply his talents to novels. As he told me, that is exactly what he did:

> You see, I was fitting myself to become a novelist, because I was a solitary soul as far as my writing was concerned. I simply didn't want to work with other people: radio and television are committee media. But I needed a mould, and I stuck with this mould, which wasn't mine, for far too long. That's the one thing I suppose I do regret, that I didn't get that advice to write a novel earlier.
>
> I can't remember his name, he was a script editor with Radio Wales in Cardiff, but in sending it to him, I wasn't relying on my Welsh connection.
>
> Most of my efforts went to the BBC, a couple to ITV, but this was a part-time hobby rather than an occupation, and with unsolicited material for radio, you need the cast of characters, the summary of the plot, the sound-effects, and so on, and samples of dialogue. So I spent vast amounts of time planning and structuring, and working out the material, but only as much time writing it as it took to have enough material to submit in the first instance. So it was that kind of hobby, instead of gardening, or keeping tropical fish, or do-it-yourself.
>
> In a way, going to the comprehensive [school, i.e. Shire Oak] and becoming a head of department, with the extra administrative and disciplinary work, drained me far more than expected, both physically and nervously. Intellectually, I was less stimulated, and less used up, and I think that, probably, I needed that kind of environment, with a certain amount of creative energy left over, to actually get a novel written.

Craig took that piece of advice very seriously, and spent the next eighteen months writing his first novel. Once he had proved he could write a 350-page typescript, he put it to one side and started another, this time finishing it in just six months: it was published as *Rat Trap*.

* * *

Trying to write while still earning a living can be a very trying business, especially when the full-time job can easily take up all the available time. Craig, though, found that his job did not tax him mentally, and he possessed the creative energy to make use of the school breaks to follow his aspirations, proving that if a writer is prepared to make the extra effort, then anything is possible.

For those who try, who have the energy and drive to get up and do something about their ambitions, life has a curious way of sometimes providing opportunities. So it was with Craig. Working hard at the school in Staffordshire precluded him from easy contacts – especially personal contacts – with publishers in London. It happened, however, that his father, Brinley Thomas, a long-serving journalist with the *Western Mail*, had had fifteen books published, and was therefore a notable author in his own right. These were all about rugby football, a far cry from fiction, but contacts are contacts, and Craig reckoned that his father simply must, by that time, know something about publishing, and whom to contact.

One of the publishing world's well-known personalities of the time, Bill Luscombe, had published his father's books, though he had, by then left to join another London publisher. However, his 'little black book' of contacts was very wide-ranging, and he knew instantly whom to put Craig in touch with.

> I never actually met Bill, and having written *Rat Trap*, I asked if he knew anybody who would look at it – and tell me what they thought of it. Though I wasn't nervous of submitting *Rat Trap*, I knew it was better than my first attempt [the novel he had 'put to one side']. I thought, ask somebody, ask my father if there was somebody he was connected with in publishing who could help. In a way, I was safeguarding myself from nepotism, because he did not write fiction, therefore he wouldn't know any fiction editors. He simply sent it to Bill Luscombe, and Bill wrote a lovely letter back saying, 'Send it to Anthea Joseph, don't send it to Michael Joseph Ltd. Send it to Anthea personally. And enclose a copy of my letter.' Which I did.
>
> I realize now, with hindsight, how important that introduction was . . .

It was early in May 1975 when Craig sent his first typescript off to Anthea Joseph. For him it was a major breakthrough, because she replied on 11 June, saying, 'subject to you agreeing to some cutting and amendments, we should be glad to make you an offer.' After all those rejections, her letter became one of his most treasured possessions, a milestone in his life. She invited Craig to visit her in London, to discuss his first novel, a meeting he greatly looked forward to, though he seldom travelled to London, and then usually only on school business. On the day, he donned his best suit, a 'CIA-style' cream outfit, and headed off to meet Anthea. He vividly remembers the first time they met, for she took him to a little Greek restaurant just off Tottenham Court Road. Later on, after lunch, they went back to her office, where she introduced Craig to a colleague, Jenny Dereham, the editor who was to look after his work.

'Was there no question of any literary agent being involved at this stage, then?' I asked.

Well, soon after this – yes. When *Rat Trap* was published, Mike Shaw of Curtis Brown, who had joined them a year before, wrote to me saying, 'I've just read your book with a great deal of interest. I think you could be very successful. But you need an agent. Could I come up and talk to you?'

So I had to take a long lunch hour from Shire Oak to take him to the local pub. I don't think he was awfully impressed with the meal, but he persisted with me, and the only reason I went to an agent was because I thought, nothing ventured, nothing gained. There's no contract with the agent to send them the next book [though nowadays some agents do ask their writers to sign an agreement with them], so if I wasn't pleased, I could have withdrawn from the experiment.

The week before, Jenny [Dereham] had telephoned me – and she's not daft, is our Jenny – she rang me up during a break in school and offered me £1,000 for *Firefox*, twice the money. [*Rat Trap* brought him an advance of £500.] 'Make your mind up now' – and I'm standing there waiting for the bell to go . . . 'Oooh, oooh, right, yes, that's wonderful. Thank you.'

If I had to do it again, I would have gone to an agent to begin with, rather than submit things to a junk-pile. I was lucky to avoid the junk-pile, but if it *had* been a junk-pile submission, then an agent is going to be of greater help. The fact of life is, because publishing is such a personal business, and the relations between publishers and authors are so personal, it is probably better to have an agent simply because somebody else talks about the vulgar subject of money.

Without an agent to help, finding a publisher at his first attempt was more than fortunate. At the time, he felt on top of the world with his advance of £500 in his pocket – not much by today's standards, perhaps, but this was 1975, well before the age of massive advances and publicity hype.

And I got £1,000 for *Firefox*. I got half on signature, and half on publication. You don't think Anthea would have given it all at once do you!

The money allowed me to give up those time-consuming evening classes, where I taught A level English for two hours a week. My fellow teachers were very good about the whole thing, but I used to say to the inquisitive, 'Well, I'm trying to write a novel.' 'Oh,' they'd say, and they would go away, but there were no silly comments. They were even very tolerant, when they discovered I was leaving [the school] because the Americans had paid a lot of money for the paperback edition of *Firefox*. At times they were certainly curious. In fact, with *Firefox*, the geography staff were very good at helping me with the background about climatic conditions and the ice-floe [crucial to the plot] . . .

A most innovative thriller in its day, *Firefox* caught the eye of American publishers, and it was the sale of the US paperback rights in that novel which earned him enough to enable him to take the plunge and 'retire' from teaching. A remarkable achievement, after only two years of writing part-time while teaching full-time, to have the confidence to take risks with his future. The advance the American publishers paid was, of course, quite substantial, but there was more to come.

The sale of the film rights in *Firefox* had, however, an air of mystery about it. A man from Warner Brothers, having driven all the way up the M1 motorway to Craig's home and induced him to sign the contract (undoubtedly by holding out another healthy advance payment, and the prospect of good earnings on top of that), would not disclose who was to play the lead role in the film, no matter how much Craig pleaded.

The plot of *Firefox*, the hijacking by a maverick American agent of a 4,000 mile-an-hour top-secret Soviet jet fighter, made a great cinema spectacle, but had the book sold well before the film came out? I wondered. And if it had, what was it that had made the book so successful? And *Rat Trap* before it?

Now, *Rat Trap* sold about 2,500 in hard-cover, so you wouldn't call it a bestseller anyway – and about 35,000 in paperback first time out.

There are a number of innovative aspects about *Firefox*, but basically, I wrote it because it seemed like a good idea at the time. Nobody had written a flying novel for years, especially a flying thriller; and nobody had used a Vietnam veteran in a thriller, and that was purely accidental, because I needed somebody who had flown in combat in the late seventies and therefore had to be a

Vietnam veteran; and lastly, which I adopted from one unsubmitted novel, was the fact that it is the first thriller set (at least for half its length) inside the Soviet Union, in Moscow.

Those elements attracted both Michael Joseph and Sphere [the British paperback publishers]; especially Sphere . . . They had been looking for a home-grown bestselling thriller writer, and they'd found somebody who had one book published, and they knew that *Wolfsbane* [his third novel] had been finished by then. They had found an author who had written a novel different enough to be attractive on a wide scale.

In terms of the book itself, I would say the flying element of the second half, rather than the plane, and perhaps especially the Moscow background in the first half. Neither of which I calculated to be different, but having read contemporary thrillers, nobody had done [i.e. written about] either, so I suppose putting them together made the difference. It's an extremely simple structure which, put simply, is a chase from Chapter One to Chapter Ten.

So that even if you are not going to be terribly interested in the Moscow background or the flying, you *can* be interested in the fact that a man is being chased for his life from start to finish. Literally from start to finish.

I remember talking to Anthea . . . on the first occasion we met, and she said the 'word-of-mouth' aspect was not that important; she didn't know how important it was, though it obviously was important. I'm sure word-of-mouth recommendation is the substance of a bestselling status. I think it has to be – this element of a loyal readership which creeps in more and more with each succeeding book.

They can ruin you in the same way. This far on in my career, it would take two or three awful books to finish me off, but they could finish me off. Publishers would be the last to react to declining sales, so as long as I'm prepared to accept smaller advances, I'd be OK. But word of mouth over a period of two or three books, or one book after your first success, can ruin you. But it can also maintain you.

The word certainly spread. *Firefox* went on to sell a quarter of a million paperbacks in the United Kingdom during the first twelve months of publication, and two million in the United States.

After the success of *Firefox* and *Rat Trap*, Craig had not only become established as a top thriller writer, but he had overcome the straitjacket that being a conventional master of English can impose upon a writer. I wondered, however, whether he agreed with Catherine Cookson (among others), that excelling at English was a prerequisite for successful authors?

> No, not at all. But I do think that I have probably learned something, whatever it is − and I wouldn't know what it is − from every book I've ever read. And I think that my grounding in and passion for English literature and the language make me a better writer in my genre than most of my peers.
>
> But I don't think that it [command of English] is even the beginning of producing a novel. It certainly wouldn't produce a bestseller, or even a literary bestseller.

By 1978, when *Wolfsbane* was published, he was well and truly established as a full-time writer. His teaching days were now history, and with three books behind him he became totally dedicated to writing, even to the extent of producing more than his publishers needed.

> I've never been commissioned for my next book, except for the first 'David Grant' book. Fontana [the paperback imprint of Collins] commissioned me for *Moscow 5000*, and then Michael Joseph decided to publish the hardback edition.
>
> By the time *Firefox* was published, I had written *Wolfsbane*, after one false start with it, and I had written the first draft of *Snow Falcon*, which is why I went on to Fontana, because my publishers only wanted to do one a year. It's why I used a pseudonym − and also because by that time I actually thought that if I wrote under two names, I could become a full-time writer all the quicker.
>
> In strict terms, I did sign up for *Sea Leopard* before I had written it, but . . . no, I have never actually been commissioned, except for *Moscow 5000*, and I don't need to do it now. Publishers get awfully nosy, and quite rightly, too, because they've paid money.*

Did he get many reviews for *Rat Trap*, or *Firefox*?

> I got a few, but, generally, I'm not an author who gets many reviews.
>
> I got a good one [for *Rat Trap*] in *The Times*, and a good one in *The Guardian*, and a couple of other smaller reviews. For *Firefox*, I got a reasonable one in *The Times*, but I didn't get one in *The Guardian*, and I got a fair number in regional papers. And then I suppose my

---

* To date, Craig Thomas has only been commissioned twice, for *Moscow 5000* and *Emerald Decision*. Furthermore, once he had become firmly established as a top author, he had the confidence to dispense with the services of a literary agent.

review status went down and down and down, until *The Bear's Tears*, [which] got very good reviews from a number of newspapers. But I long ago learned not to expect much.

I do, however, get good reviews in America. Especially for *The Bear's Tears*, which up until the new book, *All The Grey Cats*, is the book I've been proudest of. I got superb reviews in the *New York Times*, the *Washington Post*, and the *Wall Street Journal*. And I thought, yes, thank you. They were lengthy and detailed, but I got a terrible review for *Winter Hawk* in the *Boston Globe*.

At this point Craig's wife, Jill, remarked with a good deal of feeling that they both resent reviews in which it is clear that the writer has not read the book in question. This is a view held by all writers, whether bestsellers or not; besides, such reviewers manage only to diminish their own credibility.

Authors are no different from anyone else: any criticism can hurt them. Everyone likes to be praised and good reviews are like gold; conversely, bad reviews can be very painful. Some writers pay no attention to reviews at all, others, at least early on in their careers, sneak glimpses and, if they are good, read on. For an expert in English, however, and an ex-schoolmaster at that, any criticism would be doubly felt.

Did Craig suffer from any lack of confidence in his writing, perhaps to the extent of seeking professional advice from a writing school?

I suspect they [writing schools] may do a lot of good. I'm not certain, because I don't know enough about it. So I speak, in a sense, from ignorance, but I do have a terrible feeling that an awful lot of people imagine themselves as writers, without any sense as to what they've written, or what they are attempting to write. I think an awful lot of people who assume that they might become writers don't actually read an awful lot in the first place. And they don't learn enough from what they read, and don't actually have any sense of fiction, since that is what we are talking about, prose fiction, albeit in this case [writing thrillers] in a popular genre. They don't really have the sense of, if you like, the constituents of the recipe for any book - like characters, style, imagery, all the language bits, and then the plot and the structure. Now, I don't know where they should get it from, and I don't see why they shouldn't be able to get it from a writing school.

I told Craig that one of the authors I interviewed, Barbara Taylor Bradford, had said, with considerable truth, that 'Writing cannot be taught, but it can be learned.'

Now that's not a bad comment. I think the passion for language cannot be born, it can only be acquired, because you don't have any language when you are born. But there is something similar to the quality that makes a mathematician, or a musician-stroke-composer, that produces that passion for language, which is the first way in which you are going to write, without knowing anything about characterization, dialogue, and those adult things. The childish thing about writing is the language, the words. And that is acquired as early as Mozart was composing his first concertos, and so on. You acquire it when you learn to read.

Behind every successful man, it is said, there is a successful woman. Though not a publisher's reader, say, or an ex-journalist – in fact, she was formerly a secretary – Jill Thomas is now his trusted 'first editor'. Most authors, whether aspiring or established, like to get a reader's opinion before pressing on to the next chapter or section. In Craig's case, Jill had little to do with his work at first, but, as she explained:

The first one I edited was *Moscow 5000*. The reason it started was because he had a chum, John Knowler, and he was English but he worked for an American publisher. He was an extremely perceptive man, and he was the one person who could really make Craig do exactly as he wanted him to with his editing. He was very sensitive, and very good, too. He used to say things like 'This is very good, but let's make it better.' Not just that, but his comments were encouraging, too: 'I can also recommend . . .' as a note in the margin; 'We are being told something here, but you are getting a piece of information across, and it is coming across as a piece of information rather than part of the story,' which made Craig, in turn, think and do it a different way.

Well, he died, and he was one of those people we were extremely fond of, and I said to Craig, 'Would you like me to just read it through and see what I think as a second opinion, before it goes in to the agent and publisher?' It sort of went on from there. And I've got worse and worse, and harder and harder.

And Craig added: 'It allows us, when we send the book in, to defend it, doesn't it?'

I doubt very much whether he has to defend his work nowadays. His days of £500 advances must seem like aeons ago; today, he is offered six figure sums just to clinch a deal. This is good money for doing something that he always wanted to do, but to win this level of reward he has to be a workaholic. He now works for six to eight months just researching his next book, then spends approximately the same time writing it – somewhat longer than the six months he took to write *Rat Trap*. His working day starts at 9.30am through to 5.00pm, only allowing himself one coffee break in the morning and just half an hour for lunch.

It is clear from the interviews in this book that the life of a full-time writer is very a lonely one indeed. Authors who write from home, and most do, become virtual recluses, and it becomes very difficult for them to persuade friends and relatives that they really are working, and are not to be disturbed.

> We realized about five or six years ago that we were becoming a bit hermit-like. Reclusive. When people rang the door-bell at any time during the day, we kept saying 'Oh God, who's that?' instead of, 'Oh, I wonder who is at the door?' But we are more available nowadays.

One quality common to all the successful authors in this book is the attention they devote to detail; indeed, it seems that detail is critical to their success. This may seem obvious, but it is a common denominator among them. Many authors, Craig included, use cross-cutting (a technique of shifting between scenes, characters, action sequences, locations, time-frames, and back again) as a means of capturing and holding a reader's attention. It is an art that requires more planning, and more attention to detail, than a straightforward text. How does Craig cope?

> I do plan with great care now, but I didn't in the early days.
>
> The best story I can tell you about cross-cutting, as an instinctive art as opposed to a planned art – because I do plan my scenes, and I know what what's going to be in them, but I never plan where precisely, where they finish and the next one begins – [is about] when I was proof-reading *Firefox*. I got to the scene towards the end of the first half, where he [the central character] actually steals the plane. Now he is having one of his funny turns, his delayed stress [from Vietnam], he's having one of his turns while hiding in the pilots' restrooms, and I cross-cut it to that point in the hangar where they [dissidents helping with the theft] start the fire on the second prototype. Then cross-cut back to him, and as I was reading the proofs, I said, 'Oh God, I've got this wrong, come on, come on, it's taking too long, it's taking too long. And because I was saying it, I realized I hadn't got it wrong, it was right, because the reader is going 'come on, come on.'

That was the one piece in the film that wasn't exploited, the cross-cutting between those two [scenes]. In the film, the fire was more or less out and he just walked in, whereas in the book this useless individual who is supposed to be such a sky-hot pilot can't even get himself dressed in his flying suit.

The first major author to embrace the art of cross-cutting was the late Graham Greene (it is a technique drawn to a considerable extent from film making; Greene had been a notable film critic, and had written screenplays). The results, at least when it is well done, do increase the tension in a novel, but it can take up to one hundred pages for a period of twenty-four hours to elapse, while the shorter the cross-cut passages are, the greater the tension.

Firefox, as it turned out, starred Clint Eastwood, who not only played the lead, but produced and directed as well. Perhaps that was the reason why Warner Brothers' representative had declined to break the news when the contract for the film rights was signed. Hollywood's hard man must have thought very highly of Craig's work, but how had Eastwood discovered the novel?

What he told me – so therefore it must be true – is not the often misquoted story that he picked up a copy from a bookstall at Heathrow.

I gather what happened was [that] a friend of his [who] runs a small private airline in Southern California . . . read it when it came out in paperback in the States, and gave Eastwood his copy, saying, 'Read it, you'll be great in the movie.' So he actually read the book, rather than a screenplay, which is quite unusual.

Firefox was a highly successful film, and it is almost a racing certainty that most of the audience thought that the scenes in Moscow were for real. In fact, however, all the 'Russian' scenes were filmed in Vienna and elsewhere in Austria. Perhaps what is more surprising, though, is that Craig Thomas never visited Moscow during the course of his research for the novel.

This fact makes the plot and location of *Firefox* rather more significant than those found in many other thrillers, as the majority of top authors advise aspiring writers to write what they know about. This prompted me to ask, as I have other authors, whether Craig felt obliged to write novels that he believed his readers wanted to read?

I am not aware of my readers when I'm planning or writing a book. I'm aware of the reception for what I write, and the effect it will have.

Therefore obviously I am a better writer for that, simply because I understand the problems of communicating exactly the effect I want to communicate. I don't know my readers. They are a very diverse bunch, from a senior lecturer at University College, here, whom I've met [and] who is a fan, to a taxi driver in Birmingham for whom I signed a hardback copy of *The Bear's Tears*. So who should I aim for? I have a lot of women readers, too...

It is difficult to describe my readers, but since my sales held up well during the recession, I would assume that they have disposable income, and continue to have it, to spend on books. I would say that they probably are readers rather than non-readers. I think a lot of bestselling authors pick up non-habitual readers, when one of their books comes out, or when a hyped book comes out, or when a book is advertised on television, or the book is a 'tie-in' with a film.

They want to become engrossed in the book, and I think that those who don't want that will try me once or twice, and then not buy me again.

But far more readers do buy his next book, with the result that he is a very successful author, by any standards. However, as his books were all within one genre, wondered whether he had ambitions in other literary fields.

I have been asked by former colleagues when I am going to write a proper book, but I take no notice as they don't read anyway. I don't have any unfulfilled 'literary' ambition, because I don't have a theme or a story that isn't a thriller in my head at the moment.

If I did, I would write it. I have one ... one brilliant idea for a horror story, a proper old-fashioned ghost story, not a blood-and-guts horror story. But I'm still at the stage where I am very interested in the thriller genre, or the thriller-adventure genre.

Every clown wants to play *Hamlet*, but the clown ought to know he can't. If I could write *King Lear*, I would have written it, so to speak. You have got to know what you can – and can't – do.

Taking him up on this last point, as he did not seem to have many sex scenes in his books, I wondered if this was a deliberate policy, or whether he found the subject difficult to write about. He agreed that there were few such scenes, but added:

There's one sex scene between husband and wife in *Snow Falcon*, I seem to remember, but it's not a feature.

I eschew sex in novels, in the sense that it's not necessary to attract the reader if the other factors are in place. And I don't think that titillation is part of my business anyway. If a sexual relationship was germane, a hinge in the novel, I would try and write the scenes that showed why those scenes were important, but I don't see any necessity.

Looking back, and with the benefit of hindsight, what advice would he offer to someone contemplating writing a thriller?

Persistence. The virtue of persistence. Nothing else, because I can't say, not having met them, whether they have got talent, the facility, imagination, strength of character. But I do know they have to have persistence, and that can apply to anybody.

I always remember those old orange and white Penguins, and the exotic authors they had. They'd always been lumberjacks, brain surgeons, or beachcombers before they became authors. And that there was a syndrome whereby you had to experience everything before you wrote – usually – very bad books.

I would think that today's writer draws more consistently upon his imagination than upon his experience. I mean – it's no good being a monk unless you are writing a religious poem or novel, but other than that, I don't see that there's an apprenticeship to be served in the world before you can become a writer.

Apprenticeship or not, all authors are very sensitive people. And as we parted after an excellent lunch in a West London restaurant, he asked me: 'What are you going to call your book? *A Basketful of Egos*?'

Which struck me as being very apt.

POSTSCRIPT

Of all his seventeen thrillers, which have sold, in round terms, twenty million copies, *The Bear's Tears* has remained the top selling title for the longest period. When he had finished it, he felt that he had achieved all he wanted to achieve in a book. Unlike other authors, he has changed the theme with each title. *The Last Raven* was his first true 'post Cold War' novel; *Playing With Cobras* was, as he told me, his homage to Buchan, a good traditional 'adventure' story in the context of India in the 1990s; and the current thriller, *A Different War*, is based on global business and international trade.

Joseph Wambaugh

The New Centurions, The Blue Knight, The Onion Field, The Choirboys, The Black Marble, The Glitter Dome, The Delta Star, Lines and Shadows, The Secrets of Harry Bright, Echoes in the Darkness, The Blooding, The Golden Orange, Fugitive Nights, Finnegan's Week and *Floaters*. Over 15 million copies sold.

I had to fly to Los Angeles in California to meet Joseph Wambaugh, but I did not think that I would ever get to actually meet him. He had told me that it would be very difficult to find him out in the desert, and that he preferred to tell all in a telephone interview. But after I rang him from my hotel in Los Angeles, he relented, and invited me to meet him at his home in Newport Beach, some thirty miles away, later that day.

Joe, as he likes to be called, is the very epitome of the Los Angeles cop that he once was, even though he has long since given up policing the streets of that city. It is, however, still very easy to imagine him in the full LAPD uniform – he has that sort of aura.

Here, I thought, is an author, renowned for his police stories, who uses his own experiences as a basis for writing. In this respect, his approach has much in common with those of Dora Saint, James Herriot, Dick Francis and James Herbert, although Dick Francis had in fact retired from his main career before taking up writing seriously. The others started and continued to write whilst supported by their main careers. However, Joe is unique amongst those interviewed, as he was the only author to have written not one, but three bestsellers, while in full-time public service.

How did Joe manage to make the break, for usually a policeman has to dedicate his life totally to the force?

I was not only a policeman, of course, but a part-time student as well. I majored in English only because I seem to have an affinity for it. I wasn't good at anything else anyway, but I liked to read and seemed to be able to express myself. I enjoyed it all so I went on to take my Master's degree.

It wasn't something that you talked about to other policemen, and it wasn't something that any policeman ordinarily does. If they knew I was going to college, I would pretend, if anyone asked me, to be studying law, police science or criminology. I think I was the *only* serving officer studying literature. I wasn't afraid of being teased, but I did not want to appear different from the others. I certainly didn't mention I was trying to write. I was a closet writer.

Having got my degree, I did not tell anybody at work. I started fooling around writing short stories, because everybody on the face of the earth who has ever majored in English tries to write, whether he admits it or not. And you know, they all say they don't, but they do. Anyway, I was one who did and I just sent them to magazines; little short stories about police work, you know, but they were all rejected. In fact, I recall that *Playboy* magazine even sent a mean little note with one of them saying, 'This is the second time you've sent the same story to us, schmuck. Don't do it again, it's no better this time than it was last time.'

I always regretted that I didn't hang on to that letter because some years later, *Playboy* was trying to get me to do a piece for them and I would have loved to have sent it back to them in revenge.

So I kept sending stories out, and getting them rejected. In the end, I stopped sending them to ordinary magazines and *Playboy*, and I sent one to a literary magazine, the *Atlantic Monthly*. It's the oldest magazine in the country and I thought, what the hell, everybody has turned me down so why not go upmarket? They claimed to have a different readership and though they encouraged me, they never actually published any of my short stories.

His experiences with some of the cases he dealt with as a police officer were often harrowing and mentally scaring. It was quite natural for him to believe that if he could tell the story right, he might bring the horrors home to others, and writing these stories was at least a cathartic method of releasing his tensions. Most of his first efforts were sent to men's adventure-type magazines chosen at random from a reference book, rather than selectively by type of magazine. As the rejection slips mounted up, he was forced to become more selective. It was, as he said, a brave action to send one of his stories to a literary magazine.

That opportunist move, made more from frustration than as a result of careful planning, was the best thing he ever did, because it created the lucky break that every writer needs. A junior editor at *Atlantic Monthly* passed his letter and story to Edward Weeks, the former editor of the magazine. At the time, Weeks was a senior consultant and he thought that Joe's efforts were worthy of his attention.

This provided the turning point for Wambaugh. What he was writing, Weeks said, did not lend itself to short stories, but a novel – advice which Joseph Wambaugh took very seriously.

> Then I immediately started writing a book and finished in a matter of six months, even though I was working full time. Dee [his wife] helped by reading what I had written, and giving me her opinions. She had no formal training, but has an instinctive idea as to what is good. I sent it off to them, but did not hear from them for ages. In fact I got so impatient that I sent it off to another publisher, who promptly rejected it. Then I thought I'd better wait for Atlantic Monthly. Eventually, they responded and said they were going to publish it.
>
> That was the greatest thrill of my life, but it also scared me. We were supposed to have permission to do anything like this, any sort of writing. I hadn't asked, and I feared it would cost me my job. No one in the police department, though, had ever attempted to write a novel before, so far as I'm aware.
>
> I had read enough about writing to know that almost everybody makes nothing. I knew that, and I didn't think I was going to be any different. I never aspired to make money.
>
> When Weeks came to our modest policeman's home, to present us with our $4,000 advance and our contract, he must have been seventy-five or eighty. We set out to entertain him by providing lunch for this terrific literary character who knew all the great authors. Dee and I did our best, and it was one of those things, but we put out paper napkins that day. From the moment he arrived, he coughed continuously from the second he sat down until lunch. He was eating and talking non-stop. Mostly talking. Then have a bite and wipe his mouth. Talk, have another bite, and wipe his mouth. Soon, the paper napkin started to shred, and by the end of the meal there were shreds sticking to his chin, lips and nose!
>
> Dee and I looked at each other and didn't dare tell him. We have never forgotten that day.

The typescript for *The New Centurions*, Joe's first book, was large: about 145,000 words. This meant that he had driven himself to write an average of over 800 words, or more, a day, and that after a full day's work. Any aspiring writer would do well to bear that in mind.

With $4,000 in his bank account, he took off for what he thought would be a short celebratory holiday in the coastal city of Mazatlán, Mexico. He was on a high, but life has a way of dealing with people in this frame of mind. Dee and the two neighbours they took with them ended up nursing one very sick author, for he went down with a severe case of Montezuma's revenge!

The telegram that awaited him on his return more than made up for the acute discomfort, though: '. . .*The New Centurions* has been accepted as Book of the Month. A check [cheque] will be forthcoming in the amount of $75,000.' Although he received only half of that (the publisher getting the other half), it was a sum that made it all worth while.

The New Centurions, published by Atlantic-Little, Brown, appeared on the *New York Times* bestseller list for (as he recalled) thirty weeks. The results of this, and of the Book of the Month Club deal, gave him a boost both morally and financially, and the novel eventually sold well over 2 million copies, a superb achievement. It certainly brought him to the notice of the American literary world.

Joe was an energetic thirty-four year-old when his career as a writer began. He was to remain with the LAPD for another two years during which he completed two more books before 'retiring'. This was not because he was earning huge sums, but because, being employed in such a public role, he could not risk being instantly recognised by the public when he was on duty, and on the streets; a situation no well-known person had had to face before.

* * *

Joe was born into an Irish Catholic family in Pittsburgh, Pennsylvania. His father was a police chief, albeit in a small town, but he also worked as a steelworker for a time, an occupation that Joe took up while studying literature at evening classes.

Joe's affinity for English was far from evident at school. He openly admits that in his days at Chaffey High School in Ontario, California, he was a very poor student, and not just in the academic sense, either. He did, however, enjoy learning Spanish, and studied that language intensely.

His latent talent for English only surfaced at the age of twenty, after he left the Marines. In an attempt to better himself he joined Chaffey College in Alta Loma, California, where he matriculated. He gained his BA in English at California State College (California State University) when he was twenty-three, and his MA eight years later. Such academic success was in itself quite an achievement, and reflects a common trait among the top group of authors, but education and erudition are not automatic passports to bestsellerdom.

Early in his career with the Los Angeles Police, Joe had only humble aspirations:

My ambition was simply to be published. And a short story in a magazine would have been a great honour and probably have satisfied any sort of ambitions I had in the area.

It became apparent that I had some facility for reports whatever class I was in. I would turn a geology report into some sort of romantic interlude and when I was supposed to be talking about fossils, I would be waxing semi-poetic about something or other. I discovered I had an ability to communicate in an entertaining fashion.

The thought then struck me that when I retired from police work, I might write a book, but in the meantime, I'd start with a short story.

The experiences and situations he faced in his everyday life served as a complete social education in themselves. He met all kinds of people, in many different situations; the violent criminals, the drug-pushers and pimps, the con-men, all presented crises for him to handle. With his ambitions as a writer in mind, he would jot down cryptic notes to himself, recording incidents and characters for future use. Since notepads were not always to hand, he would write on anything that came his way – backs of envelopes, old police forms, scraps of wrapping-paper, even the reverse sides of official police 'hot sheets', the forms on which all known stolen car licence numbers are recorded. When he came home, he would dump his works into a convenient drawer. Most of them finished up as parts of short stories, and latterly found their way into his books. Then came the news from Atlantic Monthly Press.

The instant success of *The New Centurions* completely wrong-footed his police superiors, who had no more idea of his covert activities than had his immediate colleagues. At first his Chief, Edward M. Davis, admonished him in no uncertain terms, and Wambaugh was in genuine fear for his job. He had not sought permission to submit his work, which disclosed details of police life and methods, for publication. Perhaps it was the novel's content, rather than the bare fact of its having been published, that made Joe worry more, but as the publicity mounted so did the Chief's embarrassment; so much so that he made it clear he wanted to fire Wambaugh from the service. Then the press, like the US Cavalry, came galloping to his rescue.

The row over the book within the police department raised a constitutional issue: the American constitution encompasses freedom of speech, putting Chief Davis in an invidious position. Policemen had written books before, of course, usually on police science, but this was the first time anyone in the force had written a work of fiction – a very true-to-life work of fiction – that had become an instant bestseller.

The storyline in *The New Centurions* covers five years in the lives of three fictional policemen. The novel traces their training at the Police Academy and then follows their daily experiences on duty, which at times were just routine, and at other times, horrific. It is a story told from the Los Angeles policemen's viewpoint, and culminates with an account of how they coped with the Watts riots that took place in August 1965. Joe was one of eighty policemen who initally faced the rioters; shooting broke out and people fell all around him. According to reports, all they could do was to retreat and defend themselves as best they could.

But it was the way in which Joe told his story that made all the difference. He showed the reader how even the most honest and principled officer could become inured to the horrors of being in the front line of society's fight against every sort of violent and sordid crime. The publication in 1971 had some unexpected results.

> Immediately it came out, I was an instant celebrity. Superiors treated me differently, and my peers with a certain amount of deference, which is more difficult to handle than disapproval would have been. But my superiors were really confused.
>
> I thought I should not be sitting around apologizing for my book, but it *was* written by a moonlighting policeman. So, I immediately started another book, as I was really afraid for my job. I wasn't commissioned and finished it in forty-eight days, as far as I can remember. I thought I might well end up losing my job, and with a wife and two little children, $4,000 wasn't enough to live on then.
>
> My wage in 1970 was about $15,000 a year and giving that up for the honour of being published was a little frightening... [but] it was a such a great honour to be published, that it was worth risking a career.
>
> When I sent it [the new book] off to Atlantic Monthly, I gave them no notice at all. Nevertheless, they accepted it straight away, and *The Blue Knight* was published a year after the first.

Joe thus learned that it had been no use rushing ahead to finish his second book. Seldom does any publisher, unless they are publishers of romantic fiction, put out two books in one year from the same author – one a year, certainly, but not two.

Having one book published might have been seen as pure luck, but not two. *The Blue Knight*, published in 1972, also sold well, sales exceeding, according to one report, 1 million copies by 1980. The main character, Bumper Morgan, is an ageing cop and Joe draws on his personal experiences to build the storyline;

one which could be told well if written by a serving officer.

Though his first two books were fictional, they were truthful portrayals and accurate reflections of the real life of the police force. It also led him into a series of arguments about how police should be portrayed, for he bitterly disapproves of the 'bullet-spattered and full-of-violence' image created by television and cinema directors. His own experience had proved that the danger police faced was more emotional than physical, a point he repeatedly makes.

The particularly brutal murder of a Californian policeman in an isolated onion field, the subsequent lengthy trial of the murderers, and the fate of the policeman's partner, who survived the attack, inspired Joe to write the full story. This was his third book to be published while remaining a serving police officer. Wambaugh's 'non-fiction novel', *The Onion Field* (1975), was to be the forerunner of several others.

But his superiors, quite apart from being bemused by the appearance of a talented writer in their ranks, failed to take advantage of his literary ability. Here, on their own doorstep, was a gifted writer whose talent was instantly recognized not only by experienced publishers but, more importantly, by reviewers and the reading public. But there was to be no role for Joe as editor of a police magazine, or in public relations. The LAPD failed to take advantage of his burgeoning talent. He added:

> To this very day, the LAPD does not extol my virtues, and doesn't use me in any way. Yet police departments all over the world have offered me various honours, and are always inviting me to appear at various events, and constantly asking me to speak – to give speeches. I don't give speeches. I don't know how to give speeches. They terrify me and I never do it, but I still get, weekly, several invitations from police forces all over the world.

His runaway success might possibly owe a good deal to the fact that he was first published in America; certainly he feels that to be true. Whenever he comes to England for interviews, however, he is referred to as the author of *The Choirboys* and *The Onion Field*, although he has written many others books.

On reflection, Joseph Wambaugh attributes his sudden success essentially to good timing – and, of course, to a small element of luck. The police force had been through a turbulent time in the 1960s and its public image had taken a pounding. People were beginning to question the actions and attitudes of a force once held to be above reproach. Then, suddenly, here was a novel about the police written from the inside; a novel which told how the job acts on the man, rather than how the man acts on the job. The news that

Joe's superiors did not approve of his writing no doubt heightened his appeal in the public's eyes.

> I just think that the timing for the first book was perfect, but I don't think that explains why, ten books later, people still read them.
>
> The publishing game is old-fashioned, and the marketing is years behind the times. No one takes a great deal of trouble to find out why people read books, why they buy certain books.
>
> I wonder why a publisher doesn't just bite the bullet and spend several thousand dollars for a very good marketing survey – not just on one book, let's say on thirty books and, let's say, share the cost with other publishers; to find out why some books are bought and others not. But they never do things like that, and so it's still an old-fashioned industry.

Currently, his UK publisher is Bantam Press, and he told me that he does not retain the services of a literary agent.

> I usually give my publisher fifteen percent to handle world rights.
>
> After the first book, I asked Weeks for advice and he put me on to an elderly agent in New York, but sadly, he died of cancer shortly afterwards. I could not see that an agent could do anything for me, I just couldn't understand why I should give away ten percent to one of these people.

* * *

Joe's most successful book by far has been *The Choirboys* (also published in 1975). Again, an accurate reflection of life in the force, it differs from his earlier novels in that it is primarily humorous, though effectively realistic for all that. It was certainly a novel that could not be written by a serving police officer for it exposed too many 'practices' about which his superiors were unaware.

'Choir practice' was one, held after work and away from the eyes of authority: it was a euphemism for wild drinking sessions where the police officers would really let their hair down – all inhibitions would completely disappear. Such parties helped relieve the tensions of being in the front line of the fight against crime. Such tension, Joe points out time and time again, is not so much physical as emotional, and can be far more damaging. *The Choirboys*, for all its humour, is also a story tinged with tragedy.

* * *

One of Joe's many talents lies in writing dialogue – it is the only kind of writing that he finds easy. He has written many screenplays, an art to which novelists seldom adapt successfully. With the *The Choirboys* an instantaneous and huge success, he then turned to writing the screenplay version of it. The results were not, however, what the studio wanted, and the director, Robert Aldridge, and Lorimar Productions decided Joe's screenplay was not right. A costly error, as he explained:

> I had a horrendous problem with Hollywood. They had someone else rewrite the screenplay without my knowledge or consent, and I had a special arrangement with the production company, because the book was such a huge success, that they were not allowed to do that. So I created a big fuss and sued them. We settled out of court.

Joe shares, with many other authors, a strong dislike for the way his stories are dramatized for films or television; far too often studios seem to enjoy changing the storyline. At least Joe took positive action, rather than just bemoaning what had happened.

He then went on to buy back the film rights to *The Onion Field*, which had been sold to Columbia Pictures four years earlier. The studio never finished the film and Joe wanted to buy it back, though, again, he had to resort to litigation before they released it. Being a man who puts his money where his mouth is, he then set out to produce the film. He invested a large sum of his own money into the production, one report put it at $750,000, and Dee raised the rest, from anyone she could find provided they were not involved in Hollywood.

> I was happy with the result because we were naive. We didn't make a good business arrangement and it seems that though everyone had seen the film, we didn't make any money. But we did get our money back. I worked very hard. I wrote it. I produced it. But we didn't make any money. So the screenplay was free, the producing was free, all the hours were free, but it was stupid.
>
> We did the same for *The Black Marble* as well. Now that one we lost money on. Fortunately not too much!

This lead us to discuss writer's personalities. What followed was a healthy family 'discussion'. Joseph did not believe his personality showed in his writing, but Dee disagreed.

> It definitely does show. He quite definitely creates his own pressure, and the characters who in his books appear to be under pressure are

him. He's very impatient and sensitive, but not self-centred or ruthless.

Joe interrupted:

But writers really are a miserable bunch. They feel guilty all the time when they are not writing. They're unhappy when they are *not* writing and they are unhappy when they *are* writing.

Frankly, I normally don't do any detailed outline, I just have a vague outline of what I'm doing and then I start. I just get going and hope that it writes itself. If it doesn't, I'm in trouble!

Once or twice, I've tried to do an outline and then I'd deviate from it immediately.

Joseph Wambaugh shares this lack of liking for prepared outlines with James Herbert. It maybe that reviewers would have something to say on this lack of detailed planning. Surprisingly, Joe has a relaxed view about the media, feeling that, in the main, 'he has been more than fairly treated by the critics'.

His fourth non-fiction work, *The Blooding*, is based on two murders in the village of Narborough, Leicestershire. The detection technique based on isolating an individual's DNA, known as 'genetic fingerprinting', was invented by Professor Alec Jeffreys at Leicester University, and has shown itself to be an effective a means of identification as conventional fingerprinting. Criminals frequently leave behind minute traces of blood, semen, shreds of skin, or even a single hair, and any one of these can be used for identification, since all individuals have a unique genetic pattern. The new technique was bound to fire the imaginations of writers, and so it was with Joe; *The Blooding* is also his first book on an all-British theme.

* * *

Since he had established himself firmly both as a bestselling writer and as an author who would fight for his rights, had he become so well-known that his private life suffered? The media, which in a sense 'saved' him from disciplinary action when his first book came out, must have used his photographs, so did he, for example, find himself recognised wherever he went?

I used to enjoy the fame, but it soon wore off. Rather quickly for me, after the first five years.

Once in a while I'm recognized, but not that often. The name sometimes gets recognized, but not the face. That's OK with me.

Richard Burton once said that he'd like to be an author because the name gets recognized when you want a table at a restaurant, or when you want special service on an airline.

The fact that he was not often recognised was one aspect of bestsellerdom that he liked, but he went on to tell me that writing the sort of books he does brings other problems.

I get sued a lot, because I write non-fiction books about unsavoury people. *The Onion Field* got me a lawsuit that lasted for twelve years, and there are some threats right now.

My second non-fiction book, called *Lines and Shadows* got me a lawsuit which I've had to defend.

I've been fighting lawsuits for sixteen years, because of my non-fiction books, almost my entire writing career. Fiction, of course, does not get me lawsuits.

The actions drain me emotionally. Lawsuits do that, ask anyone who has been through a divorce. You can be thoroughly blameless and have this frivolous, scurrilous lawsuit just eating you.

The thrill has gone for me, as far as fame is concerned. I've had that and it was fine – not any more.

So be warned – the pleasures of fame may well wane after a while. Aspiring authors contemplating using a word-processor might also like to consider Joe's own experience which was a disaster. He bought the latest IBM machine of the day, complete with a printer, but had the company collect everything back after three weeks. He found sitting in front of the screen very intimidating. No sooner had he asked them to collect it than a lawyer from San Francisco telephoned to enquire why. He told Joe that no one in the history of IBM had ever asked to have their equipment returned, and he had one question: did he expect this word-processor to write the book for him? Joe thought for a moment and replied, 'Well, maybe I did, I don't know.'

Finally, Joseph Wambaugh put his success into perspective for me:

By the way, I've never had a short story published. So, in a way, I didn't really achieve my ambition. In that sense I'm still a failure.

Yes, I thought, as I took my leave, authors are not only lonely, but insecure, too. Even the best of them.

Afterword

Assuming that you have read all the interviews, you will surely have drawn your own conclusions about the intangible quality that singled these authors out for fame and fortune. If, on the other hand, you have simply read the interviews with your favourite authors, then you will have missed much.

I would not presume to draw any firm conclusions, neither would I like to colour anyone's thinking. Each reader will, I hope, have found help here, and perhaps the inspiration to pursue their dreams. For others, those who just enjoy reading and not writing, I hope they have had their interest held, and have been intrigued by the authors' own tales of their journeys along the road to bestsellerdom.

Acknowledgements

First and foremost, I am extremely grateful to all twenty-three authors interviewed for this book. They gave up their valuable writing time to talk about the subject for this book and their contributions will forever be a source of great interest.

The idea for *Bestsellers* was thought up by Jane Tatam who, as publisher at Ashford Press Publishing, also published my first book, *Michael Joseph – Master of Words*, in 1986. To her, I owe a vote of thanks, for it has been a fascinating task.

In addition to the personal information given by authors, other references were drawn upon for background material, and I readily acknowledge the help of the following sources:

> *The Writer's Handbook* for Ruth Rendell's quotation, reprinted by permission from 'How Do You Learn to Write?', by Ruth Rendell, which appeared in *The Writer's Handbook* copyright © 1988 by The Writer, Inc., Boston USA.

> *The Writer's Handbook* for Samm Sinclair Baker's quotation reprinted by permission from 'Where to Sell: A 3 Point Checklist That Works', by Samm Sinclair Baker, which appeared in *The Writer's Handbook*, copyright © 1988 by The Writer, Inc., Boston USA.

> Sheil Land Associates Limited for an extract from *Our Kate*, copyright © Catherine Cookson 1969, published by Corgi Books Ltd.

> Michael Joseph Ltd for an extract from Dora Saint's contribution in *At The Sign of the Mermaid* published in 1986. 'Miss Read' novels are published by Michael Joseph in hardback and Penguin in paperback.

> David Higham Associates for James Herriot's letter, which appeared in *The Best of James Herriot* and for the extract from Roald Dahl's *Lucky Break* in *The Wonderful World of Henry Sugar* published by Penguin Books.

> *The Guardian* for an extract about James A. Michener which appeared in the edition dated 23 February 1972.

> *Sunday Mirror* for an extract on Molly Parkin, published 9 January 1983.

I.P.C. to whom clearance has been sought for an extract from *The Barbara Cartland Story* by Gwen Robyns in *Woman*, October 1984.

H. F. Ellis for an appreciation of Dora Saint published in *The Sunday Telegraph*, February 1978.

Los Angeles Times for quotation from Betty Cuniberti's article on Tom Clancy.

Hugh Joseph for quotations from Anthea Joseph's letters, and article.

To my Elizabeth, whose patience I have stretched to the limit with my incessant questions and requests for an opinion.

Alison Lake who was press-ganged into typesetting this book. And to Peter Russell for photography.

Other sources acknowledged for assistance in the research of this book: The Naval Institute Press, *Sunday Express*, *Sunday Mirror*, *The Sunday Telegraph*, I.P.C. Magazines, *Woman*, BBC Data Enquiry Service, *The Bookseller*, The British Horse Society, *Daily Express*, David Higham Associates Limited, Deborah Owen Limited; Toby Buchan; Ian Roberts and not least, the helpful staff of the Basingstoke Public Library.